The Frontier in American History

◆ THE BARNES & NOBLE LIBRARY OF ESSENTIAL READING ◆

THE FRONTIER IN AMERICAN HISTORY

FREDERICK JACKSON TURNER

INTRODUCTION BY ANDREW TREES

BARNES & NOBLE
NEW YORK

THE BARNES & NOBLE
LIBRARY OF ESSENTIAL READING

Introduction and Suggested Reading
© 2009 by Barnes & Noble, Inc.

Originally published in 1920

This 2009 edition published by Barnes & Noble, Inc.

All rights reserved. No part of this publication may be reproduced, stored in a retrieval system, or transmitted, in any form or by any means, electronic, mechanical, photocopying, recording, or otherwise, without prior written permission from the publisher.

Barnes & Noble, Inc.
122 Fifth Avenue
New York, NY 10011

ISBN: 978-1-4351-2078-5

Printed and bound in the United States of America

1 3 5 7 9 10 8 6 4 2

Contents

INTRODUCTION   VII

PREFACE   XIII

I. THE SIGNIFICANCE OF THE FRONTIER IN AMERICAN HISTORY   1

II. THE FIRST OFFICIAL FRONTIER OF THE MASSACHUSETTS BAY   25

III. THE OLD WEST   42

IV. THE MIDDLE WEST   78

V. THE OHIO VALLEY IN AMERICAN HISTORY   100

VI. THE SIGNIFICANCE OF THE MISSISSIPPI VALLEY IN AMERICAN HISTORY   114

VII. THE PROBLEM OF THE WEST   133

VIII. DOMINANT FORCES IN WESTERN LIFE   146

IX. CONTRIBUTIONS OF THE WEST TO AMERICAN DEMOCRACY   161

X. PIONEER IDEALS AND THE STATE UNIVERSITY   180

XI. THE WEST AND AMERICAN IDEALS	195
XII. SOCIAL FORCES IN AMERICAN HISTORY	210
XIII. MIDDLE WESTERN PIONEER DEMOCRACY	227
INDEX	244
SUGGESTED READING	258

Introduction

When Frederick Jackson Turner first delivered his essay "The Significance of the Frontier in American History" no one present at the 1893 lecture could have known that he or she was listening to a revolutionary idea that would dominate the historical profession for almost half a century. Turner's "frontier thesis" offered a compelling interpretation of how the frontier played the decisive role in shaping a distinctly American identity. Although recent decades have given rise to a host of critics, Turner's thesis lives on not only in the popular imagination but as the starting point for a great deal of contemporary historical investigation. Turner's essay is, quite simply, one of the most influential works of American history ever written, and readers still find it an invaluable starting point for thinking about American identity. Although historians have discredited many of its claims, it remains, at the very least, a profound influence on how Americans imagine themselves as individuals and as a nation.

Turner was born in Portage, Wisconsin, in 1861. His parents moved to the state near the end of its frontier period, and this close proximity to frontier life clearly influenced his work. He received his B.A and M.A. from the University of Wisconsin and completed his doctorate at Johns Hopkins University in 1889. He returned that year to teach at the University of Wisconsin and later moved to Harvard University in 1910. He played a leading role in the American Historical Association, serving as its president in 1910 and on the editorial board of the Association's *American Historical Review* from 1910 to 1915. He retired from Harvard because of ill health in 1924 and died in 1932.

Despite his outsized influence, Turner wrote very little. His fame rests entirely on his essays, many of which were republished in two collections,

The Frontier in American History in 1920 and *The Significance of Sections in American History* in 1933 (for which he was posthumously awarded the Pulitzer Prize). He wrote only one book-length monograph, *The Rise of the New West, 1819–1829*, which was published in 1906, but he never managed to complete its sequel (his former students later pieced together *The United States 1830–1850: The Nation and Its Sections* and published it after his death in 1935). A number of plausible reasons have been offered for Turner's lack of productivity, including writer's block, but it seems likely that at least part of the problem was due to a failure, as one biographer put it, to buckle down. He was a social creature and said he needed both daily diversion as well as regular vacations. The ambitious nature of his projects also undermined his efforts to bring them to fruition. Given the relatively small amount of writing he completed, his influence is astounding. Turner's reach was extended through his teaching. He spent more than four decades training graduate students, although many of them came to disagree with Turner's theories. A number of them went on to have distinguished careers in their own right, including Merle Curti, an American historian who specialized in social and intellectual history, and Herbert Bolton, one of the leading authorities at the time on Spanish American history.

Turner first delivered "The Significance of the Frontier in American History" at an 1893 American Historical Association conference. He was only a thirty-two-year-old junior faculty member at the University of Wisconsin when he gave his paper in a hot, sleepy lecture room. He began by highlighting the fact that the United States of America no longer had a frontier, according to a recent bulletin of the Superintendent of the Census of 1890, which noted: "Up to and including 1880 the country had a frontier of settlement, but at present the unsettled area has been so broken into by isolated bodies of settlement that there can hardly be said to be a frontier line. In the discussion of its extent, its westward movement, etc., it cannot, therefore, any longer have a place in the census reports." That statement helped crystallize ideas that Turner had been thinking about for years. In particular, he zeroed in on the concept of the frontier as a flexible and powerful organizing concept for his thoughts about what was unique in America's historical development. In his seminal essay, Turner laid out his "frontier thesis," which made the frontier the catalyst for the development of a distinctly American national character.

At least part of the appeal of the frontier thesis lies in its simplicity. Traditionally, most historians argued that America's important institutions derived from English and European sources, and when they did look for the origins of an "American" character, they focused on eastern groups, such as the Puritans of New England. Completely rejecting the reigning orthodoxy, Turner argued that the crucial element transforming Europeans into Americans was the process of settling the continent. As he wrote in his first paragraph, "The existence of an area of free land, its continuous recession, and the advance of American settlement westward, explain American development." He suggestively outlined an evolutionary process during which the primitive conditions of the explorer gave way to a more mature agricultural stage before reaching the complexity of urban, industrial life. For Turner, the key factor in shaping America's identity was the frontier conditions the pioneers faced as they moved westward. Settling those undeveloped regions, Turner argued, unmoored settlers from their European heritage and made them into Americans. As he poetically wrote, the frontier "strips off the garments of civilization and arrays [the colonist] in the hunting shirt and the moccasin. . . . Little by little he transforms the wilderness, but the outcome is not the old Europe. . . . The fact is, that here is a new product that is American." This new American was distinguished by a number of characteristics, according to Turner. In the first place, the frontier melded the disparate people who settled in the new world into a "composite nationality." These Americans were characterized by distinct traits as well, such as self-reliance, mobility, and optimism. As he wrote more lyrically, "The result is that to the frontier the American intellect owes its striking characteristics. That coarseness and strength combined with acuteness and inquisitiveness; that practical, inventive turn of mind, quick to find expedients; that masterful grasp of material things, lacking in the artistic but powerful to effect great ends; that restless, nervous energy; that dominant individualism, working for good and for evil, and withal that buoyancy and exuberance which comes with freedom—these are traits of the frontier, or traits called out elsewhere because of the existence of the frontier." Turner also argued that "the most important effect of the frontier has been in the promotion of democracy here and in Europe." He believed that the frontier promoted individualism, which produced an "antipathy to control" and made Americans vigilant about their liberty.

According to Turner, any attempt to explain American history had to wrestle with the implications of the frontier. Ironically, despite its later importance, Turner's essay was only a suggestive beginning, and he soon turned to different questions, leaving it to other scholars to hunt for evidence for and against his theory. He himself recognized the abbreviated nature of his treatment and wrote in the essay, "This paper will make no attempt to treat the subject exhaustively; its aim is simply to call attention to the frontier as a fertile field for investigation, and to suggest some of the problems which arise in connection with it." Despite this modest disclaimer, the frontier thesis has continued to challenge historians ever since, and Turner likely also had grander ambitions in mind, for the essay reads almost as a manifesto for future historical work. Ending with a rhetorical flourish that called attention to the closing of the frontier as an epochal shift, he wrote, "And now, four centuries from the discovery of America, at the end of a hundred years of life under the Constitution, the frontier has gone, and with its going has closed the first period of American history." Although no great fanfare greeted the essay's initial publication, it was reprinted numerous times in the coming decade and seized not just the imaginations of professional historians but that of ordinary Americans as well, so much so that it remains at the core of our popular image of ourselves as a people even today.

A number of significant themes underlie "The Significance of the Frontier in American History." Like many of Turner's contemporaries, Charles Darwin influenced his thought, and the essay is filled with references to evolution to explain how Europeans were changed into Americans. Biological and organic metaphors also abound as a means of explaining how American society changed over time. For example, Turner compares the development of American civilization at one point to "the steady growth of a complex nervous system for the originally simple, inert continent." In addition, the essay's influence was increased because of its support for the idea of American exceptionalism, the belief that this country's citizens have a unique character unlike that of any other nation. Written at a time when America was becoming more assertive about its place on the world stage, the essay reinforced Americans' growing self-confidence. Finally, Turner's writing style played a role in the ongoing appeal of the "frontier thesis." His rich, evocative language imbued his words with an electrifying force.

But Turner's significance goes beyond his ideas. Today, historians consider one of his most important contributions to be his methodology, which was decidedly interdisciplinary. He used to joke that his graduate students should only read history when they were too tired to read anything else. Although interdisciplinary work is common now, it was radical when he proposed that historians should move beyond the conventional confines of disciplinary barriers and make use of the methods from the social sciences. His own work mingled politics, economics, culture, and geography to name just a few.

Although his ideas dominated American history for decades, most historians now reject Turner's claims. His critics have argued that he ignored industrial and urban history along with the class rivalries that accompanied them. Others have noted that he largely slighted groups outside the white, Protestant mainstream of his childhood, including Indians, African Americans, and southern European immigrants. Women also are absent from his work. In large part, these complaints can be made about most historians of his generation, and it is only in the last few decades that historians have turned their attention to many of these issues. But historians have also called into question central aspects of Turner's frontier thesis. For instance, far from being self-made men, many of the settlers of the frontier relied heavily on family connections and wealth from the eastern United States. In addition, some historians have found that the amount of opportunity available on the frontier was only slightly greater than it was in the East. And far from being incubators of individualism, frontier towns survived because of the rapid development of civic institutions, such as churches and political parties, according to new research. Even his argument that free land acted as a "safety valve" for American labor markets has turned out to be of less importance than first imagined.

After delivering his essay, Turner largely turned to new issues. He was no ivory-tower historian. He argued that history should be applied to real world problems. As he wrote in his first professional paper, "The Significance of History" (1891), "Each age writes the history of the past anew with reference to the conditions uppermost in its own time." For Turner, the passing of the frontier raised pressing questions about what would happen to America during this new historical era. Specifically, he worried that the Jeffersonian, agrarian ideals of the nation would soon be supplanted by industrial capitalism and that an over-crowded America would, in effect, become "Europeanized." The nation was largely rural when Turner was born, but almost half the population lived in cities by the time he wrote his essay. The appeal of Turner's ideas was, in part, due to their connection to larger anxieties. The popularity of his frontier thesis spread at the same time that the Populist revolt flowered (similar to Turner, the Populists warned about the passing agrarian nature of the country). Although the question of the frontier and its role in American history became a central topic of historical scholarship, he turned his attention to protecting the country's identity by studying regions or, as he called them, sections. In his later work, he attempted to demonstrate that those essential American values had grown to fruition in the country's various regions and that protecting those values involved defending the distinctiveness of those areas. He also moved away from the mono-causal explanation of the frontier to embrace a more complex theory of historical development that involved multiple forces interacting with the environment.

Despite the many valid criticisms of his theory, Turner's ideas live on in part because his critics have failed to capture the public imagination as Turner did—so much so that historians still find themselves writing under his shadow. Although some disagree with the theses laid out in his work, they find they cannot ignore it. While no longer holding the preeminent place among American historians, Turner remains a persuasive and poetic voice of the American character, and "The Significance of the Frontier in American History" continues to be one of the most influential works of American history ever written.

Andrew Trees holds a Ph.D. in American history from the University of Virginia. He is the author of *The Founding Fathers and the Politics of Character* (Princeton University Press, 2003) as well as a number of articles and books on American history and other subjects.

Preface

In republishing these essays in collected form, it has seemed best to issue them as they were originally printed, with the exception of a few slight corrections of slips in the text and with the omission of occasional duplication of language in the different essays. A considerable part of whatever value they may possess arises from the fact that they are commentaries in different periods on the central theme of the influence of the frontier in American history. Consequently they may have some historical significance as contemporaneous attempts of a student of American history, at successive transitions in our development during the past quarter century to interpret the relations of the present to the past. Grateful acknowledgment is made to the various societies and periodicals which have given permission to reprint the essays.

Various essays dealing with the connection of diplomatic history and the frontier and others stressing the significance of the section, or geographic province, in American history, are not included in the present collection. Neither the French nor the Spanish frontier is within the scope of the volume.

The future alone can disclose how far these interpretations are correct for the age of colonization which came gradually to an end with the disappearance of the frontier and free land. It alone can reveal how much of the courageous, creative American spirit, and how large a part of the historic American ideals are to be carried over into that new age which is replacing the era of free lands and of measurable isolation by consolidated and complex industrial development and by increasing resemblances and connections between the New World and the Old.

But the larger part of what has been distinctive and valuable in America's contribution to the history of the human spirit has been due to this nation's peculiar experience in extending its type of frontier into new regions; and in creating peaceful societies with new ideals in the successive vast and differing geographic provinces which together make up the United States. Directly or indirectly these experiences shaped the life of the eastern as well as the western states, and even reacted upon the Old World and influenced the direction of its thought and its progress. This experience has been fundamental in the economic, political and social characteristics of the American people and in their conceptions of their destiny.

Writing at the close of 1796, the French minister to the United States, M. Adet, reported to his government that Jefferson could not be relied on to be devoted to French interests, and he added: "Jefferson, I say, is American, and as such he cannot be sincerely our friend. An American is the born enemy of all European peoples." Obviously erroneous as are these words, there was an element of truth in them. If we would understand this element of truth, we must study the transforming influence of the American wilderness, remote from Europe, and by its resources and its free opportunities affording the conditions under which a new people, with new social and political types and ideals, could arise to play its own part in the world, and to influence Europe.

FREDERICK J. TURNER
HARVARD UNIVERSITY, March 1920

→ CHAPTER ONE ←

THE SIGNIFICANCE OF THE FRONTIER IN AMERICAN HISTORY

IN A RECENT BULLETIN OF THE SUPERINTENDENT OF THE CENSUS FOR 1890 appear these significant words: "Up to and including 1880 the country had a frontier of settlement, but at present the unsettled area has been so broken into by isolated bodies of settlement that there can hardly be said to be a frontier line. In the discussion of its extent, its westward movement, etc., it cannot, therefore, any longer have a place in the census reports." This brief official statement marks the closing of a great historic movement. Up to our own day American history has been in a large degree the history of the colonization of the Great West. The existence of an area of free land, its continuous recession, and the advance of American settlement westward, explain American development.

Behind institutions, behind constitutional forms and modifications, lie the vital forces that call these organs into life and shape them to meet changing conditions. The peculiarity of American institutions is the fact that they have been compelled to adapt themselves to the changes of an expanding people—to the changes involved in crossing a continent, in winning a wilderness, and in developing at each area of this progress out of the primitive economic and political conditions of the frontier into the complexity of city life. Said Calhoun in 1817, "We are great, and rapidly—I was about to say fearfully—growing!" So saying, he touched the distinguishing feature of American life. All peoples show development; the germ theory of politics has been sufficiently emphasized. In the case of most nations, however, the development has occurred in a limited area; and if the nation has expanded, it has met other growing peoples whom it has conquered. But in the case of the United States we have a different phenomenon. Limiting our attention to the Atlantic coast, we have the familiar phenomenon of the evolution of institutions in a limited area, such as the rise of representative government; the differentiation of simple colonial governments into complex organs; the progress from primitive industrial society, without division of labor, up to manufacturing civilization. But we have in addition to this a recurrence of the process of evolution in each western area reached in the process of expansion. Thus American development has exhibited not merely advance along a single line, but a return to primitive conditions on a continually advancing frontier line, and a new development for that area. American social development has been continually beginning over again on the frontier. This perennial rebirth, this fluidity of American life, this expansion westward with its new opportunities, its continuous touch with the simplicity of primitive society, furnish the forces dominating American character. The true point of view in the history of this nation is not the Atlantic coast, it is the Great West. Even the slavery struggle, which is made so exclusive an object of attention by writers like Professor von Holst, occupies its important place in American history because of its relation to westward expansion.

In this advance, the frontier is the outer edge of the wave—the meeting point between savagery and civilization. Much has been written about the frontier from the point of view of border warfare and the chase, but as a field for the serious study of the economist and the historian it has been neglected.

The American frontier is sharply distinguished from the European frontier—a fortified boundary line running through dense populations. The most significant thing about the American frontier is, that it lies at the hither edge of free land. In the census reports it is treated as the margin of that settlement which has a density of two or more to the square mile. The term is an elastic one, and for our purposes does not need sharp definition. We shall consider the whole frontier belt, including the Indian country and the outer margin of the "settled area" of the census reports. This paper will make no attempt to treat the subject exhaustively; its aim is simply to call attention to the frontier as a fertile field for investigation, and to suggest some of the problems which arise in connection with it.

In the settlement of America we have to observe how European life entered the continent, and how America modified and developed that life and reacted on Europe. Our early history is the study of European germs developing in an American environment. Too exclusive attention has been paid by institutional students to the Germanic origins, too little to the American factors. The frontier is the line of most rapid and effective Americanization. The wilderness masters the colonist. It finds him a European in dress, industries, tools, modes of travel, and thought. It takes him from the railroad car and puts him in the birch canoe. It strips off the garments of civilization and arrays him in the hunting shirt and the moccasin. It puts him in the log cabin of the Cherokee and Iroquois and runs an Indian palisade around him. Before long he has gone to planting Indian corn and plowing with a sharp stick; he shouts the war cry and takes the scalp in orthodox Indian fashion. In short, at the frontier the environment is at first too strong for the man. He must accept the conditions which it furnishes, or perish, and so he fits himself into the Indian clearings and follows the Indian trails. Little by little he transforms the wilderness, but the outcome is not the old Europe, not simply the development of Germanic germs, any more than the first phenomenon was a case of reversion to the Germanic mark. The fact is, that here is a new product that is American. At first, the frontier was the Atlantic coast. It was the frontier of Europe in a very real sense. Moving westward, the frontier became more and more American. As successive terminal moraines result from successive glaciations, so each frontier leaves its traces behind it, and when it becomes a settled area the region still partakes of the frontier characteristics. Thus the advance of the frontier has meant a steady movement away from the influence of Europe, a steady growth of independence on American lines. And to study this advance, the men who grew up under these conditions, and the political, economic, and social results of it, is to study the really American part of our history.

In the course of the seventeenth century the frontier was advanced up the Atlantic river courses, just beyond the "fall line," and the tidewater region became the settled area. In the first half of the eighteenth century another advance occurred. Traders followed the Delaware and Shawnese Indians to the Ohio as early as the end of the first quarter of the century. Gov. Spotswood, of Virginia, made an expedition in 1714 across the Blue Ridge. The end of the first quarter of the century saw the advance of the Scotch-Irish and the Palatine Germans up the Shenandoah Valley into the western part of Virginia, and along the Piedmont region of the Carolinas. The Germans in New York pushed the frontier of settlement up the Mohawk to German Flats. In Pennsylvania the town of Bedford indicates the line of settlement. Settlements soon began on the New River, or the Great Kanawha, and on the sources of the Yadkin and French Broad. The king attempted to arrest the advance by his proclamation of 1763, forbidding settlements beyond the sources of the rivers flowing into the Atlantic; but in vain. In the period of the Revolution the frontier crossed the Alleghanies into Kentucky and Tennessee, and the upper waters of the Ohio were settled. When the first census was taken in 1790, the continuous settled area was bounded by a line which ran near the coast of Maine, and included New England except a portion of Vermont and New Hampshire, New York along the Hudson and up the Mohawk about Schenectady, eastern and southern Pennsylvania, Virginia well across the Shenandoah Valley, and the Carolinas and eastern Georgia. Beyond this region of continuous settlement were the small settled areas of Kentucky and Tennessee, and the Ohio, with the mountains intervening between them and the Atlantic area, thus giving a new and important character to the frontier. The isolation of the region increased its peculiarly American tendencies, and the need of transportation facilities to connect it with the East called out important schemes of internal improvement, which will be noted farther on. The "West," as a self-conscious section, began to evolve.

From decade to decade distinct advances of the frontier occurred. By the census of 1820 the settled area included Ohio, southern Indiana and Illinois, southeastern Missouri, and about one-half of Louisiana. This settled area had surrounded Indian areas, and the management of these tribes became an object of political concern. The frontier region of the time lay along the Great Lakes, where Astor's American Fur Company operated in the Indian trade, and beyond the Mississippi, where Indian traders extended their activity even to the Rocky Mountains; Florida also furnished frontier conditions. The Mississippi River region was the scene of typical frontier settlements.

The rising steam navigation on western waters, the opening of the Erie Canal, and the westward extension of cotton culture added five frontier states to the Union in this period. Grund, writing in 1836, declares:

> It appears then that the universal disposition of Americans to emigrate to the western wilderness, in order to enlarge their dominion over inanimate nature, is the actual result of an expansive power which is inherent in them, and which by continually agitating all classes of society is constantly throwing a large portion of the whole population on the extreme confines of the state, in order to gain space for its development. Hardly is a new state or territory

formed before the same principle manifests itself again and gives rise to a further emigration; and so is it destined to go on until a physical barrier must finally obstruct its progress.

In the middle of this century the line indicated by the present eastern boundary of Indian Territory, Nebraska, and Kansas marked the frontier of the Indian country. Minnesota and Wisconsin still exhibited frontier conditions, but the distinctive frontier of the period is found in California, where the gold discoveries had sent a sudden tide of adventurous miners, and in Oregon, and the settlements in Utah. As the frontier had leaped over the Alleghanies, so now it skipped the Great Plains and the Rocky Mountains; and in the same way that the advance of the frontiersmen beyond the Alleghanies had caused the rise of important questions of transportation and internal improvement, so now the settlers beyond the Rocky Mountains needed means of communication with the East, and in the furnishing of these arose the settlement of the Great Plains and the development of still another kind of frontier life. Railroads, fostered by land grants, sent an increasing tide of immigrants into the Far West. The United States Army fought a series of Indian wars in Minnesota, Dakota, and the Indian Territory.

By 1880 the settled area had been pushed into northern Michigan, Wisconsin, and Minnesota, along Dakota rivers, and in the Black Hills region, and was ascending the rivers of Kansas and Nebraska. The development of mines in Colorado had drawn isolated frontier settlements into that region, and Montana and Idaho were receiving settlers. The frontier was found in these mining camps and the ranches of the Great Plains. The superintendent of the census for 1890 reports, as previously stated, that the settlements of the West lie so scattered over the region that there can no longer be said to be a frontier line.

In these successive frontiers we find natural boundary lines which have served to mark and to affect the characteristics of the frontiers, namely: the "fall line"; the Alleghany Mountains; the Mississippi; the Missouri where its direction approximates north and south; the line of the arid lands, approximately the ninety-ninth meridian; and the Rocky Mountains. The fall line marked the frontier of the seventeenth century; the Alleghanies that of the eighteenth; the Mississippi that of the first quarter of the nineteenth; the Missouri that of the middle of this century (omitting the California movement); and the belt of the Rocky Mountains and the arid tract, the present frontier. Each was won by a series of Indian wars.

At the Atlantic frontier one can study the germs of processes repeated at each successive frontier. We have the complex European life sharply precipitated by the wilderness into the simplicity of primitive conditions. The first frontier had to meet its Indian question, its question of the disposition of the public domain, of the means of intercourse with older settlements, of the extension of political organization, of religious and educational activity. And the settlement of these and similar questions for one frontier served as a guide for the next. The American student needs not to go to the "prim little townships of Sleswick" for illustrations of the law of continuity and development. For example, he may study the origin of our land policies in the colonial land policy; he may see how the system grew by adapting the statutes to the customs of the successive frontiers. He may see how the mining experience in the lead regions of Wisconsin, Illinois, and Iowa was applied to the mining laws of the Sierras, and how our Indian policy has been a series of experimentations on successive frontiers. Each tier of new states has found in the older ones material for its constitutions. Each frontier has made similar contributions to American character, as will be discussed farther on.

But with all these similarities there are essential differences, due to the place element and the time element. It is evident that the farming frontier of the Mississippi Valley presents different conditions from the mining frontier of the Rocky Mountains. The frontier reached by the Pacific Railroad, surveyed into rectangles, guarded by the United States Army, and recruited by the daily immigrant ship, moves forward at a swifter pace and in a different way than the frontier reached by the birch canoe or the pack horse. The geologist traces patiently the shores of ancient seas, maps their areas, and compares the older and the newer. It would be a work worth the historian's labors to mark these various frontiers and in detail compare one with another. Not only would there result a more adequate conception of American development and characteristics, but invaluable additions would be made to the history of society.

Loria, the Italian economist, has urged the study of colonial life as an aid in understanding the stages of European development, affirming that colonial settlement is for economic science what the mountain is for geology, bringing to light primitive stratifications. "America," he says, "has the key to the historical enigma which Europe has sought for centuries in vain, and the land which has no history reveals luminously the course of universal history." There is much truth in this. The United States lies like a huge page in the history of society. Line by line as we read this continental page from West to East we find the record of social evolution. It begins with the Indian and the hunter; it goes on to tell of the disintegration of savagery by the entrance of the trader, the pathfinder of civilization; we read the annals of the pastoral stage in ranch life; the exploitation of the soil by the raising of unrotated crops of corn and wheat in sparsely settled farming communities; the intensive culture of the denser farm settlement; and finally the manufacturing organization with city and factory system. This page is familiar to the student of census statistics, but how little of it has been used by our historians. Particularly in eastern states this page is a palimpsest. What is now a manufacturing state was in an earlier decade an area of intensive farming. Earlier yet it had been a wheat area, and still earlier the "range" had attracted the cattle-herder. Thus Wisconsin, now developing manufacture, is a state with varied agricultural interests. But earlier it was given over to almost exclusive grain-raising, like North Dakota at the present time.

Each of these areas has had an influence in our economic and political history; the evolution of each into a higher stage has worked political transformations. But what constitutional historian has made any adequate attempt to interpret political facts by the light of these social areas and changes?

The Atlantic frontier was compounded of fisherman, fur-trader, miner, cattle-raiser, and farmer. Excepting the fisherman, each type of industry was on the march toward the West, impelled by an irresistible attraction. Each passed in successive waves across the continent. Stand at Cumberland Gap and watch the procession of civilization, marching single file—the buffalo following the trail to the salt springs, the Indian, the fur-trader and hunter, the cattle-raiser, the pioneer farmer—and the frontier has passed by. Stand at South Pass in the Rockies a century later and see the same procession with wider intervals between. The unequal rate of advance compels us to distinguish the frontier into the trader's frontier, the rancher's frontier, or the miner's frontier, and the farmer's frontier. When the mines and the cow pens were still near the fall line the traders' pack trains were tinkling across the Alleghanies, and the French on the Great Lakes were fortifying their posts, alarmed by the British trader's birch canoe. When the trappers scaled the Rockies, the farmer was still near the mouth of the Missouri.

Why was it that the Indian trader passed so rapidly across the continent? What effects followed from the trader's frontier? The trade was coeval with American discovery. The Norsemen, Vespuccius, Verrazani, Hudson, John Smith, all trafficked for furs. The Plymouth pilgrims settled in Indian cornfields, and their first return cargo was of beaver and lumber. The records of the various New England colonies show how steadily exploration was carried into the wilderness by this trade. What is true for New England is, as would be expected, even plainer for the rest of the colonies. All along the coast from Maine to Georgia the Indian trade opened up the river courses. Steadily the trader passed westward, utilizing the older lines of French trade. The Ohio, the Great Lakes, the Mississippi, the Missouri, and the Platte, the lines of Western advance, were ascended by traders. They found the passes in the Rocky Mountains and guided Lewis and Clark, Frémont, and Bidwell. The explanation of the rapidity of this advance is connected with the effects of the trader on the Indian. The trading post left the unarmed tribes at the mercy of those that had purchased firearms—a truth which the Iroquois Indians wrote in blood, and so the remote and unvisited tribes gave eager welcome to the trader. "The savages," wrote La Salle, "take better care of us French than of their own children; from us only can they get guns and goods." This accounts for the trader's power and the rapidity of his advance. Thus the disintegrating forces of civilization entered the wilderness. Every river valley and Indian trail became a fissure in Indian society, and so that society became honeycombed. Long before the pioneer farmer appeared on the scene, primitive Indian life had passed away. The farmers met Indians armed with guns. The trading frontier, while steadily undermining Indian power by making the tribes ultimately dependent on the whites, yet, through its sale of guns, gave to the Indian increased power of resistance to the farming frontier. French colonization was dominated by its trading frontier; English colonization by its farming frontier. There was an antagonism between the two frontiers as between the two nations. Said Duquesne to the Iroquois,

> Are you ignorant of the difference between the king of England and the king of France? Go see the forts that our king has established and you will see that you can still hunt under their very walls. They have been placed for your advantage in places which you frequent. The English, on the contrary, are no sooner in possession of a place than the game is driven away. The forest falls before them as they advance, and the soil is laid bare so that you can scarce find the wherewithal to erect a shelter for the night.

And yet, in spite of this opposition of the interests of the trader and the farmer, the Indian trade pioneered the way for civilization. The buffalo trail became the Indian trail, and this became the trader's "trace"; the trails widened into roads, and the roads into turnpikes, and these in turn were transformed into railroads. The same origin can be shown for the railroads of the South, the Far West, and the Dominion of Canada. The trading posts reached by these trails were on the sites of Indian villages which had been placed in positions suggested by nature; and these trading posts, situated so as to command the water systems of the country, have grown into such cities as Albany, Pittsburgh, Detroit, Chicago, St. Louis, Council Bluffs, and Kansas City. Thus civilization in America has followed the arteries made by geology, pouring an ever richer tide through them, until at last the slender paths of aboriginal intercourse have been broadened and interwoven into the complex mazes of modern commercial lines; the wilderness has been interpenetrated by lines of civilization growing ever more numerous. It is like the steady growth of a complex nervous system for the originally simple, inert continent. If one would understand why we are today one nation, rather than a collection of isolated states, he must study this economic and social consolidation of the country. In this progress from savage conditions lie topics for the evolutionist.

The effect of the Indian frontier as a consolidating agent in our history is important. From the close of the seventeenth century various intercolonial congresses have been called to treat with Indians and establish common measures of defense. Particularism was strongest in colonies with no Indian frontier. This frontier stretched along the western border like a cord of union. The Indian was a common danger, demanding united action. Most celebrated of these conferences was the Albany congress of 1754, called to treat with the Six Nations, and to consider plans of union. Even a cursory reading of the plan proposed by the congress reveals the importance of the frontier. The powers of the general council and the officers were, chiefly, the determination of peace and war with the Indians, the regulation of Indian trade, the purchase of Indian lands, and the creation and government of new settlements as a security against the Indians. It is evident that the unifying tendencies of the Revolutionary period were facilitated by the previous coöperation in the regulation of the frontier. In this connection may be mentioned the importance of the frontier, from that day to this, as a military training school, keeping alive the power of resistance to aggression, and developing the stalwart and rugged qualities of the frontiersman.

It would not be possible in the limits of this paper to trace the other frontiers across the continent. Travelers of the eighteenth century found the "cow pens" among the cane-brakes and peavine pastures of the South, and the "cow drivers" took their droves to Charleston, Philadelphia, and New York. Travelers at the close of the War of 1812 met droves of more than a thousand cattle and swine from the interior of Ohio going to Pennsylvania to fatten for the Philadelphia market. The ranges of the Great Plains, with ranch and cowboy and nomadic life, are things of yesterday and of today. The experience of the Carolina cow pens guided the ranchers of Texas. One element favoring the rapid extension of the rancher's frontier is the fact that in a remote country lacking transportation facilities the product must be in small bulk, or must be able to transport itself, and the cattle raiser could easily drive his product to market. The effect of these great ranches on the subsequent agrarian history of the localities in which they existed should be studied.

The maps of the census reports show an uneven advance of the farmer's frontier, with tongues of settlement pushed forward and with indentations of wilderness. In part this is due to Indian resistance, in part to the location of river valleys and passes, in part to the unequal force of the centers of frontier attraction. Among the important centers of attraction may be mentioned the following: fertile and favorably situated soils, salt springs, mines, and army posts.

The frontier army post, serving to protect the settlers from the Indians, has also acted as a wedge to open the Indian country, and has been a nucleus for settlement. In this connection mention should also be made of the government military and exploring expeditions in determining the lines of settlement. But all the more important expeditions were greatly indebted to the earliest pathmakers, the Indian guides, the traders and trappers, and the French voyageurs, who were inevitable parts of governmental expeditions from the days of Lewis and Clark. Each expedition was an epitome of the previous factors in Western advance.

In an interesting monograph, Victor Hehn has traced the effect of salt upon early European development, and has pointed out how it affected the lines of settlement and the form of administration. A similar study might be made for the salt springs of the United States. The early settlers were tied to the coast by the need of salt, without which they could not preserve their meats or live in comfort. Writing in 1752, Bishop Spangenburg says of a colony for which he was seeking lands in North Carolina, "They will require salt & other necessaries which they can neither manufacture nor raise. Either they must go to Charleston, which is 300 miles distant. . . . Or else they must go to Boling's Point in VA on a branch of the James & is also 300 miles from here. . . . Or else they must go down the Roanoke—I know not how many miles—where salt is brought up from the Cape Fear." This may serve as a typical illustration. An annual pilgrimage to the coast for salt thus became essential. Taking flocks or furs and ginseng root, the early settlers sent their pack trains after seeding time each year to the coast. This proved to be an important educational influence, since it was almost the only way in which the pioneer learned what was going on in the East. But when discovery was made of the salt springs of the Kanawha, and the Holston, and Kentucky, and central New York, the West began to be freed from dependence on the coast. It was in part the effect of finding these salt springs that enabled settlement to cross the mountains.

From the time the mountains rose between the pioneer and the seaboard, a new order of Americanism arose. The West and the East began to get out of touch of each other. The settlements from the sea to the mountains kept connection with the rear and had a certain solidarity. But the over-mountain men grew more and more independent. The East took a narrow view of American advance, and nearly lost these men. Kentucky and Tennessee history bears abundant witness to the truth of this statement. The East began to try to hedge and limit westward expansion. Though Webster could declare that there were no Alleghanies in his politics, yet in politics in general they were a very solid factor.

The exploitation of the beasts took hunter and trader to the West, the exploitation of the grasses took the rancher West, and the exploitation of the virgin soil of the river valleys and prairies attracted the farmer. Good soils have been the most continuous attraction to the farmer's frontier. The land hunger of the Virginians drew them down the rivers into Carolina, in early colonial days; the search for soils took the Massachusetts men to Pennsylvania and to New York. As the eastern lands were taken up migration flowed across them to the west. Daniel Boone, the great backwoodsman, who combined the occupations of hunter, trader, cattle-raiser, farmer, and surveyor—learning, probably from the traders, of the fertility of the lands of the upper Yadkin, where the traders were wont to rest as they took their way to the Indians, left his Pennsylvania home with his father, and passed down the Great Valley road to that stream. Learning from a trader of the game and rich pastures of Kentucky, he pioneered the way for the farmers to that region. Thence he passed to the frontier of Missouri, where his settlement was long a landmark on the frontier. Here again he helped to open the way for civilization, finding salt licks, and trails, and land. His son was among the earliest trappers in the passes of the Rocky Mountains, and his party are said to have been the first to camp on the present site of Denver. His grandson, Col. A. J. Boone, of Colorado, was a power among the Indians of the Rocky Mountains, and was appointed an agent by the government. Kit Carson's mother was a Boone. Thus this family epitomizes the backwoodsman's advance across the continent.

The farmer's advance came in a distinct series of waves. In Peck's *New Guide to the West*, published in Boston in 1837, occurs this suggestive passage:

> Generally, in all the western settlements, three classes, like the waves of the ocean, have rolled one after the other. First comes the pioneer, who depends for the subsistence of his family chiefly upon the natural growth of vegetation, called the "range," and the proceeds of hunting. His implements of agriculture are rude, chiefly of his own make, and his efforts directed mainly to a crop of corn and a "truck patch." The last is a rude garden for growing cabbage, beans, corn for roasting ears, cucumbers, and potatoes. A log cabin, and, occasionally, a stable and corn-crib, and a field of a dozen acres, the timber girdled or "deadened," and fenced, are enough for his occupancy. It is quite immaterial whether he ever becomes the owner of the soil. He is the occupant for the time being, pays no rent, and feels as independent as the "lord of the manor." With a horse, cow, and one or two breeders of swine, he strikes into the woods with his family, and becomes the founder of a new county, or perhaps state. He builds his cabin, gathers around him a few other families of similar tastes and habits, and occupies till the range is somewhat subdued, and hunting a little precarious, or, which is more frequently the case, till the neighbors crowd around, roads, bridges, and fields annoy him, and he lacks elbow room. The preëmption law enables him to dispose of his cabin and cornfield to the next class of emigrants; and, to employ his own figures, he "breaks for the high timber," "clears out for the New Purchase," or migrates to Arkansas or Texas, to work the same process over.
>
> The next class of emigrants purchase the lands, add field to field, clear out the roads, throw rough bridges over the streams, put up hewn log houses with glass windows and brick or stone

chimneys, occasionally plant orchards, build mills, schoolhouses, courthouses, etc., and exhibit the picture and forms of plain, frugal, civilized life.

Another wave rolls on. The men of capital and enterprise come. The settler is ready to sell out and take the advantage of the rise in property, push farther into the interior and become, himself, a man of capital and enterprise in turn. The small village rises to a spacious town or city; substantial edifices of brick, extensive fields, orchards, gardens, colleges, and churches are seen. Broadcloths, silks, leghorns, crapes, and all the refinements, luxuries, elegancies, frivolities, and fashions are in vogue. Thus wave after wave is rolling westward; the real Eldorado is still farther on.

A portion of the two first classes remain stationary amidst the general movement, improve their habits and condition, and rise in the scale of society.

The writer has traveled much amongst the first class, the real pioneers. He has lived many years in connection with the second grade; and now the third wave is sweeping over large districts of Indiana, Illinois, and Missouri. Migration has become almost a habit in the West. Hundreds of men can be found, not over fifty years of age, who have settled for the fourth, fifth, or sixth time on a new spot. To sell out and remove only a few hundred miles makes up a portion of the variety of backwoods life and manners.

Omitting those of the pioneer farmers who move from the love of adventure, the advance of the more steady farmer is easy to understand. Obviously the immigrant was attracted by the cheap lands of the frontier, and even the native farmer felt their influence strongly. Year by year the farmers who lived on soil whose returns were diminished by unrotated crops were offered the virgin soil of the frontier at nominal prices. Their growing families demanded more lands, and these were dear. The competition of the unexhausted, cheap, and easily tilled prairie lands compelled the farmer either to go west and continue the exhaustion of the soil on a new frontier, or to adopt intensive culture. Thus the census of 1890 shows, in the Northwest, many counties in which there is an absolute or a relative decrease of population. These states have been sending farmers to advance the frontier on the plains, and have themselves begun to turn to intensive farming and to manufacture. A decade before this, Ohio had shown the same transition stage. Thus the demand for land and the love of wilderness freedom drew the frontier ever onward.

Having now roughly outlined the various kinds of frontiers, and their modes of advance, chiefly from the point of view of the frontier itself, we may next inquire what were the influences on the East and on the Old World. A rapid enumeration of some of the more noteworthy effects is all that I have time for.

First, we note that the frontier promoted the formation of a composite nationality for the American people. The coast was preponderantly English, but the later tides of continental immigration flowed across to the free lands. This was the case from the early colonial days. The Scotch-Irish and the Palatine Germans, or Pennsylvania Dutch, furnished the dominant element in the stock of the colonial frontier. With these peoples were also the freed indented servants, or redemptioners, who at the expiration of their time of service passed to the frontier. Governor Spotswood of Virginia writes in 1717, "The inhabitants of our frontiers are composed generally of such as have been transported hither as servants, and, being out of their time, settle themselves where land is to be taken up and that will produce the necessarys of life with little labor." Very generally these redemptioners were of non-English stock. In the crucible of the frontier the immigrants were Americanized, liberated, and fused into a mixed race, English in neither nationality nor characteristics. The process has gone on from the early days to our own. Burke and other writers in the middle of the eighteenth century believed that Pennsylvania was "threatened with the danger of being wholly foreign in language, manners, and perhaps even inclinations." The German and Scotch-Irish elements in the frontier of the South were only less great. In the middle of the present century the German element in Wisconsin was already so considerable that leading publicists looked to the creation of a German state out of the commonwealth by concentrating their colonization. Such examples teach us to beware of misinterpreting the fact that there is a common English speech in America into a belief that the stock is also English.

In another way the advance of the frontier decreased our dependence on England. The coast, particularly of the South, lacked diversified industries, and was dependent on England for the bulk of its supplies. In the South there was even a dependence on the northern colonies for articles of food. Governor Glenn, of South Carolina, writes in the middle of the eighteenth century: "Our trade with New York and Philadelphia was of this sort, draining us of all the little money and bills we could gather from other places for their bread, flour, beer, hams, bacon, and other things of their produce, all which, except beer, our new townships begin to supply us with, which are settled with very industrious and thriving Germans. This no doubt diminishes the number of shipping and the appearance of our trade, but it is far from being a detriment to us." Before long the frontier created a demand for merchants. As it retreated from the coast it became less and less possible for England to bring her supplies directly to the consumer's wharfs, and carry away staple crops, and staple crops began to give way to diversified agriculture for a time. The effect of this phase of the frontier action upon the northern section is perceived when we realize how the advance of the frontier aroused seaboard cities like Boston, New York, and Baltimore, to engage in rivalry for what Washington called "the extensive and valuable trade of a rising empire."

The legislation which most developed the powers of the national government, and played the largest part in its activity, was conditioned on the frontier. Writers have discussed the subjects of tariff, land, and internal improvement, as subsidiary to the slavery question. But when American history comes to be rightly viewed it will be seen that the slavery question is an incident. In the period from the end of the first half of the present century to the close of the Civil War slavery rose to primary, but far from exclusive, importance. But this does not justify Dr. von Holst (to take an example) in treating our constitutional history in its formative period down to 1828 in a single volume, giving six volumes chiefly to the history of slavery from 1828 to 1861, under the title *Constitutional History of the United States*. The growth of nationalism and the evolution of American political institutions were dependent on the advance of the frontier. Even so recent a writer as Rhodes, in his *History of the United States since the Compromise of 1850*, has treated the legislation called out by the Western advance as incidental to the slavery struggle.

This is a wrong perspective. The pioneer needed the goods of the coast, and so the grand series of internal improvement and railroad legislation began, with potent nationalizing effects. Over internal improvements occurred great debates, in which grave constitutional questions were discussed. Sectional groupings appear in the votes, profoundly significant for the historian. Loose construction increased as the nation marched westward. But the West was not content with bringing the farm to the factory. Under the lead of Clay—"Harry of the West"—protective tariffs were passed, with the cry of bringing the factory to the farm. The disposition of the public lands was a third important subject of national legislation influenced by the frontier.

The public domain has been a force of profound importance in the nationalization and development of the government. The effects of the struggle of the landed and the landless states, and of the Ordinance of 1787, need no discussion. Administratively the frontier called out some of the highest and most vitalizing activities of the general government. The purchase of Louisiana was perhaps the constitutional turning point in the history of the republic, inasmuch as it afforded both a new area for national legislation and the occasion of the downfall of the policy of strict construction. But the purchase of Louisiana was called out by frontier needs and demands. As frontier states accrued to the Union the national power grew. In a speech on the dedication of the Calhoun monument Mr. Lamar explained: "In 1789 the states were the creators of the federal government; in 1861 the federal government was the creator of a large majority of the states."

When we consider the public domain from the point of view of the sale and disposal of the public lands we are again brought face-to-face with the frontier. The policy of the United States in dealing with its lands is in sharp contrast with the European system of scientific administration. Efforts to make this domain a source of revenue, and to withhold it from emigrants in order that settlement might be compact, were in vain. The jealousy and the fears of the East were powerless in the face of the demands of the frontiersmen. John Quincy Adams was obliged to confess: "My own system of administration, which was to make the national domain the inexhaustible fund for progressive and unceasing internal improvement, has failed." The reason is obvious; a system of administration was not what the West demanded; it wanted land. Adams states the situation as follows: "The slaveholders of the South have bought the coöperation of the western country by the bribe of the western lands, abandoning to the new western states their own proportion of the public property and aiding them in the design of grasping all the lands into their own hands. Thomas H. Benton was the author of this system, which he brought forward as a substitute for the American system of Mr. Clay, and to supplant him as the leading statesman of the West. Mr. Clay, by his tariff compromise with Mr. Calhoun, abandoned his own American system. At the same time he brought forward a plan for distributing among all the states of the Union the proceeds of the sales of the public lands. His bill for that purpose passed both Houses of Congress, but was vetoed by President Jackson, who, in his annual message of December 1832 formally recommended that all public lands should be gratuitously given away to individual adventurers and to the states in which the lands are situated."

"No subject," said Henry Clay, "which has presented itself to the present, or perhaps any preceding, Congress, is of greater magnitude than that of the public lands." When we consider the far-reaching effects of the government's land policy upon political, economic, and social aspects of American life, we are disposed to agree with him. But this legislation was framed under frontier influences, and under the lead of western statesmen like Benton and Jackson. Said Senator Scott of Indiana in 1841: "I consider the preëmption law merely declaratory of the custom or common law of the settlers."

It is safe to say that the legislation with regard to land, tariff, and internal improvements—the American system of the nationalizing Whig party—was conditioned on frontier ideas and needs. But it was not merely in legislative action that the frontier worked against the sectionalism of the coast. The economic and social characteristics of the frontier worked against sectionalism. The men of the frontier had closer resemblances to the Middle region than to either of the other sections. Pennsylvania had been the seed-plot of frontier emigration, and, although she passed on her settlers along the Great Valley into the west of Virginia and the Carolinas, yet the industrial society of these southern frontiersmen was always more like that of the Middle region than like that of the tidewater portion of the South, which later came to spread its industrial type throughout the South.

The Middle region, entered by New York harbor, was an open door to all Europe. The tidewater part of the South represented typical Englishmen, modified by a warm climate and servile labor, and living in baronial fashion on great plantations; New England stood for a special English movement—Puritanism. The Middle region was less English than the other sections. It had a wide mixture of nationalities, a varied society, the mixed town and county system of local government, a varied economic life, many religious sects. In short, it was a region mediating between New England and the South, and the East and the West. It represented that composite nationality which the contemporary United States exhibits, that juxtaposition of non-English groups, occupying a valley or a little settlement, and presenting reflections of the map of Europe in their variety. It was democratic and nonsectional, if not national; "easy, tolerant, and contented"; rooted strongly in material prosperity. It was typical of the modern United States. It was least sectional, not only because it lay between North and South, but also because with no barriers to shut out its frontiers from its settled region, and with a system of connecting waterways, the Middle region mediated between East and West as well as between North and South. Thus it became the typically American region. Even the New Englander, who was shut out from the frontier by the Middle region, tarrying in New York or Pennsylvania on his westward march, lost the acuteness of his sectionalism on the way.

The spread of cotton culture into the interior of the South finally broke down the contrast between the "tidewater" region and the rest of the state, and based southern interests on slavery. Before this process revealed its results the western portion of the South, which was akin to Pennsylvania in stock, society, and industry, showed tendencies to fall away from the faith of the fathers into internal improvement legislation and nationalism. In the Virginia convention of 1829–30, called to revise the constitution, Mr. Leigh, of Chesterfield, one of the tidewater counties, declared:

> One of the main causes of discontent which led to this convention, that which had the strongest influence in overcoming our veneration for the work of our fathers, which taught us to contemn the sentiments of Henry and Mason and Pendleton, which weaned us from our reverence for the constituted authorities of the state, was an overweening passion for internal improvement. I say this with perfect knowledge, for it has been avowed to me by gentlemen from the West over and over again. And let me tell the gentleman from Albemarle (Mr. Gordon) that it has been another principal object of those who set this ball of revolution in motion, to overturn the doctrine of state rights, of which Virginia has been the very pillar, and to remove the barrier she has interposed to the interference of the federal government in that same work of internal improvement, by so reorganizing the legislature that Virginia, too, may be hitched to the federal car.

It was this nationalizing tendency of the West that transformed the democracy of Jefferson into the national republicanism of Monroe and the democracy of Andrew Jackson. The West of the War of 1812, the West of Clay, and Benton and Harrison, and Andrew Jackson, shut off by the Middle states and the mountains from the coast sections, had a solidarity of its own with national tendencies. On the tide of the Father of Waters,

North and South met and mingled into a nation. Interstate migration went steadily on—a process of cross-fertilization of ideas and institutions. The fierce struggle of the sections over slavery on the western frontier does not diminish the truth of this statement; it proves the truth of it. Slavery was a sectional trait that would not down, but in the West it could not remain sectional. It was the greatest of frontiersmen who declared: "I believe this government can not endure permanently half slave and half free. It will become all of one thing or all of the other." Nothing works for nationalism like intercourse within the nation. Mobility of population is death to localism, and the western frontier worked irresistibly in unsettling population. The effect reached back from the frontier and affected profoundly the Atlantic coast and even the Old World.

But the most important effect of the frontier has been in the promotion of democracy here and in Europe. As has been indicated, the frontier is productive of individualism. Complex society is precipitated by the wilderness into a kind of primitive organization based on the family. The tendency is antisocial. It produces antipathy to control, and particularly to any direct control. The tax-gatherer is viewed as a representative of oppression. Prof. Osgood, in an able article, has pointed out that the frontier conditions prevalent in the colonies are important factors in the explanation of the American Revolution, where individual liberty was sometimes confused with absence of all effective government. The same conditions aid in explaining the difficulty of instituting a strong government in the period of the confederacy. The frontier individualism has from the beginning promoted democracy.

The frontier states that came into the Union in the first quarter of a century of its existence came in with democratic suffrage provisions, and had reactive effects of the highest importance upon the older states whose peoples were being attracted there. An extension of the franchise became essential. It was *western* New York that forced an extension of suffrage in the constitutional convention of that state in 1821; and it was *western* Virginia that compelled the tidewater region to put a more liberal suffrage provision in the constitution framed in 1830, and to give to the frontier region a more nearly proportionate representation with the tidewater aristocracy. The rise of democracy as an effective force in the nation came in with western preponderance under Jackson and William Henry Harrison, and it meant the triumph of the frontier—with all of its good and with all of its evil elements. An interesting illustration of the tone of frontier democracy in 1830 comes from the same debates in the Virginia convention already referred to. A representative from western Virginia declared:

> But, sir, it is not the increase of population in the West which this gentleman ought to fear. It is the energy which the mountain breeze and western habits impart to those emigrants. They are regenerated, politically I mean, sir. They soon become *working politicians;* and the difference, sir, between a *talking* and a *working* politician is immense. The Old Dominion has long been celebrated for producing great orators; the ablest metaphysicians in policy; men that can split hairs in all abstruse questions of political economy. But at home, or when they return from Congress, they have Negroes to fan them asleep. But a Pennsylvania, a New York, an Ohio, or a western Virginia statesman, though far inferior in logic, metaphysics, and rhetoric to an old Virginia statesman, has this advantage, that when he returns home he takes off his coat and takes hold of the plow. This gives him bone and muscle, sir, and preserves his republican principles pure and uncontaminated.

So long as free land exists, the opportunity for a competency exists, and economic power secures political power. But the democracy born of free land, strong in selfishness and individualism, intolerant of administrative experience and education, and pressing individual liberty beyond its proper bounds, has its dangers as well as its benefits. Individualism in America has allowed a laxity in regard to governmental affairs which has rendered possible the spoils system and all the manifest evils that follow from the lack of a highly developed civic spirit. In this connection may be noted also the influence of frontier conditions in permitting lax business honor, inflated paper currency and wildcat banking. The colonial and revolutionary frontier was the region whence emanated many of the worst forms of an evil currency. The West in the War of 1812 repeated the phenomenon on the frontier of that day, while the speculation and wildcat banking of the period of the crisis of 1837 occurred on the new frontier belt of the next tier of states. Thus each one of the periods of lax financial integrity coincides with periods when a new set of frontier communities had arisen, and coincides in area with these successive frontiers, for the most part. The recent Populist agitation is a case in point. Many a state that now declines any connection with the tenets of the Populists, itself adhered to such ideas in an earlier stage of the development of the state. A primitive society can hardly be expected to show the intelligent appreciation of the complexity of business interests in a developed society. The continual recurrence of these areas of paper-money agitation is another evidence that the frontier can be isolated and studied as a factor in American history of the highest importance.

The East has always feared the result of an unregulated advance of the frontier, and has tried to check and guide it. The English authorities would have checked settlement at the headwaters of the Atlantic tributaries and allowed the "savages to enjoy their deserts in quiet lest the peltry trade should decrease." This called out Burke's splendid protest:

> If you stopped your grants, what would be the consequence? The people would occupy without grants. They have already so occupied in many places. You can not station garrisons in every part of these deserts. If you drive the people from one place, they will carry on their annual tillage and remove with their flocks and herds to another. Many of the people in the back settlements are already little attached to particular situations. Already they have topped the Appalachian Mountains. From thence they behold before them an immense plain, one vast, rich, level meadow; a square of five hundred miles. Over this they would wander without a possibility of restraint; they would change their manners with their habits of life; would soon forget a government by which they were disowned; would become hordes of English Tartars; and, pouring down upon your unfortified frontiers a fierce and irresistible cavalry, become masters of your governors and your counselers, your collectors and comptrollers, and of all the slaves that adhered to them. Such would, and in no long time must, be the effect of attempting to forbid as a crime and to suppress as an evil the command and blessing of Providence, "Increase and multiply." Such would be the happy result of an endeavor to keep as a lair of wild beasts that earth which God, by an express charter, has given to the children of men.

But the English government was not alone in its desire to limit the advance of the frontier and guide its destinies. Tidewater Virginia and South Carolina gerrymandered those colonies to insure the dominance of the coast in their legislatures. Washington desired to settle a state at a time in the Northwest; Jefferson would reserve from settlement the territory of his Louisiana Purchase north of the thirty-second parallel, in order to offer it to the Indians in exchange for their settlements east of the Mississippi. "When we shall be full on this side," he writes, "we may lay off a range of states on the western bank from the head to the mouth, and so range after range, advancing compactly as we multiply." Madison went so far as to argue to the French minister that the United States had no interest in seeing population extend itself on the right bank of the Mississippi, but should rather fear it. When the Oregon question was under debate, in 1824, Smyth, of Virginia, would draw an unchangeable line for the limits of the United States at the outer limit of two tiers of states beyond the Mississippi, complaining that the seaboard states were being drained of the flower of their population by the bringing of too much land into market. Even Thomas Benton, the man of widest views of the destiny of the West, at this stage of his career declared that along the ridge of the Rocky mountains "the western limits of the Republic should be drawn, and the statue of the fabled god Terminus should be raised upon its highest peak, never to be thrown down." But the attempts to limit the boundaries, to restrict land sales and settlement, and to deprive the West of its share of political power were all in vain. Steadily the frontier of settlement advanced and carried with it individualism, democracy, and nationalism, and powerfully affected the East and the Old World.

The most effective efforts of the East to regulate the frontier came through its educational and religious activity, exerted by interstate migration and by organized societies. Speaking in 1835, Dr. Lyman Beecher declared: "It is equally plain that the religious and political destiny of our nation is to be decided in the West," and he pointed out that the population of the West

> . . . is assembled from all the states of the Union and from all the nations of Europe, and is rushing in like the waters of the flood, demanding for its moral preservation the immediate and universal action of those institutions which discipline the mind and arm the conscience and the heart. And so various are the opinions and habits, and so recent and imperfect is the acquaintance, and so sparse are the settlements of the West, that no homogeneous public sentiment can be formed to legislate immediately into being the requisite institutions. And yet they are all needed immediately in their utmost perfection and power. A nation is being "born in a day." . . . But what will become of the West if her prosperity rushes

up to such a majesty of power, while those great institutions linger which are necessary to form the mind and the conscience and the heart of that vast world. It must not be permitted. . . . Let no man at the East quiet himself and dream of liberty, whatever may become of the West. . . . Her destiny is our destiny.

With the appeal to the conscience of New England, he adds appeals to her fears lest other religious sects anticipate her own. The New England preacher and school teacher left their mark on the West. The dread of western emancipation from New England's political and economic control was paralleled by her fears lest the West cut loose from her religion. Commenting in 1850 on reports that settlement was rapidly extending northward in Wisconsin, the editor of the *Home Missionary* writes: "We scarcely know whether to rejoice or mourn over this extension of our settlements. While we sympathize in whatever tends to increase the physical resources and prosperity of our country, we can not forget that with all these dispersions into remote and still remoter corners of the land the supply of the means of grace is becoming relatively less and less." Acting in accordance with such ideas, home missions were established and western colleges were erected. As seaboard cities like Philadelphia, New York, and Baltimore strove for the mastery of western trade, so the various denominations strove for the possession of the West. Thus an intellectual stream from New England sources fertilized the West. Other sections sent their missionaries; but the real struggle was between sects. The contest for power and the expansive tendency furnished to the various sects by the existence of a moving frontier must have had important results on the character of religious organization in the United States. The multiplication of rival churches in the little frontier towns had deep and lasting social effects. The religious aspects of the frontier make a chapter in our history which needs study.

From the conditions of frontier life came intellectual traits of profound importance. The works of travelers along each frontier from colonial days onward describe certain common traits, and these traits have, while softening down, still persisted as survivals in the place of their origin, even when a higher social organization succeeded. The result is that to the frontier the American intellect owes its striking characteristics. That coarseness and strength combined with acuteness and inquisitiveness; that practical, inventive turn of mind, quick to find expedients; that masterful grasp of material things, lacking in the artistic but powerful to effect great ends; that restless, nervous energy; that dominant individualism, working for good and for evil, and withal that buoyancy and exuberance which comes with freedom—these are traits of the frontier, or traits called out elsewhere because of the existence of the frontier. Since the days when the fleet of Columbus sailed into the waters of the New World, America has been another name for opportunity, and the people of the United States have taken their tone from the incessant expansion which has not only been open but has even been forced upon them. He would be a rash prophet who should assert that the expansive character of American life has now entirely ceased. Movement has been its dominant fact, and, unless this training has no effect upon a people, the American energy will continually demand a wider field for its exercise. But never again will such gifts of free land offer themselves. For a moment, at the frontier, the bonds of custom are broken and unrestraint is triumphant. There is not *tabula rasa*. The stubborn American environment is there with its imperious summons to accept its conditions; the inherited ways of doing things are also there; and yet, in spite of environment, and in spite of custom, each frontier did indeed furnish a new field of opportunity, a gate of escape from the bondage of the past; and freshness, and confidence, and scorn of older society, impatience of its restraints and its ideas, and indifference to its lessons, have accompanied the frontier. What the Mediterranean Sea was to the Greeks, breaking the bond of custom, offering new experiences, calling out new institutions and activities, that, and more, the ever retreating frontier has been to the United States directly, and to the nations of Europe more remotely. And now, four centuries from the discovery of America, at the end of a hundred years of life under the Constitution, the frontier has gone, and with its going has closed the first period of American history.

→ CHAPTER TWO ←

THE FIRST OFFICIAL FRONTIER OF THE MASSACHUSETTS BAY

IN THE *SIGNIFICANCE OF THE FRONTIER IN AMERICAN HISTORY*, I TOOK FOR MY text the following announcement of the Superintendent of the Census of 1890:

> Up to and including 1880 the country had a frontier of settlement but at present the unsettled area has been so broken into by isolated bodies of settlement that there can hardly be said to be a frontier line. In the discussion of its extent, the westward movement, etc., it cannot therefore any longer have a place in the census reports.

Two centuries prior to this announcement, in 1690, a committee of the General Court of Massachusetts recommended the Court to order what shall be the frontier and to maintain a committee to settle garrisons on the frontier with forty soldiers to each frontier town as a main guard. In the two hundred years between this official attempt to locate the Massachusetts frontier line, and the official announcement of the ending of the national frontier line, westward expansion was the most important single process in American history.

The designation "frontier town" was not, however, a new one. As early as 1645 inhabitants of Concord, Sudbury, and Dedham, "being inland townes & but thinly peopled," were forbidden to remove without authority; in 1669, certain towns had been the subject of legislation as "frontier towns"; and in the period of King Philip's War there were various enactments regarding frontier towns. In the session of 1675–6 it had been proposed to build a fence of stockades or stone eight feet high from the Charles "where it is navigable" to the Concord at Billerica and thence to the Merrimac and down the river to the Bay, "by which meanes that whole tract will [be] environed, for the security & safty (vnder God) of the people, their houses, goods & cattel; from the rage & fury of the enemy." This project, however, of a kind of Roman Wall did not appeal to the frontiersmen of the time. It was a part of the antiquated ideas of defense which had been illustrated by the impossible equipment of the heavily armored soldier of the early Puritan régime whose corslets and head pieces, pikes, matchlocks, fourquettes and bandoleers, went out of use about the period of King Philip's War. The fifty-seven postures provided in the approved manual of arms for loading and firing the matchlock proved too great a handicap in the chase of the nimble savage. In this era the frontier fighter adapted himself to a more open order, and lighter equipment suggested by the Indian warrior's practice.

The settler on the outskirts of Puritan civilization took up the task of bearing the brunt of attack and pushing forward the line of advance which year after year carried American settlements into the wilderness. In American thought and speech the term "frontier" has come to mean the edge of settlement, rather than, as in Europe, the political boundary. By 1690 it was already evident that the frontier of settlement and the frontier of military defense were coinciding. As population advanced into the wilderness and thus successively brought new exposed areas between the settlements on the one side and the Indians with their European backers on the other, the military frontier ceased to be thought of as the Atlantic coast, but rather as a moving line bounding the un-won wilderness. It could not be a fortified boundary along the charter limits, for those limits extended to the South Sea, and conflicted with the bounds of sister colonies. The thing to be defended was the outer edge of this expanding society, a changing frontier, one that needed designation and restatement with the changing location of the "West."

It will help to illustrate the significance of this new frontier when we see that Virginia at about the same time as Massachusetts underwent a similar change and attempted to establish frontier towns, or "co-habitations," at the "heads," that is the first falls, the vicinity of Richmond, Petersburg, etc., of her rivers.

The Virginia system of "particular plantations" introduced along the James at the close of the London Company's activity had furnished a type for the New England town. In recompense, at this later day the New

England town may have furnished a model for Virginia's efforts to create frontier settlements by legislation.

An act of March 12, 1694–5, by the General Court of Massachusetts enumerated the "Frontier Towns" which the inhabitants were forbidden to desert on pain of loss of their lands (if landholders) or of imprisonment (if not landholders), unless permission to remove were first obtained. These eleven frontier towns included Wells, York, and Kittery on the eastern frontier, and Amesbury, Haverhill, Dunstable, Chelmsford, Groton, Lancaster, Marlborough, and Deerfield. In March 1699–1700 the law was reënacted with the addition of Brookfield, Mendon, and Woodstock, together with seven others, Salisbury, Andover, Billerica, Hatfield, Hadley, Westfield, and Northampton, which, "tho' they be not frontiers as those towns first named, yet lye more open than many others to an attack of an Enemy."

In the spring of 1704 the General Court of Connecticut, following closely the act of Massachusetts, named as her frontier towns, not to be deserted, Symsbury, Waterbury, Danbury, Colchester, Windham, Mansfield, and Plainfield.

Thus about the close of the seventeenth and the beginning of the eighteenth century there was an officially designated frontier line for New England. The line passing through these enumerated towns represents: (1) the outskirts of settlement along the eastern coast and up the Merrimac and its tributaries, a region threatened from the Indian country by way of the Winnepesaukee Lake; (2) the end of the ribbon of settlement up the Connecticut Valley, menaced by the Canadian Indians by way of the Lake Champlain and Winooski River route to the Connecticut; (3) boundary towns which marked the edges of that inferior agricultural region, where the hard crystalline rocks furnished a later foundation for Shays' Rebellion, opposition to the adoption of the federal Constitution, and the abandoned farm; and (4) the isolated intervale of Brookfield which lay intermediate between these frontiers.

Besides this New England frontier there was a belt of settlement in New York, ascending the Hudson to where Albany and Schenectady served as outposts against the Five Nations, who menaced the Mohawk, and against the French and the Canadian Indians, who threatened the Hudson by way of Lake Champlain and Lake George. The sinister relations of leading citizens of Albany engaged in the fur trade with these Indians, even during time of war, tended to protect the Hudson River frontier at the expense of the frontier towns of New England.

The common sequence of frontier types (fur trader, cattle-raising pioneer, small primitive farmer, and the farmer engaged in intensive varied agriculture to produce a surplus for export) had appeared, though confusedly, in New England. The traders and their posts had prepared the way for the frontier towns, and the cattle industry was most important to the early farmers. But the stages succeeded rapidly and intermingled. After King Philip's War, while Albany was still in the fur-trading stage, the New England frontier towns were rather like mark colonies, military-agricultural outposts against the Indian enemy.

The story of the border warfare between Canada and the frontier towns furnishes ample material for studying frontier life and institutions; but I shall not attempt to deal with the narrative of the wars. The palisaded meeting-house square, the fortified isolated garrison houses, the massacres and captivities are familiar features of New England's history. The Indian was a very real influence upon the mind and morals as well as upon the institutions of frontier New England. The occasional instances of Puritans returning from captivity to visit the frontier towns, Catholic in religion, painted and garbed as Indians and speaking the Indian tongue, and the half-breed children of captive Puritan mothers, tell a sensational part of the story; but in the normal, as well as in such exceptional relations of the frontier townsmen to the Indians, there are clear evidences of the transforming influence of the Indian frontier upon the Puritan type of English colonist.

In 1703–4, for example, the General Court of Massachusetts ordered five hundred pairs of snowshoes and an equal number of moccasins for use in specified counties "lying Frontier next to the Wilderness." Connecticut in 1704 after referring to her frontier towns and garrisons ordered that "said company of English and Indians shall, from time to time at the discretion of their chief comander, range the woods to indevour the discovery of an approaching enemy, and in especiall manner from Westfield to Ousatunnuck. . . . And for the incouragement of our forces gone or going against the enemy, this Court will allow out of the publick treasurie the sume of five pounds for every mans scalp of the enemy killed in this Colonie." Massachusetts offered bounties for scalps, varying in amount according to whether the scalp was of men, or women and youths, and whether it was taken by regular forces under pay, volunteers in service, or volunteers without pay. One of the most striking phases of frontier adjustment, was the proposal of the Rev. Solomon Stoddard of Northampton in the fall of 1703, urging the use of dogs "to hunt

Indians as they do Bears." The argument was that the dogs would catch many an Indian who would be too light of foot for the townsmen, nor was it to be thought of as inhuman; for the Indians "act like wolves and are to be dealt with as wolves." In fact Massachusetts passed an act in 1706 for the raising and increasing of dogs for the better security of the frontiers, and both Massachusetts and Connecticut in 1708 paid money from their treasury for the trailing of dogs.

Thus we come to familiar ground: the Massachusetts frontiersman like his western successor hated the Indians; the "tawney serpents," of Cotton Mather's phrase, were to be hunted down and scalped in accord with law and, in at least one instance by the chaplain himself, a Harvard graduate, the hero of the Ballad of Pigwacket, who

> many Indians slew,
> And some of them he scalp'd when bullets round him flew.

Within the area bounded by the frontier line, were the broken fragments of Indians defeated in the era of King Philip's War, restrained within reservations, drunken and degenerate survivors, among whom the missionaries worked with small results, a vexation to the border towns, as they were in the case of later frontiers. Although, as has been said, the frontier towns had scattered garrison houses, and palisaded enclosures similar to the neighborhood forts, or stations, of Kentucky in the Revolution, and of Indiana and Illinois in the War of 1812, one difference is particularly noteworthy. In the case of frontiersmen who came down from Pennsylvania into the Upland South along the eastern edge of the Alleghanies, as well as in the more obvious case of the backwoodsmen of Kentucky and Tennessee, the frontier towns were too isolated from the main settled regions to allow much military protection by the older areas. On the New England frontier, because it was adjacent to the coast towns, this was not the case, and here, as in seventeenth century Virginia, great activity in protecting the frontier was evinced by the colonial authorities, and the frontier towns themselves called loudly for assistance. This phase of frontier defense needs a special study, but at present it is sufficient to recall that the colony sent garrisons to the frontier besides using the militia of the frontier towns; and that it employed rangers to patrol from garrison to garrison.

These were prototypes of the regular army post, and of rangers, dragoons, cavalry and mounted police who have carried the remoter military frontier forward. It is possible to trace this military cordon from New England to the Carolinas early in the eighteenth century, still neighboring the coast; by 1840 it ran from Fort Snelling on the upper Mississippi through various posts to the Sabine boundary of Texas, and so it passed forward until today it lies at the edge of Mexico and the Pacific Ocean.

A few examples of frontier appeals for garrison aid will help to an understanding of the early form of the military frontier. Wells asks, June 30, 1689:

1. That yor Hon^{rs} will please to send us speedily twenty Eight good brisk men that may be serviceable as a guard to us whilest we get in our Harvest of Hay & Corn, (we being unable to Defend ourselves & to Do our work), & also to Persue & destroy the Enemy as occasion may require.
2. That these men may be compleatly furnished with Arms, Amunition & Provision, and that upon the Countrys account, it being a Generall War.

Dunstable, "still weak and unable both to keep our Garrisons and to send out men to get hay for our Cattle; without doeing which wee cannot subsist," petitioned July 23, 1639, for twenty footmen for a month "to scout about the towne while wee get our hay." Otherwise, they say, they must be forced to leave. Still more indicative of this temper is the petition of Lancaster, March 11, 1675–6, to the governor and Council: "As God has made you father over us so you will have a father's pity to us." They asked a guard of men and aid, without which they must leave. Deerfield pled in 1678 to the General Court, "unlest you will be pleased to take us (out of your falherlike pitty) and Cherish us in yor Bosomes we are like Suddainly to breathe out o^r Last Breath."

The perils of the time, the hardships of the frontier towns and readiness of this particular frontier to ask appropriations for losses and wounds, are abundantly illustrated in similar petitions from other towns. One is tempted at times to attribute the very frank self-pity and dependent attitude to a minister's phrasing, and to the desire to secure remission of taxes, the latter a frontier trait more often associated with riot than with religion in other regions.

As an example of various petitions the following from Groton in 1704 is suggestive. Here the minister's hand is probably absent:

1. That wharas by the all dessposing hand of god who orders all things in infinit wisdom it is our portion to liue In such a part of the land which by reson of the enemy Is becom vary dangras as by wofull experiants

we haue falt both formarly and of late to our grat damidg & discoridgment and espashaly this last yere hauing lost so many parsons som killed som captauated and som remoued and allso much corn & cattell and horses & hay wharby wee ar gratly Impouerrished and brought uary low & in a uary pore capasity to subsist any longer As the barers her of can inform your honors.

2. And more then all this our paster mr hobard is & hath been for aboue a yere uncapable of desspansing the ordinances of god amongst us & we haue advised with th Raurant Elders of our nayboring churches and they aduise to hyare another minister and to saport mr hobard and to make our adras to your honors (we haue but litel laft to pay our deus with being so pore and few In numbr ather to town or cuntrey & we being a frantere town & lyable to dangor there being no safty in going out nor coming in but for a long time we haue got our brad with the parel of our liues & allso broght uery low by so grat a charg of bilding garisons & fortefycations by ordur of athorety & thar is saural of our Inhabitants ramoued out of town & others are prouiding to remoue, axcapt somthing be don for our Incoridgment for we are so few & so por that we canot pay two ministors nathar ar we wiling to liue without any we spand so much time in waching and warding that we can doe but litel els & truly we haue liued allmost 2 yers more like soulders then other wise & accapt your honars can find out some bater way for our safty and support we cannot uphold as a town ather by remitting our tax or tow alow pay for building the sauarall forts alowed and ordred by athority or alls to alow the one half of our own Inhabitants to be under pay or to grant liberty for our remufe Into our naiburing towns to tak cer for oursalfs all which if your honors shall se meet to grant you will hereby gratly incoridg your humble pateceners to conflect with th many trubls we are ensadant unto.

Forced together into houses for protection, getting in their crops at the peril of their lives, the frontier townsmen felt it a hardship to contribute also to the taxes of the province while they helped to protect the exposed frontier. In addition there were grievances of absentee proprietors who paid no town taxes and yet profited by the exertions of the frontiersmen; of that I shall speak later.

If we were to trust to these petitions asking favors from the government of the colony, we might impute to these early frontiersmen a degree of submission to authority unlike that of other frontiersmen, and indeed not wholly warranted by the facts. Reading carefully, we find that, however prudently phrased, the petitions are in fact complaints against taxation; demands for expenditures by the colony in their behalf; criticisms of absentee proprietors; intimations that they may be forced to abandon the frontier position so essential to the defense of the settled eastern country.

The spirit of military insubordination characteristic of the frontier is evident in the accounts of these towns, such as Pynchon's in 1694, complaining of the decay of the fortifications at Hatfield, Hadley, and Springfield: "the people a little wilful. Inclined to doe when and how they please or not at all." Saltonstall writes from Haverhill about the same time regarding his ill success in recruiting: "I will never plead for an Haverhill man more," and he begs that some meet person be sent "to tell us what we should, may or must do. I have labored in vain: some go this, and that, and the other way at pleasure, and do what they list." This has a familiar ring to the student of the frontier.

As in the case of the later frontier also, the existence of a common danger on the borders of settlement tended to consolidate not only the towns of Massachusetts into united action for defense, but also the various colonies. The frontier was an incentive to sectional combination then as it was to nationalism afterward. When in 1692 Connecticut sent soldiers from her own colony to aid the Massachusetts towns on the Connecticut River, she showed a realization that the Deerfield people, who were "in a sense in the enemy's Mouth almost," as Pynchon wrote, constituted her own frontier and that the facts of geography were more compelling than arbitrary colonial boundaries. Thereby she also took a step that helped to break down provincial antagonisms. When in 1639 Massachusetts and Connecticut sent agents to Albany to join with New York in making presents to the Indians of that colony in order to engage their aid against the French, they recognized (as their leaders put it) that Albany was "the hinge" of the frontier in this exposed quarter. In thanking Connecticut for the assistance furnished in 1690 Livingston said: "I hope your honors do not look upon Albany as Albany, but as the frontier of your honor's Colony and of all their Majesties countries."

The very essence of the American frontier is that it is the graphic line which records the expansive energies of the people behind it, and which by the law of its own being continually draws that advance after it to new conquests. This is one of the most significant things about New England's frontier in these years. That long bloodstained line of the eastern frontier which skirted the Maine coast was of great importance, for it imparted a western tone to the life and characteristics of the Maine people which endures to this day, and it was one line of advance for New England toward the mouth of the St. Lawrence, leading again and again to diplomatic negotiations with the powers that held that river. The line of the towns that occupied the waters of the Merrimac, tempted the province continually into the wilderness of New Hampshire. The Connecticut river towns pressed steadily up that stream, along its tributaries into the Hoosatonic valleys, and into the valleys between the Green Mountains of Vermont. By the end of 1723, the General Court of Massachusetts enacted—

> That It will be of Great Service to all the western Frontiers, both in this and the Neighboring Government of Conn., to Build a Block House above Northfield, in the most convenient Place on the Lands called the Equivilant Lands, & to post in it forty Able Men, English & western Indians, to be employed in Scouting at a Good Distance up Conn. River, West River, Otter Creek, and sometimes Eastwardly above the Great Manadnuck, for the Discovery of the Enemy Coming towards anny of the frontier Towns.

The "frontier Towns" were preparing to swarm. It was not long before Fort Dummer replaced "the Block House," and the Berkshires and Vermont became new frontiers.

The Hudson River likewise was recognized as another line of advance pointing the way to Lake Champlain and Montreal, calling out demands that protection should be secured by means of an aggressive advance of the frontier. *Canada delenda est* became the rallying cry in New England as well as in New York, and combined diplomatic pressure and military expeditions followed in the French and Indian wars and in the Revolution, in which the children of the Connecticut and Massachusetts frontier towns, acclimated to Indian fighting, followed Ethan Allen and his fellows to the north.

Having touched upon some of the military and expansive tendencies of this first official frontier, let us next turn to its social, economic, and political aspects. How far was this first frontier a field for the investment of eastern capital and for political control by it? Were there evidences of antagonism between the frontier and the settled, property-holding classes of the coast? Restless democracy, resentfulness over taxation and control, and recriminations between the western pioneer and the eastern capitalist, have been characteristic features of other frontiers: were similar phenomena in evidence here? Did "Populistic" tendencies appear in this frontier, and were there grievances which explained these tendencies?

In such colonies as New York and Virginia the land grants were often made to members of the Council and their influential friends, even when there were actual settlers already on the grants. In the case of New England the land system is usually so described as to give the impression that it was based on a non-commercial policy, creating new Puritan towns by free grants of land made in advance to approved settlers. This description does not completely fit the case. That there was an economic interest on the part of absentee proprietors, and that men of political influence with the government were often among the grantees seems also to be true. Melville Egleston states the case thus: "The court was careful not to authorize new plantations unless they were to be in a measure under the influence of men in whom confidence could be placed, and commonly acted upon their application." The frontier, as we shall observe later, was not always disposed to see the practice in so favorable a light.

New towns seem to have been the result in some cases of the aggregation of settlers upon and about a large private grant; more often they resulted from settlers in older towns, where the town limits were extensive, spreading out to the good lands of the outskirts, beyond easy access to the meeting-house, and then asking recognition as a separate town. In some cases they may have been due to squatting on unassigned lands, or purchasing the Indian title and then asking confirmation. In others grants were made in advance of settlement.

As early as 1636 the General Court had ordered that none go to new plantations without leave of a majority of the magistrates. This made the legal situation clear, but it would be dangerous to conclude that it represented the actual situation. In any case there would be a necessity for the settlers finally to secure the assent of the Court. This could be facilitated by a grant to leading men having political influence with the magistrates. The complaints of absentee proprietors which find expression in the frontier petitions of the seventeenth and early eighteenth century seem to indicate that this happened. In the succeeding years of the eighteenth century the grants to leading men and the economic and political motives in the grants are increasingly evident. This whole topic should be made the subject of special study. What is here offered is merely suggestive of a problem.

The frontier settlers criticized the absentee proprietors, who profited by the pioneers' expenditure of labor and blood upon their farms, while they themselves enjoyed security in an eastern town. A few examples from town historians will illustrate this. Among the towns of the Merrimac Valley, Salisbury was planted on the basis of a grant to a dozen proprietors including such men as Mr. Bradstreet and the younger Dudley, only two of whom actually lived and died in Salisbury. Amesbury was set off from Salisbury by division, one half of the signers of the agreement signing by mark. Haverhill was first seated in 1641, following petitions from Mr. Ward, the Ipswich minister, his son-in-law, Giles Firmin, and others. Firmin's letter to Governor Winthrop, in 1640, complains that Ipswich had given him his ground in that town on condition that he should stay in the town three years or else he could not sell it, "whenas others have no business but range from place to place on purpose to live upon the countrey."

Dunstable's large grant was brought about by a combination of leading men who had received grants after the survey of 1652; among such grants was one to the Ancient and Honorable Artillery Company and another to Thomas Brattle of Boston. Apparently it was settled chiefly by others than the original grantees. Groton voted in 1685 to sue the "non-Residenc" to assist in paying the rate, and in 1679 the General Court had ordered non-residents having land at Groton to pay rates for their lands as residents did. Lancaster (Nashaway) was granted to proprietors including various craftsmen in iron, indicating, perhaps, an expectation of iron works, and few of the original proprietors actually settled in the town. The grant of 1653–4 was made by the Court after reciting: (1) that it had ordered in 1647 that the "ordering and disposeing of the Plantation at Nashaway is wholly in the Courts power"; (2) "Considering that there is allredy at Nashaway about nine Families and that severall both freemen and others intend to goe and setle there, some whereof are named in this Petition," etc.

Mendon, begun in 1660 by Braintree people, is a particularly significant example. In 1681 the inhabitants petitioned that while they are not "of the number of those who dwell in their ceiled houses & yet say the time is not come that the Lord's house should be built," yet they have gone outside of their strength "unless others who are proprietors as well as ourselves, (the price of whose lands is much raysed by our carrying on public work & will be nothing worth if we are forced to quit the place) doo beare an equal share in Town charges with us. Those who are not yet come up to us are a great and far yet abler part of our Proprietors. . . ." In 1684 the selectmen inform the General Court that one half of proprietors, two only excepted, are dwelling in other places, "Our proprietors, abroad," say they, "object that they see no reason why they should pay as much for thayer lands as we do for our Land and stock, which we answer that if their be not a noff of reason for it, we are sure there is more than enough of necessity to supply that is wanting in reason." This is the authentic voice of the frontier.

Deerfield furnishes another type, inasmuch as a considerable part of its land was first held by Dedham, to which the grant was made as a recompense for the location of the Natick Indian reservation. Dedham shares in the town often fell into the hands of speculators, and Sheldon, the careful historian of Deerfield, declares that not a single Dedham man became a permanent resident of the grant. In 1678 Deerfield petitioned the General Court as follows:

> You may be pleased to know that the very principle & best of the land; the best for soile; the best for situation; as lying in ye center & midle of the town: & as to quantity, nere half, belongs unto eight or nine proprietors each and every of which, are never like to come to a settlement amongst us, which we have formerly found grievous & doe Judge for the future will be found intollerable if not altered. O^r minister, Mr. Mather . . . & we ourselves are much discouraged as judging the Plantation will be spoiled if thes proprietors may not be begged, or will not be bought up on very easy terms outt of their Right. . . . Butt as long as the maine of the plantation Lies in men's hands that can't improve it themselves, neither are ever like to putt such tenants on to it as shall be likely to advance the good of ye place in Civill or sacred Respects; he, ourselves, and all others that think of going to it, are much discouraged.

Woodstock, later a Connecticut town, was settled under a grant in the Nipmuc country made to the town of Roxbury. The settlers, who located their farms near the trading post about which the Indians still collected, were called the "go-ers," while the "stayers" were those who remained in Roxbury, and retained half of the new grant; but it should be added that they paid the go-ers a sum of money to facilitate the settlement.

This absentee proprietorship and the commercial attitude toward the lands of new towns became more evident in succeeding years of the eighteenth century. Leicester, for example, was confirmed by the General Court in 1713. The twenty shares were divided among twenty-two proprietors, including Jeremiah Dummer, Paul Dudley (Attorney-General),

William Dudley (like Paul a son of the Governor, Joseph Dudley), Thomas Hutchinson (father of the later governor), John Clark (the political leader), and Samuel Sewall (son of the Chief Justice). These were all men of influence, and none of the proprietors became inhabitants of Leicester. The proprietors tried to induce the fifty families, whose settlement was one of the conditions on which the grant was made, to occupy the eastern half of the township reserving the rest as their absolute property.

The author of a currency tract, in 1716, entitled *Some Considerations upon the Several Sorts of Banks*, remarks that formerly, when land was easy to be obtained, good men came over as indentured servants; but now, he says, they are runaways, thieves, and disorderly persons. The remedy for this, in his opinion, would be to induce servants to come over by offering them homes when the terms of indenture should expire. He therefore advocates that townships should be laid out four or five miles square in which grants of fifty or sixty acres could be made to servants. Concern over the increase of Negro slaves in Massachusetts seems to have been the reason for this proposal. It indicates that the current practice in disposing of the lands did not provide for the poorer people.

But Massachusetts did not follow this suggestion of a homestead policy. On the contrary, the desire to locate towns to create continuous lines of settlement along the roads between the disconnected frontiers and to protect boundary claims by granting tiers of towns in the disputed tract, as well, no doubt, as pressure from financial interests, led the General Court between 1715 and 1762 to dispose of the remaining public domain of Massachusetts under conditions that made speculation and colonization by capitalists important factors. When in 1762 Massachusetts sold a group of townships in the Berkshires to the highest bidders (by whole townships), the transfer from the social-religious to the economic conception was complete, and the frontier was deeply influenced by the change to "land mongering."

In one respect, however, there was an increasing recognition of the religious and social element in settling the frontier, due in part, no doubt, to a desire to provide for the preservation of eastern ideals and influences in the West. Provisions for reserving lands within the granted townships for the support of an approved minister, and for schools, appear in the seventeenth century and become a common feature of the grants for frontier towns in the eighteenth. This practice with respect to the New England frontier became the foundation for the system of grants of land from the public domain for the support of common schools and state universities by the federal government from its beginning, and has been profoundly influential in later western states.

Another ground for discontent over land questions was furnished by the system of granting lands within the town by the commoners. The principle which in many, if not all, cases guided the proprietors in distributing the town lots is familiar and is well stated in the Lancaster town records (1653):

> And, whereas Lotts are Now Laid out for the most part Equally to Rich and poore, Partly to keepe the Towne from Scatering to farr, and partly out of Charitie and Respect to men of meaner estate, yet that Equallitie (which is the rule of God) may be observed, we Covenant and Agree, That in a second Devition and so through all other Devitions of Land the mater shall be drawne as neere to *equallitie according to mens estates* as wee are able to doe, That he which hath now more then his estate Deserveth in home Lotts and entervale Lotts shall haue so much Less: and he that hath Less then his estate Deserveth shall haue so much more.

This peculiar doctrine of "equality" had early in the history of the colony created discontents. Winthrop explained the principle which governed himself and his colleagues in the case of the Boston committee of 1634 by saying that their divisions were arranged "partly to prevent the neglect of trades." This is a pregnant idea; it underlay much of the later opposition of New England as a manufacturing section to the free homestead or cheap land policy, demanded by the West and by the labor party, in the national public domain. The migration of labor to free lands meant that higher wages must be paid to those who remained. The use of the town lands by the established classes to promote an approved form of society naturally must have had some effect on migration.

But a more effective source of disputes was with respect to the relation of the town proprietors to the public domain of the town in contrast with the non-proprietors as a class. The need of keeping the town meeting and the proprietors' meeting separate in the old towns in earlier years was not so great as it was when the newcomers became numerous. In an increasing degree these newcomers were either not granted lands at all, or were not admitted to the body of proprietors with rights in the possession of the undivided town lands. Contentions on the part of the town meeting that it had the right of dealing with the town lands occasionally appear, significantly, in the frontier towns of Haverhill, Massachusetts, Simsbury, Connecticut, and in the towns of the Connecticut Valley. Jonathan Edwards, in 1751, declared that there had been in Northampton for forty or fifty years "two parties somewhat like the court and country parties of England. . . . The first party embraced the great proprietors of land, and the parties concerned about land and other matters." The tendency to divide up the common lands among the proprietors in individual possession did not become marked until the eighteenth century; but the exclusion of some from possession of the town lands and the "equality" in allotment favoring men with already large estates must have attracted ambitious men who were not of the favored class to join in the movement to new towns. Religious dissensions would combine to make frontier society as it formed early in the eighteenth century more and more democratic, dissatisfied with the existing order, and less respectful of authority. We shall not understand the relative radicalism of parts of the Berkshires, Vermont and interior New Hampshire without enquiry into the degree in which the control over the lands by a proprietary monopoly affected the men who settled on the frontier.

The final aspect of this frontier to be examined, is the attitude of the conservatives of the older sections towards this movement of westward advance. President Dwight in the era of the War of 1812 was very critical of the "foresters," but saw in such a movement a safety valve to the institutions of New England by allowing the escape of the explosive advocates of "Innovation."

Cotton Mather is perhaps not a typical representative of the conservative sentiment at the close of the seventeenth century, but his writings may partly reflect the attitude of Boston Bay toward New England's first western frontier. Writing in 1694 of "Wonderful Passages which have Occurred, First in the Protections and then in the Afflictions of New England," he says:

> One while the Enclosing of *Commons* hath made Neighbors, that should have been like Sheep, to *Bite and devour one another*. . . . Again, Do our *Old* People, any of them *Go Out* from the Institutions of God, Swarming into New Settlements, where they and their Untaught Families are like to *Perish for Lack of Vision?* They that have done so, heretofore, have to their Cost found, that they were got unto the *Wrong side of the Hedge*, in their doing so. Think, here *Should this be done any more?* We read of Balaam, in Num. 22, 23.

He was to his Damage, *driven to the* Wall, when he would needs make an unlawful Salley forth after the *Gain* of this World. . . . Why, when men, for the Sake of Earthly Gain, would be *going out* into the *Warm* Sun, they drive *Through the Wall,* and the *Angel of the Lord* becomes their Enemy.

In his essay on *Frontiers Well-Defended* (1707) Mather assures the pioneers that they "dwell in a Hatsarmaneth," a place of "tawney serpents," are "inhabitants of the Valley of Achor," and are "the Poor of this World." There may be significance in his assertion: "It is remarkable to see that when the Unchurched Villages, have been so many of them, *utterly broken up,* in the *War,* that has been upon us, those that have had *Churches* regularly formed in them, have generally been under a more *sensible Protection* of Heaven." "Sirs," he says, "a *Church-State* well form'd may fortify you wonderfully!" He recommends abstention from profane swearing, furious cursing, Sabbath breaking, unchastity, dishonesty, robbing of God by defrauding the ministers of their dues, drunkenness, and revels and he reminds them that even the Indians have family prayers! Like his successors who solicited missionary contributions for the salvation of the frontier in the Mississippi Valley during the forties of the nineteenth century, this early spokesman for New England laid stress upon teaching anti-popery, particularly in view of the captivity that might await them.

In summing up, we find many of the traits of later frontiers in this early prototype, the Massachusetts frontier. It lies at the edge of the Indian country and tends to advance. It calls out militant qualities and reveals the imprint of wilderness conditions upon the psychology and morals as well as upon the institutions of the people. It demands common defense and thus becomes a factor for consolidation. It is built on the basis of a preliminary fur trade, and is settled by the combined and sometimes antagonistic forces of eastern men of property (the absentee proprietors) and the democratic pioneers. The East attempted to regulate and control it. Individualistic and democratic tendencies were emphasized both by the wilderness conditions and, probably, by the prior contentions between the proprietors and non-proprietors of the towns from which settlers moved to the frontier. Removal away from the control of the customary usages of the older communities and from the conservative influence of the body of the clergy, increased the innovating tendency. Finally the towns were regarded by at least one prominent representative of the established order in the East, as an undesirable place for the relocation of the pillars of society. The temptation to look upon the frontier as a field for investment was viewed by the clergy as a danger to the "institutions of God." The frontier was "the Wrong side of the Hedge."

But to this "wrong side of the hedge" New England men continued to migrate. The frontier towns of 1695 were hardly more than suburbs of Boston. The frontier of a century later included New England's colonies in Vermont, western New York, the Wyoming Valley, the Connecticut Reserve, and the Ohio Company's settlement in the Old Northwest Territory. By the time of the Civil War the frontier towns of New England had occupied the great prairie zone of the Middle West and were even planted in Mormon Utah and in parts of the Pacific Coast. New England's sons had become the organizers of a Greater New England in the West, captains of industry, political leaders, founders of educational systems, and prophets of religion, in a section that was to influence the ideals and shape the destiny of the nation in ways to which the eyes of men like Cotton Mather were sealed.

→ CHAPTER THREE ←

THE OLD WEST

IT IS NOT THE OLDEST WEST WITH WHICH THIS CHAPTER DEALS. THE oldest West was the Atlantic coast. Roughly speaking, it took a century of Indian fighting and forest felling for the colonial settlements to expand into the interior to a distance of about a hundred miles from the coast. Indeed, some stretches were hardly touched in that period. This conquest of the nearest wilderness in the course of the seventeenth century and in the early years of the eighteenth, gave control of the maritime section of the nation and made way for the new movement of westward expansion which I propose to discuss.

In his *Winning of the West*, Roosevelt dealt chiefly with the region beyond the Alleghanies, and with the period of the later eighteenth century, although he prefaced his account with an excellent chapter describing the backwoodsmen of the Alleghanies and their social conditions from 1769 to 1774. It is important to notice, however, that he is concerned with a backwoods society already formed; that he ignores the New England frontier and its part in the winning of the West, and does not recognize that there was a West to be won between New England and the Great Lakes. In short, he is interested in the winning of the West beyond the Alleghanies by the southern half of the frontier folk.

There is, then, a western area intermediate between the coastal colonial settlements of the seventeenth century and the trans-Alleghany settlements of the latter portion of the eighteenth century. This section I propose to isolate and discuss under the name of the Old West, and in the period from about 1676 to 1763. It includes the back country of New England, the Mohawk Valley, the Great Valley of Pennsylvania, the

Shenandoah Valley, and the Piedmont—that is, the interior or upland portion of the South, lying between the Alleghanies and the head of navigation of the Atlantic rivers marked by the "fall line."

In this region, and in these years, are to be found the beginnings of much that is characteristic in western society, for the Atlantic coast was in such close touch with Europe that its frontier experience was soon counteracted, and it developed along other lines. It is unfortunate that the colonial back country appealed so long to historians solely in connection with the colonial wars, for the development of its society, its institutions and mental attitude all need study. Its history has been dealt with in separate fragments, by states, or towns, or in discussions of special phases, such as German and Scotch-Irish immigration. The Old West as a whole can be appreciated only by obliterating the state boundaries which conceal its unity, by correlating the special and fragmentary studies, and by filling the gaps in the material for understanding the formation of its society. The present paper is rather a reconnaissance than a conquest of the field, a program for study of the Old West rather than an exposition of it.

The end of the period proposed may be placed about 1763, and the beginning between 1676 and 1700. The termination of the period is marked by the Peace of Paris in 1763, and the royal proclamation of that year forbidding settlement beyond the Alleghanies. By this time the settlement of the Old West was fairly accomplished, and new advances were soon made into the "Western Waters" beyond the mountains and into the interior of Vermont and New Hampshire. The isolation of the transmontane settlements, and the special conditions and doctrines of the Revolutionary era during which they were formed, make a natural distinction between the period of which I am to speak and the later extension of the West.

The beginning of the period is necessarily an indeterminate date, owing to the different times of colonizing the coastal areas which served as bases of operations in the westward advance. The most active movements into the Old West occurred after 1730. But in 1676 New England, having closed the exhausting struggle with the Indians, known as King Philip's War, could regard her established settlements as secure, and go on to complete her possession of the interior. This she did in the midst of conflicts with the exterior Indian tribes which invaded her frontiers from New York and Canada during the French and Indian wars from 1690 to 1760, and under frontier conditions different from the conditions of the earlier Puritan colonization. In 1676, Virginia was passing through Indian fighting—keenest along the fall line, where the frontier lay—and also experiencing a social revolt which resulted in the defeat of the democratic forces that sought to stay the progress of aristocratic control in the colony. The date marks the end of the period when the Virginia tidewater could itself be regarded as a frontier region, and consequently the beginning of a more special interest in the interior.

Let us first examine the northern part of the movement into the back country. The expansion of New England into the vacant spaces of its own section, in the period we have chosen for discussion, resulted in the formation of an interior society which contrasted in many ways with that of the coast, and which has a special significance in western history, in that it was this interior New England people who settled the Greater New England in central and western New York, the Wyoming Valley, the Connecticut Reserve of Ohio, and much of the prairie areas of the Old Northwest. It is important to realize that the Old West included interior New England.

The situation in New England at the close of the seventeenth century is indicated by the Massachusetts act of 1694 enumerating eleven towns, then on the frontier and exposed to raids, none of which might be voluntarily deserted without leave of the governor and council, on penalty of loss of their freeholds by the landowners, or fine of other inhabitants.

Thus these frontier settlers were made substantially garrisons, or "mark colonies." Crowded into the palisades of the town, and obliged in spite of their poverty to bear the brunt of Indian attack, their hardships are illustrated in the manly but pathetic letters of Deerfield's minister, Mr. Williams, in 1704. Parkman succinctly describes the general conditions in these words:

> The exposed frontier of New England was between two and three hundred miles long, and consisted of farms and hamlets loosely scattered through an almost impervious forest. . . . Even in so-called villages the houses were far apart, because, except on the seashore, the people lived by farming. Such as were able to do so fenced their dwellings with palisades, or built them of solid timber, with loopholes, a projecting upper story like a block house, and sometimes a flanker at one or more of the corners. In the more considerable settlements the largest of these fortified houses was occupied in time of danger by armed men and served as a place of refuge for the neighbors.

Into these places, in days of alarm, were crowded the outlying settlers, just as was the case in later times in the Kentucky "stations."

In spite of such frontier conditions, the outlying towns continued to multiply. Between 1720 and the middle of the century, settlement crept up the Housatonic and its lateral valley into the Berkshires. About 1720 Litchfield was established; in 1725, Sheffield; in 1730, Great Barrington; and in 1735 a road was cut and towns soon established between Westfield and these Housatonic settlements, thus uniting them with the older extensions along the Connecticut and its tributaries.

In this period, scattered and sometimes unwelcome Scotch-Irish settlements were established, such as that at Londonderry, New Hampshire, and in the Berkshires, as well as in the region won in King Philip's War from the Nipmucks, whither there came also Huguenots.

In King George's War, the Connecticut River settlers found their frontier protection in such rude stockades as those at the sites of Keene, of Charlestown, New Hampshire (Number Four), Fort Shirley at the head of Deerfield River (Heath), and Fort Pelham (Rowe); while Fort Massachusetts (Adams) guarded the Hoosac gateway to the Hoosatonic Valley. These frontier garrisons and the self-defense of the backwoodsmen of New England are well portrayed in the pages of Parkman. At the close of the war, settlement again expanded into the Berkshires, where Lennox, West Hoosac (Williamstown), and Pittsfield were established in the middle of the century. Checked by the fighting in the last French and Indian War, the frontier went forward after the Peace of Paris (1763) at an exceptional rate, especially into Vermont and interior New Hampshire. An anonymous writer gives a contemporary view of the situation on the eve of the Revolution:

> The richest parts remaining to be granted are on the northern branches of the Connecticut river, towards Crown Point where are great districts of fertile soil still unsettled. The North part of New Hampshire, the province of Maine, and the territory of Sagadahock have but few settlements in them compared with the tracts yet unsettled. . . .
>
> I should further observe that these tracts have since the peace [i.e., 1763], been settling pretty fast: farms on the river Connecticut are every day extending beyond the old fort Dummer, for near thirty miles; and will in a few years reach to Kohasser which is nearly two hundred miles; not that such an extent will be one-tenth

settled, but the newcomers do not fix near their neighbors, and go on regularly, but take spots that please them best, though twenty or thirty miles beyond any others. This to people of a sociable disposition in Europe would appear very strange, but the Americans do not regard the near neighborhood of other farmers; twenty or thirty miles by water they esteem no distance in matters of this sort; besides in a country that promises well the intermediate space is not long in filling up. Between Connecticut river and Lake Champlain upon Otter Creek, and all along Lake Sacrament [George] and the rivers that fall into it, and the whole length of Wood Creek, are numerous settlements made since the peace.

For nearly a hundred years, therefore, New England communities had been pushed out to new frontiers in the intervals between the almost continuous wars with the French and Indians. Probably the most distinctive feature in this frontier was the importance of the community type of settlement; in other words, of the towns, with their Puritan ideals in education, morals, and religion. This has always been a matter of pride to the statesmen and annalists of New England, as is illustrated by these words of Holland in his *Western Massachusetts*, commenting on the settlement of the Connecticut Valley in villages, whereby in his judgment morality, education, and urbanity were preserved:

The influence of this policy can only be fully appreciated when standing by the side of the solitary settler's hut in the West, where even an eastern man has degenerated to a boor in manners, where his children have grown up uneducated, and where the Sabbath has become an unknown day, and religion and its obligations have ceased to exercise control upon the heart and life.

Whatever may be the real value of the community type of settlement, its establishment in New England was intimately connected both with the Congregational religious organization and with the land system of the colonies of that section, under which the colonial governments made grants—not in tracts to individuals, but in townships to groups of proprietors who in turn assigned lands to the inhabitants without cost. The typical form of establishing a town was as follows: On application of an approved body of men, desiring to establish a new settlement, the colonial General Court would appoint a committee to view the desired land and report on its fitness; an order for the grant would then issue, in varying areas, not far from the equivalent of six miles square. In the eighteenth century especially, it was common to reserve certain lots of the town for the support of schools and the ministry. This was the origin of that very important feature of western society, federal land grants for schools and colleges. The General Courts also made regulations regarding the common lands, the terms for admitting inhabitants, etc., and thus kept a firm hand upon the social structure of the new settlements as they formed on the frontier.

This practice, seen in its purity in the seventeenth century especially, was markedly different from the practices of other colonies in the settlement of their back lands. For during most of the period New England did not use her wild lands, or public domain, as a source of revenue by sale to individuals or to companies, with the reservation of quit-rents; nor attract individual settlers by "head rights," or fifty-acre grants, after the Virginia type; nor did the colonies of the New England group often make extensive grants to individuals, on the ground of special services, or because of influence with the government, or on the theory that the grantee would introduce settlers on his grant. They donated their lands to groups of men who became town proprietors for the purpose of establishing communities. These proprietors were supposed to hold the lands in trust, to be assigned to inhabitants under restraints to ensure the persistence of Puritan ideals.

During most of the seventeenth century the proprietors awarded lands to the newcomers in accordance with this theory. But as density of settlement increased, and lands grew scarce in the older towns, the proprietors began to assert their legal right to the unoccupied lands and to refuse to share them with inhabitants who were not of the body of proprietors. The distinction resulted in class conflicts in the towns, especially in the eighteenth century, over the ownership and disposal of the common lands.

The new settlements, by a process of natural selection, would afford opportunity to the least contented, whether because of grievances, or ambitions, to establish themselves. This tended to produce a western flavor in the towns on the frontier. But it was not until the original ideals of the land system began to change, that the opportunity to make new settlements for such reasons became common. As the economic and political ideal replaced the religious and social ideal, in the conditions under which new towns could be established, this became more possible.

Such a change was in progress in the latter part of the seventeenth century and during the eighteenth. In 1713, 1715, and 1727, Massachusetts determined upon a policy of locating towns in advance of settlement, to protect her boundary claims. In 1736 she laid out five towns near the New Hampshire border, and a year earlier opened four contiguous towns to connect her Housatonic and Connecticut Valley settlements. Grants in non-adjacent regions were sometimes made to old towns, the proprietors of which sold them to those who wished to move.

The history of the town of Litchfield illustrates the increasing importance of the economic factor. At a time when Connecticut feared that Andros might dispose of the public lands to the disadvantage of the colony, the legislature granted a large part of western Connecticut to the towns of Hartford and Windsor, *pro forma*, as a means of withdrawing the lands from his hands. But these towns refused to give up the lands after the danger had passed, and proceeded to sell part of them. Riots occurred when the colonial authorities attempted to assert possession, and the matter was at length compromised in 1719 by allowing Litchfield to be settled in accordance with the town grants, while the colony reserved the larger part of northwestern Connecticut. In 1737 the colony disposed of its last unlocated lands by sale in lots. In 1762 Massachusetts sold a group of entire townships in the Berkshires to the highest bidders.

But the most striking illustration of the tendency, is afforded by the "New Hampshire grants" of Governor Wentworth, who, chiefly in the years about 1760, made grants of a hundred and thirty towns west of the Connecticut, in what is now the state of Vermont, but which was then in dispute between New Hampshire and New York. These grants, while in form much like other town grants, were disposed of for cash, chiefly to speculators who hastened to sell their rights to the throngs of land-seekers who, after the peace, began to pour into the Green Mountain region.

It is needless to point out how this would affect the movement of western settlement in respect to individualistic speculation in public lands; how it would open a career to the land jobbers, as well as to the natural leaders in the competitive movement for acquiring the best lands, for laying out town sites and building up new communities under "boom" conditions. The migratory tendency of New Englanders was increased by this gradual change in its land policy; the attachment to a locality was diminished. The later years showed increasing emphasis by New England upon individual success, greater respect for the self-made man who, in the midst of opportunities under competitive conditions, achieved superiority. The old dominance of town settlement, village moral police, and traditional class control gave way slowly. Settlement in communities and rooted

Puritan habits and ideals had enduring influences in the regions settled by New Englanders; but it was in this Old West, in the years just before the Revolution, that individualism began to play an important rôle, along with the traditional habit of expanding in organized communities.

The opening of the Vermont towns revealed more fully than before, the capability of New Englanders to become democratic pioneers, under characteristic frontier conditions. Their economic life was simple and self-sufficing. They readily adopted lynch law (the use of the "birch seal" is familiar to readers of Vermont history) to protect their land titles in the troubled times when these "Green Mountain Boys" resisted New York's assertion of authority. They later became an independent Revolutionary state with frontier directness, and in very many respects their history in the Revolutionary epoch is similar to that of settlers in Kentucky and Tennessee, both in assertion of the right to independent self government and in a frontier separatism. Vermont may be regarded as the culmination of the frontier movement which I have been describing in New England.

By this time two distinct New Englands existed—the one coastal, and dominated by commercial interests and the established congregational churches; the other a primitive agricultural area, democratic in principle, and with various sects increasingly indifferent to the fear of "innovation" which the dominant classes of the old communities felt. Already speculative land companies had begun New England settlements in the Wyoming Valley of Pennsylvania, as well as on the lower Mississippi; and New England missions among the Indians, such as that at Stockbridge, were beginning the noteworthy religious and educational expansion of the section to the west.

That this movement of expansion had been chiefly from south to north, along the river valleys, should not conceal from us the fact that it was in essential characteristics a western movement, especially in the social traits that were developing. Even the men who lived in the long line of settlements on the Maine coast, under frontier conditions, and remote from the older centers of New England, developed traits and a democratic spirit that relate them closely to the westerners, in spite of the fact that Maine is "down east" by preëminence.

The frontier of the Middle region in this period of the formation of the Old West, was divided into two parts, which happen to coincide with the colonies of New York and Pennsylvania. In the latter colony the trend of settlement was into the Great Valley, and so on to the southern uplands; while the advance of settlement in New York was like that of New England, chiefly northward, following the line of Hudson River.

The Hudson and the Mohawk constituted the area of the Old West in this part of the eighteenth century. With them were associated the Wallkill, tributary to the Hudson, and Cherry Valley near the Mohawk, along the sources of the Susquehanna. The Berkshires walled the Hudson in to the east; the Adirondacks and the Catskills to the west. Where the Mohawk Valley penetrated between the mountainous areas, the Iroquois Indians were too formidable for advance on such a slender line. Nothing but dense settlement along the narrow strip of the Hudson, if even that, could have furnished the necessary momentum for overcoming the Indian barrier; and this pressure was lacking, for the population was comparatively sparse in contrast with the task to be performed. What most needs discussion in the case of New York, therefore, is not the history of expansion as in other sections, but the absence of expansive power.

The fur-trade had led the way up the Hudson, and made beginnings of settlements at strategic points near the confluence of the Mohawk. But the fur-trader was not followed by a tide of pioneers. One of the most important factors in restraining density of population in New York, in retarding the settlement of its frontier, and in determining the conditions there, was the land system of that colony.

From the time of the patroon grants along the lower Hudson, great estates had been the common form of land tenure. Rensselaerswyck reached at one time over seven hundred thousand acres. These great patroon estates were confirmed by the English governors, who in their turn followed a similar policy. By 1732 two and one-half million acres were engrossed in manorial grants. In 1764, Governor Colden wrote that three of the extravagant grants contain,

> . . . as the proprietors claim, above a million acres each, several others above 200,000. * * * Although these grants contain a great part of the province, they are made in trifling acknowledgements. The far greater part of them still remain uncultivated, without any benefit to the community, and are likewise a discouragement to the settling and improving the lands in the neighborhood of them, for from the uncertainty of their boundaries, the patentees of these great tracts are daily enlarging their pretensions, and by tedious and most expensive law suits, distress and ruin poor families who have taken out grants near them.

He adds that "the proprietors of the great tracts are not only freed from the quit-rents, which the other landholders in the province pay, but by their influence in the assembly are freed from every other public tax on their lands."

In 1769 it was estimated that at least five-sixths of the inhabitants of Westchester County lived within the bounds of the great manors there. In Albany County the Livingston manor spread over seven modern townships, and the great Van Rensselaer manor stretched twenty-four by twenty-eight miles along the Hudson; while still farther, on the Mohawk, were the vast possessions of Sir William Johnson.

It was not simply that the grants were extensive, but that the policy of the proprietors favored the leasing rather than the sale of the lands—frequently also of the stock, and taking payment in shares. It followed that settlers preferred to go to frontiers where a more liberal land policy prevailed. At one time it seemed possible that the tide of German settlement, which finally sought Pennsylvania and the up-country of the South, might flow into New York. In 1710, Governor Hunter purchased a tract in Livingston's manor and located nearly fifteen hundred Palatines on it to produce naval stores. But the attempt soon failed; the Germans applied to the Indians on Schoharie Creek, a branch of the Mohawk, for a grant of land and migrated there, only to find that the governor had already granted the land. Again were the villages broken up, some remaining and some moving farther up the Mohawk, where they and accessions to their number established the frontier settlements about Palatine Bridge, in the region where, in the Revolution, Herkimer led these German frontiersmen to stem the British attack in the battle of Oriskany. They constituted the most effective military defense of Mohawk Valley. Still another portion took their way across to the waters of the Susquehanna, and at Tulpehockon Creek began an important center of German settlement in the Great Valley of Pennsylvania.

The most important aspect of the history of the movement into the frontier of New York at this period, therefore, was the evidence which it afforded that in the competition for settlement between colonies possessing a vast area of vacant land, those which imposed feudal tenures and undemocratic restraints, and which exploited settlers, were certain to lose.

The manorial practice gave a bad name to New York as a region for settlement, which not even the actual opportunities in certain parts of the colony could counteract. The diplomacy of New York governors during this period of the Old West, in securing a protectorate over the Six Nations and a consequent claim to their territory, and in holding them aloof from France, constituted the most effective contribution of that colony to the movement of American expansion. When lands of these tribes were obtained after Sullivan's expedition in the Revolution (in which New England soldiers played a prominent part), it was by the New England inundation into this interior that they were colonized. And it was under conditions like those prevailing in the later years of the expansion of settlements in New England itself, that this settlement of interior and western New York was effected.

The result was, that New York became divided into two distinct peoples: the dwellers along Hudson Valley, and the Yankee pioneers of the interior. But the settlement of central and western New York, like the settlement of Vermont, is a story that belongs to the era in which the trans-Alleghany West was occupied.

We can best consider the settlement of the share of the Old West which is located in Pennsylvania as a part of the migration which occupied the southern Uplands, and before entering upon this it will be advantageous to survey that part of the movement toward the interior which proceeded westward from the coast. First let us observe the conditions at the eastern edge of these uplands, along the fall line in Virginia, in the latter part of the seventeenth century, in order that the process and the significance of the movement may be better understood.

About the time of Bacon's Rebellion, in Virginia, strenuous efforts were made to protect the frontier line which ran along the falls of the river, against the attacks of Indians. This "fall line," as the geographers call it, marking the head of navigation, and thus the boundary of the maritime or lowland South, runs from the site of Washington, through Richmond, and on to Raleigh, North Carolina, and Columbia, South Carolina. Virginia having earliest advanced thus far to the interior, found it necessary in the closing years of the seventeenth century to draw a military frontier along this line. As early as 1675 a statute was enacted, providing that paid troops of five hundred men should be drawn from the midland and most secure parts of the country and placed on the "heads of the rivers" and other places fronting upon the Indians. What was meant by the "heads of the rivers," is shown by the fact that several of these forts were located either at the falls of the rivers or just above tidewater, as follows: one on the lower Potomac in Stafford County; one near the falls of the Rappahannock; one on the Mattapony; one on the Pamunky; one at the falls of the

James (near the site of Richmond); one near the falls of the Appomattox, and others on the Blackwater, the Nansemond, and the Accomac peninsula, all in the eastern part of Virginia.

Again, in 1679, similar provision was made, and an especially interesting act was passed, making *quasi* manorial grants to Major Lawrence Smith and Captain William Byrd, "to seate certain lands at the head [falls] of Rappahannock and James river" respectively. This scheme failed for lack of approval by the authorities in England. But Byrd at the falls of the James near the present site of Richmond, Robert Beverley on the Rappahannock, and other frontier commanders on the York and Potomac, continued to undertake colonial defense. The system of mounted rangers was established in 1691, by which a lieutenant, eleven soldiers, and two Indians at the "heads" or falls of each great river were to scout for enemy, and the Indian boundary line was strictly defined.

By the opening years of the eighteenth century (1701), the assembly of Virginia had reached the conclusion that settlement would be the best means of protecting the frontiers, and that the best way of "settling in cohabitations upon the said land frontiers within this government will be by encouragements to induce societies of men to undertake the same." It was declared to be inexpedient to have less than twenty fighting men in each "society," and provision was made for a land grant to be given to these societies (or towns) not less than 10,000 nor more than 30,000 acres upon any of the frontiers, to be held in common by the society. The power of ordering and managing these lands, and the settling and planting of them, was to remain in the society. Virginia was to pay the cost of survey, also quit-rents for the first twenty years for the two-hundred-acre tract as the site of the "co-habitation." Within this two hundred acres each member was to have a half-acre lot for living upon, and a right to two hundred acres next adjacent, until the thirty thousand acres were taken up. The members of the society were exempt from taxes for twenty years, and from the requirements of military duty except such as they imposed upon themselves. The resemblance to the New England town is obvious.

"Provided alwayes," ran the quaint statute,

> . . . and it is the true intent and meaning of this act that for every five hundred acres of land to be granted in pursuance of this act there shall be and shall be continually kept upon the said land one christian man between sixteen and sixty years of age perfect of limb, able and fitt for service who shall alsoe be continually

provided with a well fixed musquett or fuzee, a good pistoll, sharp simeter, tomahawk and five pounds of good clean pistoll powder and twenty pounds of sizable leaden bullets or swan or goose shott to be kept within the fort directed by this act besides the powder and shott for his necessary or useful shooting at game. Provided also that the said warlike christian man shall have his dwelling and continual abode within the space of two hundred acres of land to be laid out in a geometricall square or as near that figure as conveniency will admit, etc.

Within two years the society was required to cause a half acre in the middle of the "co-habitation" to be palisaded "with good sound pallisadoes at least thirteen foot long and six inches diameter in the middle of the length thereof, and set double and at least three foot within the ground."

Such in 1701 was the idea of the Virginia tidewater assembly of a frontiersman, and of the frontier towns by which the Old Dominion should spread her population into the upland South. But the "warlike christian man" who actually came to furnish the firing line for Virginia, was destined to be the Scotch-Irishman and the German with long rifle in place of "fuzee" and "simeter," and altogether too restless to have his continual abode within the space of two hundred acres. Nevertheless there are points of resemblance between this idea of societies settled about a fortified town and the later "stations" of Kentucky.

By the beginning of the eighteenth century the engrossing of the lands of lowland Virginia had progressed so far, the practice of holding large tracts of wasteland for reserves in the great plantations had become so common, that the authorities of Virginia reported to the home government that the best lands were all taken up, and settlers were passing into North Carolina seeking cheap lands near navigable rivers. Attention was directed also to the Piedmont portions of Virginia, for by this time the Indians were conquered in this region. It was now possible to acquire land by purchase at five shillings sterling for fifty acres, as well as by head-rights for importation or settlement, and land speculation soon turned to the new area.

Already the Piedmont had been somewhat explored. Even by the middle of the seventeenth century, fur-traders had followed the trail southwest from the James more than four hundred miles to the Catawbas and later to the Cherokees. Col. William Byrd had, as we have seen, not only been absorbing good lands in the lowlands, and defending his post at the falls of the James, like a Count of the Border, but he also engaged in this fur-trade and sent his pack trains along this trail through the Piedmont of the Carolinas, and took note of the rich savannas of that region. Charleston traders engaged in rivalry for this trade.

It was not long before cattle raisers from the older settlements, learning from the traders of the fertile plains and pea-vine pastures of this land, followed the fur-traders and erected scattered "cow-pens" or ranches beyond the line of plantations in the Piedmont. Even at the close of the seventeenth century, herds of wild horses and cattle ranged at the outskirts of the Virginia settlements, and were hunted by the planters, driven into pens, and branded somewhat after the manner of the later ranching on the Great Plains. Now the cow-drovers and the cow-pens began to enter the uplands. The Indians had by this time been reduced to submission in most of the Virginia Piedmont—as Governor Spotswood reported in 1712, living "quietly on our frontiers, trafficking with the Inhabitants."

After the defeat of the Tuscaroras and Yemassees about this time in the Carolinas, similar opportunities for expansion existed there. The cattle drovers sometimes took their herds from range to range; sometimes they were gathered permanently near the pens, finding the range sufficient throughout the year. They were driven to Charleston, or later sometimes even to Philadelphia and Baltimore markets. By the middle of the century, disease worked havoc with them in South Carolina and destroyed seven-eighths of those in North Carolina; Virginia made regulations governing the driving of cattle through her frontier counties to avoid the disease, just as in our own time the northern cattlemen attempted to protect their herds against the Texas fever.

Thus cattle raisers from the coast followed the fur-traders toward the uplands, and already pioneer farmers were straggling into the same region, soon to be outnumbered by the tide of settlement that flowed into the region from Pennsylvania.

The descriptions of the uplands by contemporaneous writers are in glowing terms. Makemie, in his *Plain and Friendly Persuasion* (1705), declared "The best, richest, and most healthy part of your Country is yet to be inhabited, above the falls of every River, to the Mountains." Jones, in his *Present State of Virginia* (1724), comments on the convenience of tidewater transportation, etc., but declares that section "not nearly so healthy as the uplands and Barrens which serve for Ranges for Slock," although he speaks less enthusiastically of the savannas and marshes which lay in the midst of the forest areas. In fact, the Piedmont was by no means the unbroken forest that might have been imagined, for in addition to natural meadows, the Indians had burned over large tracts. It was a rare combination of woodland and pasture, with clear running streams and mild climate.

The occupation of the Virginia Piedmont received a special impetus from the interest which Governor Spotswood took in the frontier. In 1710 he proposed a plan for intercepting the French in their occupation of the interior, by inducing Virginia settlement to proceed along one side of James River only, until this column of advancing pioneers should strike the attenuated line of French posts in the center. In the same year he sent a body of horsemen to the top of the Blue Ridge, where they could overlook the Valley of Virginia. By 1714 he became active as a colonizer himself. Thirty miles above the falls of the Rappahannock, on the Rapidan at Germanna, he settled a little village of German redemptioners (who in return for having the passage paid agreed to serve without wages for a term of years), to engage in his iron works, also to act as rangers on the frontier. From here, in 1716, with two companies of rangers and four Indians, Governor Spotswood and a band of Virginia gentlemen made a summer picnic excursion of two weeks across the Blue Ridge into the Shenandoah Valley. *Sic juvat transcendere montes* was the motto of these Knights of the Golden Horse Shoe, as the governor dubbed them. But they were not the "warlike christian men" destined to occupy the frontier.

Spotswood's interest in the advance along the Rappahannock, probably accounts for the fact that in 1720 Spotsylvania and Brunswick were organized as frontier counties of Virginia. Five hundred dollars were contributed by the colony to the church, and a thousand dollars for arms and ammunition for the settlers in these counties. The fears of the French and Indians beyond the high mountains, were alleged as reasons for this advance. To attract settlers to these new counties, they were (1723) exempt from purchasing the lands under the system of head rights, and from payment of quit-rents for seven years after 1721. The free grants so obtained were not to exceed a thousand acres. This was soon extended to six thousand acres, but with provision requiring the settlement of a certain number of families upon the grant within a certain time. In 1729 Spotswood was ordered by the Council to produce "rights" and pay the quit-rents for the 59,786 acres which he claimed in this county.

Other similar actions by the Council show that large holdings were developing there, also that the difficulty of establishing a frontier democracy in contact with the area of expanding plantations, was very real. By the time of the occupation of the Shenandoah Valley, therefore, the custom was established in this part of Virginia, of making grants of a thousand acres for each family settled. Speculative planters, influential With the governor and Council secured grants of many thousand acres, conditioned upon seating a certain number of families, and satisfying the requirements of planting. Thus what had originally been intended as direct grants to the actual settler, frequently became grants to great planters like Beverley, who promoted the coming of Scotch-Irish and German settlers, or took advantage of the natural drift into the Valley, to sell lands in their grants, as a rule, reserving quit-rents. The liberal grants per family enabled these speculative planters, while satisfying the terms of settlement, to hold large portions of the grant for themselves. Under the lax requirements, and probably still more lax enforcement, of the provisions for actual cultivation or cattle-raising, it was not difficult to hold such wild land. These conditions rendered possible the extension of a measure of aristocratic planter life in the course of time to the Piedmont and Valley lands of Virginia. It must be added, however, that some of the newcomers, both Germans and Scotch-Irish, like the Van Meters, Stover, and Lewis, also showed an ability to act as promoters in locating settlers and securing grants to themselves.

In the northern part of the Shenandoah Valley, lay part of the estate of Lord Fairfax, some six million acres in extent, which came to the family by dower from the old Culpeper and Arlington grant of northern Neck. In 1748, the youthful Washington was surveying this estate along the upper waters of the Potomac, finding a bed under the stars and learning the life of the frontier.

Lord Fairfax established his own Greenway manor, and divided his domain into other manors, giving ninety-nine-year leases to settlers already on the ground at twenty shillings annually per hundred acres; while of the newcomers he exacted two shillings annual quit-rent for this amount of land in fee simple. Litigation kept land titles uncertain here, for many years. Similarly, Beverley's manor, about Staunton, represented a grant of 118,000 acres to Beverley and his associates on condition of placing the proper number of families on the tract. Thus speculative planters on this frontier shared in the movement of occupation and made an aristocratic element in the up-country; but the increasing proportion of Scotch-Irish immigrants, as well as German settlers, together with the contrast in natural conditions, made the interior a different Virginia from that of the tidewater.

As settlement ascended the Rappahannock, and emigrants began to enter the Valley from the north, so, contemporaneously, settlement ascended the James above the falls, succeeding to the posts of the fur-traders. Goochland County was set off in 1728, and the growth of population led, as early as 1729, to proposals for establishing a city (Richmond) at the falls. Along the upper James, as on the Rappahannock, speculative planters bought headrights and located settlers and tenants to hold their grants. Into this region came natives of Virginia, emigrants from the British isles, and scattered representatives of other lands, some of them coming up the James, others up the York, and still others arriving with the southward-moving current along both sides of the Blue Ridge.

Before 1730 few settlers lived above the mouth of the Rivanna. In 1732 Peter Jefferson patented a thousand acres at the eastern opening of its mountain gap, and here, under frontier conditions, Thomas Jefferson was born in 1743 near his later estate of Monticello. About him were pioneer farmers, as well as foresighted engrossers of the land. In the main his country was that of a democratic frontier people—Scotch-Irish Presbyterians, Quakers, Baptists, and other sects, out of sympathy with the established church and the landed gentry of the lowlands. This society in which he was born, was to find in Jefferson a powerful exponent of its ideals. Patrick Henry was born in 1736 above the falls, not far from Richmond, and he also was a mouthpiece of interior Virginia in the Revolutionary era. In short, a society was already forming in the Virginia Piedmont which was composed of many sects, of independent yeomen as well as their great planter leaders—a society naturally expansive, seeing its opportunity to deal in unoccupied lands along the frontier which continually moved toward the West, and in this era of the eighteenth century dominated by the democratic ideals of pioneers rather than by the aristocratic tendencies of slaveholding planters. As there were two New Englands, so there were by this time two Virginias, and the uplands belonged with the Old West.

The advance across the fall line from the coast was, in North Carolina, much slower than in Virginia. After the Tuscarora War (1712–13) an extensive region west from Pamlico Sound was opened (1724). The region to the north, about the Roanoke, had before this begun to receive frontier settlers, largely from Virginia. Their traits are interestingly portrayed in Byrd's *Dividing Line.* By 1728 the farthest inhabitants along the Virginia boundary were frontiersmen about Great Creek, a branch of the Roanoke. The North Carolina commissioners desired to stop running the line after going a hundred and seventy miles, on the plea that they were already fifty miles beyond the outermost inhabitant, and there would be no need for an age or two to carry the line farther; but the Virginia surveyors pointed out that already speculators were taking up the land. A line from Weldon to Fayetteville would roughly mark the western boundary of North Carolina's sparse population of forty thousand souls.

The slower advance is explained, partly because of the later settlement of the Carolinas, partly because the Indians continued to be troublesome on the flanks of the advancing population, as seen in the Tuscarora and Yemassee wars, and partly because the pine barrens running parallel with the fall line made a zone of infertile land not attractive to settlers. The North Carolina low country, indeed, had from the end of the seventeenth century been a kind of southern frontier for overflow from Virginia; and in many ways was assimilated to the type of the up-country in its turbulent democracy, its variety of sects and peoples, and its primitive conditions. But under the lax management of the public lands, the use of "blank patents" and other evasions made possible the development of large landholding, side by side with headrights to settlers. Here, as in Virginia, a great proprietary grant extended across the colony—Lord Granville's proprietary was a zone embracing the northern half of North Carolina. Within the area, sales and quit-rents were administered by the agents of the owner, with the result that uncertainty and disorder of an agrarian nature extended down to the Revolution. There were likewise great speculative holdings, conditioned on seating a certain proportion of settlers, into which the frontiersmen were drifting. But this system also made it possible for agents of later migrating congregations to establish colonies like that of the Moravians at Wachovia. Thus, by the time settlers came into the uplands from the north, a land system existed similar to that of Virginia. A common holding was a square mile (640 acres), but in practice this did not prevent the accumulation of great estates. Whereas Virginia's Piedmont area was to a large extent entered by extensions from the coast, that of North Carolina remained almost untouched by 1730.

The same is true of South Carolina. By 1730, settlement had progressed hardly eighty miles from the coast, even in the settled area of the lowlands. The tendency to engross the lowlands for large plantations was clear, here as elsewhere. The surveyor-general reports in 1732 that not as many as a thousand acres within a hundred miles of Charleston, or within twenty miles of a river or navigable creek, were unpossessed. In

1729 the crown ordered eleven townships of twenty thousand acres each to be laid out in rectangles, divided into fifty acres for each actual settler under a quit-rent of four shillings a year for every hundred acres, or proportionally, to be paid after the first ten years. By 1732 these townships, designed to attract foreign Protestants, were laid out on the great rivers of the colony. As they were located in the middle region, east of the fall line, among pine barrens, or in malarial lands in the southern corner of the colony, they all proved abortive as towns, except Orangeburg on the North Edisto, where German redemptioners made a settlement. The Scotch-Irish Presbyterians who came to Williamsburg, on Black River, suffered hardships; as did the Swiss who, under the visionary leadership of Purry, settled in the deadly climate of Purrysburg, on the lower Savannah. To Welsh colonists from Pennsylvania there was made a grant—known as the "Welsh tract," embracing over 173,000 acres on the Great Pedee (Marion County) under headrights of fifty acres, also a bounty in provisions, tools, and livestock.

These attempts, east of the fall line, are interesting as showing the colonial policy of marking out towns (which were to be politically organized parishes, with representation in the legislature), and attracting foreigners thereto, prior to the coming of settlers from the North.

The settlement of Georgia, in 1732, completed the southern line of colonization toward the Piedmont. Among the objects of the colony, as specified in the charters, were the relief of the poor and the protection of the frontiers. To guard against the tendency to engross the lands in great estates, already so clearly revealed in the older colonies, the Georgia trustees provided that the grants of fifty acres should not be alienated or divided, but should pass to the male heirs and revert to the trustees in case heirs were lacking. No grant greater than five hundred acres was permitted, and even this was made conditionally upon the holder settling ten colonists. However, under local conditions and the competition and example of neighboring colonies, this attempt to restrict land tenure in the interest of democracy broke down by 1750, and Georgia's land system became not unlike that of the other southern colonies.

In 1734, Salzburgers had been located above Savannah, and within seven years some twelve hundred German Protestants were dwelling on the Georgia frontier; while a settlement of Scotch Highlanders at Darien, near the mouth of the Altamaha, protected the southern frontier. At Augusta, an Indian trading fort (1735), whence the dealers in peltry visited the Cherokee, completed the familiar picture of frontier advance.

We have now hastily surveyed the movement of the frontier of settlement westward from the lowlands, in the later years of the seventeenth and early part of the eighteenth century. There is much that is common in the whole line of advance. The original settlers engross the desirable lands of the older area. Indented servants and newcomers pass to the frontier seeking a place to locate their headrights, or plant new towns. Adventurous and speculative wealthy planters acquire large holdings in the new areas, and bring over settlers to satisfy the requirements of seating and cultivating their extensive grants, thus building up a yeomanry of small landholders side by side with the holders of large estates. The most farsighted of the newcomers follow the example of the planters, and petition for increasing extensive grants. Meanwhile, pioneers like Abraham Wood, himself once an indented servant, and gentlemen like Col. William Byrd—prosecuting the Indian trade from their posts at the "heads" of the rivers, and combining frontier protection, exploring, and surveying—make known the more distant fertile soils of the Piedmont. Already in the first part of the eighteenth century, the frontier population tended to be a rude democracy, with a large representation of Scotch-Irish, Germans, Welsh, and Huguenot French settlers, holding religious faiths unlike that of the followers of the established church in the lowlands. The movement of slaves into the region was unimportant, but not unknown.

The Virginia Valley was practically unsettled in 1730, as was much of Virginia's Piedmont area and all the Piedmont area of the Carolinas. The significance of the movement of settlers from the North into this vacant Valley and Piedmont, behind the area occupied by expansion from the coast is, that it was geographically separated from the westward movement from the coast, and that it was sufficient in volume to recruit the democratic forces and postpone for a long time the process of social assimilation to the type of the lowlands.

As has been pointed out, especially in the Carolinas a belt of pine barrens, roughly eighty miles in breadth, ran parallel with the fall line and thus discouraged Western advance across this belt, even before the head of navigation was reached. In Virginia, the Blue Ridge made an almost equally effective barrier, walling off the Shenandoah Valley from the westward advance. At the same time this valley was but a continuation of the Great Valley, that ran along the eastern edge of the Alleghanies in southeastern Pennsylvania, and included in its mountain trough the Cumberland and Hagerstown valleys. In short, a broad limestone band of fertile soil was stretched within mountain walls, southerly from Pennsylvania to southwestern Virginia; and here the watergaps opened the way to descend to the Carolina Piedmont. This whole area, a kind of peninsula thrust down from Pennsylvania, was rendered comparatively inaccessible to the westward movement from the lowlands, and was equally accessible to the population which was entering Pennsylvania.

Thus it happened that from about 1730 to 1760 a generation of settlers poured along this mountain trough into the southern uplands, or Piedmont, creating a new continuous social and economic area, which cut across the artificial colonial boundary lines, disarranged the regular extension of local government from the coast westward, and built up a new Pennsylvania in contrast with the old Quaker colonies, and a new South in contrast with the tidewater South. This New South composed the southern half of the Old West.

From its beginning, Pennsylvania was advertised as a home for dissenting sects seeking freedom in the wilderness. But it was not until the exodus of German redemptioners, from about 1717, that the Palatinate and neighboring areas sent the great tide of Germans which by the time of the Revolution made them nearly a third of the total population of Pennsylvania. It has been carefully estimated that in 1775 over two hundred thousand Germans lived in the thirteen colonies, chiefly along the frontier zone of the Old West. Of these, a hundred thousand had their home in Pennsylvania, mainly in the Great Valley, in the region which is still so notably the abode of the Pennsylvania Dutch.

Space does not permit us to describe this movement of colonization. The entrance to the fertile limestone soils of the Great Valley of Pennsylvania was easy, in view of the low elevation of the South Mountain ridge, and the watergaps thereto. The continuation along the similar valley to the south, in Maryland and Virginia, was a natural one, especially as the increasing tide of emigrants raised the price of lands. In 1719 the proprietor's price for Pennsylvania lands was ten pounds per hundred acres, and two shillings quit-rents. In 1732 this became fifteen and one-half pounds, with a quit-rent of a half penny per acre. During the period 1718 to 1732, when the Germans were coming in great numbers, the management of the lands fell into confusion, and many seated themselves as squatters, without title. This was a fortunate possibility for the poor redemptioners, who had sold their service for a term of years in order to secure their transportation to America.

By 1726 it was estimated that there were one hundred thousand squatters; and of the 670,000 acres occupied between 1732 and 1740, it is estimated that 400,000 acres were settled without grants. Nevertheless these must ultimately be paid for, with interest, and the concession of the right of preëmption to squatters made this easier. But it was not until 1755 that the governor offered land free from purchase, and this was to be taken only west of the Alleghanies.

Although the credit system relieved the difficulty in Pennsylvania, the lands of that colony were in competition with the Maryland lands, offered between 1717 and 1738 at forty shillings sterling per hundred acres, which in 1738 was raised to five pounds sterling. At the same time, in the Virginia Valley, as will be recalled, free grants were being made of a thousand acres per family. Although large tracts of the Shenandoah Valley had been granted to speculators like Beverley, Borden, and the Carters, as well as to Lord Fairfax, the owners sold six or seven pounds cheaper per hundred acres than did the Pennsylvania land office. Between 1726 and 1734, therefore, the Germans began to enter this valley, and before long they extended their settlements into the Piedmont of the Carolinas, being recruited in South Carolina by emigrants coming by way of Charleston—especially after Governor Glenn's purchase from the Cherokee in 1755, of the extreme western portion of the colony. Between 1750 and the Revolution, these settlers in the Carolinas greatly increased in numbers.

Thus a zone of almost continuous German settlements had been established, running from the head of the Mohawk in New York to the Savannah in Georgia. They had found the best soils, and they knew how to till them intensively and thriftily, as attested by their large, well-filled barns, good stock, and big canvas-covered Conestoga wagons. They preferred to dwell in groups, often of the same religious denomination—Lutherans, Reformed, Moravians, Mennonites, and many lesser sects. The diaries of Moravian missionaries from Pennsylvania, who visited them, show how the parent congregations kept in touch with their colonies and how intimate, in general, was the bond of connection between this whole German frontier zone and that of Pennsylvania.

Side by side with this German occupation of Valley and Piedmont, went the migration of the Scotch-Irish. These lowland Scots had been planted in Ulster early in the seventeenth century. Followers of John Knox, they had the contentious individualism and revolutionary temper that seem natural to Scotch Presbyterianism. They were brought up on the Old Testament, and in the doctrine of government by covenant or compact. In Ireland their fighting qualities had been revealed in the siege of Londonderry, where their stubborn resistance balked the hopes of James II. However, religious and political disabilities were imposed upon these Ulstermen, which made them discontented, and hard times contributed to detach them from their homes. Their movement to America was contemporaneous with the heavy German migration. By the Revolution, it is believed that a third of the population of Pennsylvania was Scotch-Irish; and it has been estimated, probably too liberally, that a half million came to the United States between 1730 and 1770. Especially after the Rebellion of 1745, large numbers of Highlanders came to increase the Scotch blood in the nation. Some of the Scotch-Irish went to New England. Given the cold shoulder by congregational Puritans, they passed to unsettled lands about Worcester, to the frontier in the Berkshires, and in southern New Hampshire at Londonderry—whence came John Stark, a frontier leader in the French and Indian War, and the hero of Bennington in the Revolution, as well as the ancestors of Horace Greeley and S. P. Chase. In New York, a Scotch-Irish settlement was planted on the frontier at Cherry Valley. Scotch Highlanders came to the Mohawk, where they followed Sir William Johnson and became Tory raiders in the Revolution.

But it was in Pennsylvania that the center of Scotch-Irish power lay. "These bold and indigent strangers, saying as their excuse when challenged for titles that we had solicited for colonists and they had come accordingly," and asserting that "it was against the laws of God and nature that so much land should be idle while so many christians wanted it to work on and to raise their bread," squatted on the vacant lands, especially in the region disputed between Pennsylvania and Maryland, and remained in spite of efforts to drive them off. Finding the Great Valley in the hands of the Germans, they planted their own outposts along the line of the Indian trading path from Lancaster to Bedford; they occupied Cumberland Valley, and before 1760 pressed up the Juniata somewhat beyond the narrows, spreading out along its tributaries, and by 1768 had to be warned off from the Redstone country to avoid Indian trouble. By the time of the Revolution, their settlements made Pittsburgh a center from which was to come a new era in Pennsylvania history. It was the Scotch-Irish and German fur-traders whose pack trains pioneered into the Ohio Valley in the days before the French and Indian wars. The messengers between civilization and savagery were such men, as the Irish Croghan, and the Germans Conrad Weiser and Christian Post.

Like the Germans, the Scotch-Irish passed into the Shenandoah Valley, and on to the uplands of the South. In 1738 a delegation of the

Philadelphia Presbyterian synod was sent to the Virginia governor and received assurances of security of religious freedom; the same policy was followed by the Carolinas. By 1760 a zone of Scotch-Irish Presbyterian churches extended from the frontiers of New England to the frontiers of South Carolina. This zone combined in part with the German zone, but in general Scotch-Irishmen tended to follow the valleys farther toward the mountains, to be the outer edge of this frontier. Along with this combined frontier stream were English, Welsh and Irish Quakers, and French Huguenots.

Among this moving mass, as it passed along the Valley into the Piedmont, in the middle of the eighteenth century, were Daniel Boone, John Sevier, James Robertson, and the ancestors of John C. Calhoun, Abraham Lincoln, Jefferson Davis, Stonewall Jackson, James K. Polk, Sam Houston, and Davy Crockett, while the father of Andrew Jackson came to the Carolina Piedmont at the same time from the coast. Recalling that Thomas Jefferson's home was on the frontier, at the edge of the Blue Ridge, we perceive that these names represent the militant expansive movement in American life. They foretell the settlement across the Alleghanies in Kentucky and Tennessee; the Louisiana Purchase, and Lewis and Clark's transcontinental exploration; the conquest of the Gulf Plains in the War of 1812–15; the annexation of Texas; the acquisition of California and the Spanish Southwest. They represent, too, frontier democracy in its two aspects personified in Andrew Jackson and Abraham Lincoln. It was a democracy responsive to leadership, susceptible to waves of emotion, of a "high religious voltage"—quick and direct in action.

The volume of this northern movement into the southern uplands is illustrated by the statement of Governor Tryon, of North Carolina, that in the summer and winter of 1765 more than a thousand immigrant wagons passed through Salisbury, in that colony. Coming by families, or groups of families or congregations, they often drove their herds with them. Whereas in 1746 scarce a hundred fighting men were found in Orange and the western counties of North Carolina, there were in 1753 fully three thousand, in addition to over a thousand Scotch in the Cumberland; and they covered the province more or less thickly, from Hillsboro and Fayetteville to the mountains. Bassett remarks that the Presbyterians received their first ministers from the synod of New York and Pennsylvania, and later on sent their ministerial students to Princeton College. "Indeed it is likely that the inhabitants of this region knew more about Philadelphia at that time than about Newbern or Edenton."

We are now in a position to note briefly, in conclusion, some of the results of the occupation of this new frontier during the first half of the eighteenth century—some of the consequences of this formation of the Old West.

I. A fighting frontier had been created all along the line from New England to Georgia, which bore the brunt of French and Indian attacks and gave indispensable service during the Revolution. The significance of this fact could only be developed by an extended survey of the scattered border warfare of this era. We should have to see Rogers leading his New England Rangers, and Washington defending interior Virginia with his frontiersmen in their hunting shirts, in the French and Indian War. When all of the campaigns about the region of Canada, Lake Champlain, and the Hudson, central New York (Oriskany, Cherry Valley, Sullivan's expedition against the Iroquois), Wyoming Valley, western Pennsylvania, the Virginia Valley, and the back country of the South are considered as a whole from this point of view, the meaning of the Old West will become more apparent.

II. A new society had been established, differing in essentials from the colonial society of the coast. It was a democratic self-sufficing, primitive agricultural society, in which individualism was more pronounced than the community life of the lowlands. The indented servant and the slave were not a normal part of its labor system. It was engaged in grain and cattle raising, not in producing staples, and it found a partial means of supplying its scarcity of specie by the peltries which it shipped to the coast. But the hunter folk were already pushing farther on; the cow-pens and the range were giving place to the small farm, as in our own day they have done in the cattle country. It was a region of hard work and poverty, not of wealth and leisure. Schools and churches were secured under serious difficulty, if at all; but in spite of the natural tendencies of a frontier life, a large portion of the interior showed a distinctly religious atmosphere.

III. The Old West began the movement of internal trade which developed home markets and diminished that colonial dependence on Europe in industrial matters shown by the maritime and staple-raising sections. Not only did Boston and other New England towns increase as trading centers when the back country settled up, but an even more significant interchange occurred along the Valley and Piedmont. The German farmers of the Great Valley brought their woven linen, knitted stockings, firkins of butter, dried apples, grain, etc., to Philadelphia and especially to

Baltimore, which was laid out in 1730. To this city also came trade from the Shenandoah Valley, and even from the Piedmont came peltry trains and droves of cattle and hogs to the same market. The increase of settlement on the upper James resulted in the establishment of the city of Richmond at the falls of the river in 1737. Already the tobacco-planting aristocracy of the lowlands were finding rivals in the grain-raising area of interior Virginia and Maryland. Charleston prospered as the up-country of the Carolinas grew. Writing in the middle of the eighteenth century, Governor Glenn, of South Carolina, explained the apparent diminution of the colony's shipping thus:

> Our trade with New York and Philadelphia was of this sort, draining us of all the little money and bills that we could gather from other places, for their bread, flour, beer, hams, bacon, and other things of their produce, all which, except beer, our new townships begin to supply us with which are settled with very industrious and consequently thriving Germans.

It was not long before this interior trade produced those rivalries for commercial ascendancy, between the coastwise cities, which still continue. The problem of internal improvements became a pressing one, and the statutes show increasing provision for roads, ferries, bridges, river improvements, etc. The basis was being laid for a national economy, and at the same time a new source for foreign export was created.

IV. The Old West raised the issues of nativism and a lower standard of comfort. In New England, Scotch-Irish Presbyterians had been frowned upon and pushed away by the Puritan townsmen. In Pennsylvania, the coming of the Germans and the Scotch-Irish in such numbers caused grave anxiety. Indeed, a bill was passed to limit the importation of the Palatines, but it was vetoed. Such astute observers as Franklin feared in 1753 that Pennsylvania would be unable to preserve its language and that even its government would become precarious. "I remember," he declares, "when they modestly declined intermeddling in our elections, but now they come in droves and carry all before them, except in one or two counties"; and he lamented that the English could not remove their prejudices by addressing them in German. Dr. Douglas apprehended that Pennsylvania would "degenerate into a foreign colony" and endanger the quiet of the adjacent provinces. Edmund Burke, regretting that the Germans adhered to their own schools, literature, and language, and that they possessed great tracts without admixture of English, feared that they would not blend and become one people with the British colonists, and that the colony was threatened with the danger of being wholly foreign. He also noted that "these foreigners by their industry, frugality, and a hard way of living, in which they greatly exceed our people, have in a manner thrust them out in several places." This is a phenomenon with which a succession of later frontiers has familiarized us. In point of fact the Pennsylvania Dutch remained through our history a very stubborn area to assimilate, with corresponding effect upon Pennsylvania politics.

It should be noted also that this coming of non-English stock to the frontier raised in all the colonies affected, questions of naturalization and land tenure by aliens.

V. The creation of this frontier society—of which so large a portion differed from that of the coast in language and religion as well as in economic life, social structure, and ideals—produced an antagonism between interior and coast, which worked itself out in interesting fashion. In general this took these forms: contests between the property-holding class of the coast and the debtor class of the interior, where specie was lacking, and where paper money and a readjustment of the basis of taxation were demanded; contests over defective or unjust local government in the administration of taxes, fees, lands, and the courts; contests over apportionment in the legislature, whereby the coast was able to dominate, even when its white population was in the minority; contests to secure the complete separation of church and state; and, later, contests over slavery, internal improvements, and party politics in general. These contests are also intimately connected with the political philosophy of the Revolution and with the development of American democracy. In nearly every colony prior to the Revolution, struggles had been in progress between the party of privilege, chiefly the eastern men of property allied with the English authorities, and the democratic classes, strongest in the West and the cities.

This theme deserves more space than can here be allotted to it; but a rapid survey of conditions in this respect, along the whole frontier, will at least serve to bring out the point.

In New England as a whole, the contest is less in evidence. That part of the friction elsewhere seen as the result of defective local government in the back country, was met by the efficiency of the town system; but between the interior and the coast there were struggles over apportionment and religious freedom. The former is illustrated by the convention that met in Dracut, Massachusetts, in 1776, to petition the states of Massachusetts and New Hampshire to relieve the financial distress and unfair legislative representation. Sixteen of the border towns of New Hampshire sent delegates to this convention. Two years later, these New Hampshire towns attempted to join Vermont. As a Revolutionary state, Vermont itself was an illustration of the same tendency of the interior to break away from the coast. Massachusetts in this period witnessed a campaign between the paper money party which was entrenched in the more recently and thinly settled areas of the interior and west, and the property-holding classes of the coast. The opposition to the constitutions of 1778 and 1780 is tinctured with the same antagonism between the ideas of the newer part of the interior and of the coast. Shays' Rebellion and the anti-federal opposition of 1787–88 found its stronghold in the same interior areas.

The religious struggles continued until the democratic interior, where dissenting sects were strong, and where there was antagonism to the privileges of the congregational church, finally secured complete disestablishment in New Hampshire, Connecticut, and Massachusetts. But this belongs to a later period.

Pennsylvania affords a clear illustration of these sectional antagonisms. The memorial of the frontier *Paxton Boys*, in 1764, demanded a right to share in political privileges with the older part of the colony, and protested against the apportionment by which the counties of Chester, Bucks, and Philadelphia, together with the city of Philadelphia, elected twenty-six delegates, while the five frontier counties had but ten. The frontier complained against the failure of the dominant Quaker party of the coast to protect the interior against the Indians. The three old wealthy counties under Quaker rule feared the growth of the West, therefore made few new counties, and carefully restricted the representation in each to preserve the majority in the old section. At the same time, by a property qualification they met the danger of the democratic city population. Among the points of grievance in this colony, in addition to apportionment and representation, was the difficulty of access to the county seat, owing to the size of the back counties. Dr. Lincoln has well set forth the struggle of the back country, culminating in its triumph in the constitutional convention of 1776, which was chiefly the work of the Presbyterian counties. Indeed, there were two revolutions in Pennsylvania, which went on side by side: one a revolt against the coastal property-holding classes, the old dominant Quaker party, and the other a revolt against

Great Britain, which was in this colony made possible only by the triumph of the interior.

In Virginia, as early as 1710, Governor Spotswood had complained that the old counties remained small while the new ones were sometimes ninety miles long, the inhabitants being obliged to travel thirty or forty miles to their own courthouse. Some of the counties had one thousand seven hundred tithables, while others only a dozen miles square had five hundred. Justices of the peace disliked to ride forty or fifty miles to their monthly courts. Likewise there was disparity in the size of parishes—for example, that of Varina, on the upper James, had nine hundred tithables, many of whom lived fifty miles from their church. But the vestry refused to allow the remote parishioners to separate, because it would increase the parish levy of those that remained. He feared lest this would afford "opportunity to Sectarys to establish their opinions among 'em, and thereby shake that happy establishment of the Church of England which this colony enjoys with less mixture of Dissenters than any other of her Maj'tie's plantations, and when once Schism has crept into the Church, it will soon create faction in the Civil government."

That Spotswood's fears were well founded, we have already seen. As the sectaries of the back country increased, dissatisfaction with the established church grew. After the Revolution came, Jefferson, with the back country behind him, was able finally to destroy the establishment, and to break down the system of entails and primogeniture behind which the tobacco-planting aristocracy of the coast was entrenched. The desire of Jefferson to see slavery gradually abolished and popular education provided, is a further illustration of the attitude of the interior. In short, Jeffersonian democracy, with its idea of separation of church and state, its wish to popularize education, and its dislike for special privilege, was deeply affected by the western society of the Old Dominion.

The Virginian reform movement, however, was unable to redress the grievance of unequal apportionment. In 1780 Jefferson pointed out that the practice of allowing each county an equal representation in the legislature gave control to the numerous small counties of the tidewater, while the large populous counties of the up-country suffered. "Thus," he wrote, "the nineteen thousand men below the falls give law to more than thirty thousand living in other parts of the state, and appoint all their chief officers, executive and judiciary." This led to a long struggle between coast and interior, terminated only when the slave population passed across the fall line, and more nearly assimilated coast and up-country. In the mountain areas which did not undergo this change, the independent state of West Virginia remains as a monument of the contest. In the convention of 1829–30, the whole philosophy of representation was discussed, and the coast defended its control as necessary to protect property from the assaults of a numerical majority. They feared that the interior would tax their slaves in order to secure funds for internal improvements.

As Doddridge put the case:

> The principle is that the owners of slave property must be possessed of all the powers of government, however small their own numbers may be, to secure that property from the rapacity of an overgrown majority of white men. This principle admits of no relaxation, because the weaker the minority becomes, the greater will their need for power be according to their own doctrines.

Leigh of Chesterfield county declared:

> It is remarkable—I mention it for the curiosity of the fact—that if any evil, physical or moral, arise in any of the states south of us, it never takes a northerly direction, or taints the southern breeze; whereas, if any plague originate in the North, it is sure to spread to the South and to invade us sooner or later; the influenza—the smallpox—the varioloid—the Hessian fly—the Circuit Court system—Universal Suffrage—all come from the North, *and they always cross above the falls of the great rivers;* below, it seems, the broad expanse of waters interposing, effectually arrests their progress.

Nothing could more clearly bring out the sense of contrast between upland and lowland Virginia, and the continued intimacy of the bond of connection between the North and its Valley and Piedmont colonies, than this unconscious testimony.

In North and South Carolina the upland South, beyond the pine barrens and the fall line, had similar grievances against the coast; but as the zone of separation was more strongly marked, the grievances were more acute. The tide of backwoods settlement flowing down the Piedmont from the north, had cut across the lines of local government and disarranged the regular course of development of the colonies from the seacoast. Under the common practice, large counties in North Carolina and parishes in South Carolina had been projected into the unoccupied interior from the older settlements along their eastern edge.

But the Piedmont settlers brought their own social order, and could not be well governed by the older planters living far away toward the seaboard. This may be illustrated by conditions in South Carolina. The general court in Charleston had absorbed county and precinct courts, except the minor jurisdiction of justices of the peace. This was well enough for the great planters who made their regular residence there for a part of each year; but it was a source of oppression to the up-country settlers, remote from the court. The difficulty of bringing witnesses, the delay of the law, and the costs all resulted in the escape of criminals as well as in the immunity of reckless debtors. The extortions of officials, and their occasional collusion with horse and cattle thieves, and the lack of regular administration of the law, led the South Carolina up-country men to take affairs in their own hands, and in 1764 to establish associations to administer lynch law under the name of "Regulators." The "Scovillites," or government party, and the Regulators met in arms on the Saluda in 1769, but hostilities were averted and remedial measures passed, which alleviated the difficulty until the Revolution. There still remained, however, the grievance of unjust legislative representation. Calhoun stated the condition in these words:

> The upper country had no representation in the government and no political existence as a constituent portion of the state until a period near the commencement of the revolution. Indeed, during the revolution, and until the formation of the present constitution, in 1790, its political weight was scarcely felt in the government. Even then although it had become the most populous section, power was so distributed under the constitution as to leave it in a minority in every department of government.

Even in 1794 it was claimed by the up-country leaders that four-fifths of the people were governed by one-fifth. Nor was the difficulty met until the constitutional amendment of 1808, the effect of which was to give the control of the senate to the lower section and of the house of representatives to the upper section, thus providing a mutual veto. This South Carolina experience furnished the historical basis for Calhoun's argument for nullification, and for the political philosophy underlying his theory of the "concurrent majority." This adjustment was effected, however, only after the advance of the black belt toward the interior had assimilated portions of the Piedmont to lowland ideals.

When we turn to North Carolina's upper country we find the familiar story, but with a more tragic ending. The local officials owed their selection to the governor and the council whom he appointed. Thus power was all concentrated in the official "ring" of the lowland area. The men of the interior resented the extortionate fees and the poll tax, which bore with unequal weight upon the poor settlers of the back country. This tax had been continued after sufficient funds had been collected to extinguish the debt for which it was originally levied, but venal sheriffs had failed to pay it into the treasury. A report of 1770 showed at least one defaulting sheriff in every county of the province. This tax, which was almost the sole tax of the colony, was to be collected in specie, for the warehouse system, by which staples might be accepted, while familiar on the coast, did not apply to the interior. The specie was exceedingly difficult to obtain; in lack of it, the farmer saw the sheriff, who owed his appointment to the dominant lowland planters, sell the lands of the delinquent to his speculative friends. Lawyers and court fees followed.

In short, the interior felt that it was being exploited. and it had no redress, for the legislature was so apportioned that all power rested in the old lowland region. Efforts to secure paper money failed by reason of the governor's opposition under instructions from the crown, and the currency was contracting at the very time when population was rapidly increasing in the interior. As in New England, in the days of Shays' Rebellion, violent prejudice existed against the judiciary and the lawyers, and it must, of course, be understood that the movement was not free from frontier dislike of taxation and the restraints of law and order in general. In 1766 and 1768, meetings were held in the upper counties to organize the opposition, and an "association" was formed, the members of which pledged themselves to pay no more taxes or fees until they satisfied themselves that these were agreeable to law.

The Regulators, as they called themselves, assembled in the autumn of 1768 to the number of nearly four thousand, and tried to secure terms of adjustment. In 1770 the courthouse at Hillsboro was broken into by a mob. The assembly passed some measures designed to conciliate the back country; but before they became operative, Governor Tryon's militia, about twelve hundred men, largely from the lowlands, and led by the gentry whose privileges were involved, met the motley army of the Regulators, who numbered about two thousand, in the battle of the Alamance (May 1771). Many were killed and wounded, the Regulators dispersed, and over six thousand men came into camp and took the oath of submission to the colonial authorities. The battle was not the first battle of the Revolution, as it has been sometimes called, for it had little or no relation to the stamp act; and many of the frontiersmen involved, later refused to fight against England because of the very hatred which had been inspired for the lowland Revolutionary leaders in this battle of the Alamance. The interior of the Carolinas was a region where neighbors, during the Revolution, engaged in internecine conflicts of Tories against Whigs.

But in the sense that the battle of Alamance was a conflict against privilege, and for equality of political rights and power, it was indeed a preliminary battle of the Revolution, although fought against many of the very men who later professed Revolutionary doctrines in North Carolina. The need of recognizing the importance of the interior led to concessions in the convention of 1776 in that state. "Of the forty-four sections of the constitution, thirteen are embodiments of reforms sought by the Regulators." But it was in this period that hundreds of North Carolina backwoodsmen crossed the mountains to Tennessee and Kentucky, many of them coming from the heart of the Regulator region. They used the device of "associations" to provide for government in their communities.

In the matter of apportionment, North Carolina showed the same lodgment of power in the hands of the coast, even after population preponderated in the Piedmont.

It is needless to comment on the uniformity of the evidence which has been adduced, to show that the Old West, the interior region from New England to Georgia, had a common grievance against the coast; that it was deprived throughout most of the region of its due share of representation, and neglected and oppressed in local government in large portions of the section. The familiar struggle of West against East, of democracy against privileged classes, was exhibited along the entire line. The phenomenon must be considered as a unit, not in the fragments of state histories. It was a struggle of interior against coast.

VI. Perhaps the most noteworthy western activity in the Revolutionary era, aside from the aspects already mentioned, was in the part which the multitude of sects in the Old West played in securing the great contribution which the United States made to civilization by providing for complete religious liberty, a secular state with free churches. Particularly the Revolutionary constitutions of Pennsylvania and Virginia, under the influence of the back country, insured religious freedom. The effects of the North Carolina upland area to secure a similar result were noteworthy, though for the time ineffective.

VII. As population increased in these years, the coast gradually yielded to the up-country's demands. This may be illustrated by the transfer of the capitals from the lowlands to the fall line and Valley. In 1779, Virginia changed her seat of government from Williamsburg to Richmond; in 1790, South Carolina, from Charleston to Columbia; in 1791, North Carolina, from Edenton to Raleigh; in 1797, New York, from New York City to Albany; in 1799, Pennsylvania, from Philadelphia to Lancaster.

VIII. The democratic aspect of the new constitutions was also influenced by the frontier as well as by the prevalent Revolutionary philosophy; and the demands for paper money, stay and tender laws, etc., of this period were strongest in the interior. It was this region that supported Shays' Rebellion; it was (with some important exceptions) the same area that resisted the ratification of the federal constitution, fearful of a stronger government and of the loss of paper money.

IX. The interior later showed its opposition to the coast by the persistent contest against slavery, carried on in the up-country of Virginia, and North and South Carolina. Until the decade 1830–40, it was not certain that both Virginia and North Carolina would not find some means of gradual abolition. The same influence accounts for much of the exodus of the Piedmont pioneers into Indiana and Illinois, in the first half of the nineteenth century.

X. These were the regions, also, in which were developed the desire of the pioneers who crossed the mountains, and settled on the "Western waters," to establish new states free from control by the lowlands, owning their own lands, able to determine their own currency, and in general to govern themselves in accordance with the ideals of the Old West. They were ready also, if need be, to become independent of the Old Thirteen. Vermont must be considered in this aspect, as well as Kentucky and Tennessee.

XI. The land system of the Old West furnished precedents which developed into the land system of the trans-Alleghany West. The squatters of Pennsylvania and the Carolinas found it easy to repeat the operation on another frontier. Preemption laws became established features. The Revolution gave opportunity to confiscate the claims of Lord Fairfax, Lord Granville, and McCulloh to their vast estates, as well as the remaining lands of the Pennsylvania proprietors. The 640 acre (or one square mile) unit of North Carolina for preemptions, and frontier land bounties, became the area awarded to frontier stations by Virginia in 1779, and the "section" of the later federal land system. The Virginia preëmption right of four hundred acres on the western waters, or a thousand for those who came prior to 1778, was, in substance, the continuation of a system familiar in the Old West.

The grants to Beverley, of over a hundred thousand acres in the Valley, conditioned on seating a family for every thousand acres, and the similar grants to Borden, Carter, and Lewis, were followed by the great grant to the Ohio Company. This company, including leading Virginia planters and some frontiersmen, asked in 1749 for two hundred thousand acres on the upper Ohio, conditioned on seating a hundred families in seven years, and for an additional grant of three hundred thousand acres after this should be accomplished. It was proposed to settle Germans on these lands.

The Loyal Land Company, by order of the Virginia council (1749), was authorized to take up eight hundred thousand acres west and north of the southern boundary of Virginia, on condition of purchasing "rights" for the amount within four years. The company sold many tracts for £3 per hundred acres to settlers, but finally lost its claim. The Mississippi Company, including in its membership the Lees, Washingtons, and other great Virginia planters, applied for two and one-half million acres in the West in 1769. Similar land companies of New England origin, like the Susquehanna Company and Lyman's Mississippi Company, exhibit the same tendency of the Old West on the northern side. New England's Ohio Company of Associates, which settled Marietta, had striking resemblances to town proprietors.

These were only the most noteworthy of many companies of this period, and it is evident that they were a natural outgrowth of speculations in the Old West. Washington, securing military bounty land claims of soldiers of the French and Indian War, and selecting lands in West Virginia until he controlled over seventy thousand acres for speculation, is an excellent illustration of the tendency. He also thought of colonizing German Palatines upon his lands. The formation of the Transylvania and Vandalia companies were natural developments on a still vaster scale.

XII. The final phase of the Old West, which I wish merely to mention, in conclusion, is its colonization of areas beyond the mountains. The essential unity of the movement is brought out by a study of how New England's Old West settled northern Maine, New Hampshire and Vermont, the Adirondacks, central and western New York, the Wyoming Valley (once organized as a part of Litchfield, Connecticut), the Ohio Company's region about Marietta, and Connecticut's western Reserve on the shores of Lake Erie; and how the pioneers of the Great Valley and the Piedmont region of the South crossed the Alleghanies and settled on the Western Waters. Daniel Boone, going from his Pennsylvania home to the Yadkin, and from the Yadkin to Tennessee and Kentucky, took part in the whole process, and later in its continuation into Missouri. The social conditions and ideals of the Old West powerfully shaped those of the trans-Alleghany West.

The important contrast between the spirit of individual colonization, resentful of control, which the southern frontiersmen showed, and the spirit of community colonization and control to which the New England pioneers inclined, left deep traces on the later history of the West. The Old West diminished the importance of the town as a colonizing unit, even in New England. In the southern area, efforts to legislate towns into existence, as in Virginia, South Carolina, and Georgia, failed. They faded away before wilderness conditions. But in general, the northern stream of migration was communal, and the southern individual. The difference which existed between that portion of the Old West which was formed by the northward colonization, chiefly of the New England Plateau (including New York), and that portion formed by the southward colonization of the Virginia Valley and the southern Piedmont was reflected in the history of the Middle West and the Mississippi Valley.

→ CHAPTER FOUR ←

THE MIDDLE WEST

AMERICAN SECTIONAL NOMENCLATURE IS STILL CONFUSED. ONCE "THE West" described the whole region beyond the Alleghanies; but the term has hopelessly lost its definiteness. The rapidity of the spread of settlement has broken down old usage, and as yet no substitute has been generally accepted. The "Middle West" is a term variously used by the public, but for the purpose of the present paper, it will be applied to that region of the United States included in the census reports under the name of the North Central division, comprising the states of Ohio, Indiana, Illinois, Michigan, and Wisconsin (the old "Territory Northwest of the River Ohio"), and their trans-Mississippi sisters of the Louisiana Purchase, Missouri, Iowa, Minnesota, Kansas, Nebraska, North Dakota, and South Dakota. It is an imperial domain. If the greater countries of Central Europe, France, Germany, Italy, and Austro-Hungary, were laid down upon this area, the Middle West would still show a margin of spare territory. Pittsburgh, Cleveland, and Buffalo constitute its gateways to the eastern states; Kansas City, Omaha, St. Paul-Minneapolis, and Duluth-Superior dominate its western areas; Cincinnati and St. Louis stand on its southern borders; and Chicago reigns at the center. What Boston, New York, Philadelphia, and Baltimore are to the Atlantic seaboard these cities are to the Middle West. The Great Lakes and the Mississippi, with the Ohio and the Missouri as laterals, constitute the vast water system that binds the Middle West together. It is the economic and political center of the Republic. At one edge is the Populism of the prairies; at the other, the capitalism that is typified in Pittsburgh. Great as are the local differences within the Middle West, it possesses, in its physiography, in the history of its settlement, and in its economic and social life, a unity and interdependence which warrant a study of the area as an entity. Within the limits of this article, treatment of so vast a region, however, can at best afford no more than an outline sketch, in which old and well-known facts must, if possible, be so grouped as to explain the position of the section in American history.

In spite of the difficulties of the task, there is a definite advantage in so large a view. By fixing our attention too exclusively upon the artificial boundary lines of the states, we have failed to perceive much that is significant in the westward development of the United States. For instance, our colonial system did not begin with the Spanish War; the United States has had a colonial history and policy from the beginning of the Republic; but they have been hidden under the phraseology of "interstate migration" and "territorial organization."

The American people have occupied a spacious wilderness; vast physiographic provinces, each with its own peculiarities, have lain across the path of this migration, and each has furnished a special environment for economic and social transformation. It is possible to underestimate the importance of state lines, but if we direct our gaze rather to the physiographic province than to the state area, we shall be able to see some facts in a new light. Then it becomes clear that these physiographic provinces of America are in some respects comparable to the countries of Europe, and that each has its own history of occupation and development. General Francis A. Walker once remarked that "the course of settlement has called upon our people to occupy territory as extensive as Switzerland, as England, as Italy, and latterly, as France or Germany, every ten years." It is this element of vastness in the achievements of American democracy that gives a peculiar interest to the conquest and development of the Middle West. The effects of this conquest and development upon the present United States have been of fundamental importance.

Geographically the Middle West is almost conterminous with the Provinces of the Lake and Prairie Plains; but the larger share of Kansas and Nebraska, and the western part of the two Dakotas belong to the Great Plains; the Ozark Mountains occupy a portion of Missouri, and the southern parts of Ohio and Indiana merge into the Alleghany Plateau. The relation of the Provinces of the Lake and Prairie Plains to the rest of the United States is an important element in the significance of the Middle West. On the north lies the similar region of Canada: the Great Lakes are in the center of the whole eastern and more thickly settled half of North America, and they bind the Canadian and Middle Western people together. On the south, the provinces meet the apex of that of the Gulf Plains, and the Mississippi unites them. To the west, they merge gradually into the Great Plains; the Missouri and its tributaries and the Pacific railroads make for them a bond of union; another rather effective bond is the interdependence of the cattle of the plains and the corn of the prairies. To the east, the province meets the Alleghany and New England Plateaus, and is connected with them by the upper Ohio and by the line of the Erie Canal. Here the interaction of industrial life and the historical facts of settlement have produced a close relationship. The intimate connection between the larger part of the North Central and the North Atlantic divisions of the United States will impress any one who examines the industrial and social maps of the census atlas. By reason of these interprovincial relationships, the Middle West is the mediator between Canada and the United States, and between the concentrated wealth and manufactures of the North Atlantic states and the sparsely settled western mining, cattle-raising, and agricultural states. It has a connection with the South that was once still closer, and is likely before long to reassert itself with new power. Within the limits of the United States, therefore, we have problems of interprovincial trade and commerce similar to those that exist between the nations of the Old World.

Over most of the Province of the Lake and Prairie Plains the Laurentide glacier spread its drift, rich in loess and other rock powder, which farmers in less favored sections must purchase to replenish the soil. The alluvial deposit from primeval lakes contributed to fatten the soil of other parts of the prairies. Taken as a whole, the Prairie Plains surpass in fertility any other region of America or Europe, unless we except some territory about the Black Sea. It is a land marked out as the granary of the nation; but it is more than a granary. On the rocky shores of Lake Superior were concealed copper mines rivaled only by those of Montana, and iron fields which now furnish the ore for the production of eighty percent of the pig iron of the United States. The Great Lakes afford a highway between these iron fields and the coal areas of the Ohio Valley. The gas and oil deposits of the Ohio Valley, the coal of Illinois, Iowa, Michigan, and eastern Kansas, the lead and zinc of the Ozark region and of the upper Mississippi Valley, and the gold of the black Hills, all contribute underground wealth to the Middle West.

The primeval American forest once spread its shade over vast portions of the same province. Ohio, Indiana, southern Michigan, and central Wisconsin were almost covered with a growth of noble deciduous trees. In southern Illinois, along the broad bottom lands of the Mississippi and the Illinois, and in southern and southwestern Missouri, similar forests prevailed. To the north, in Michigan, Wisconsin, and Minnesota, appeared the somber white pine wilderness, interlaced with hard woods, which swept in ample zone along the Great Lakes, till the deciduous forests triumphed again, and, in their turn, faded into the treeless expanse of the prairies. In the remaining portions were openings in the midst of the forested area, and then the grassy ocean of prairie that rolled to west and northwest, until it passed beyond the line of sufficient rainfall for agriculture without irrigation, into the semi-arid stretches of the Great Plains.

In the middle of the eighteenth century, the forested region of this province was occupied by the wigwams of many different tribes of the Algonquin tongue, sparsely scattered in villages along the water courses, warring and trading through the vast wilderness. The western edge of the prairie and the Great Plains were held by the Sioux, chasing herds of bison across these far-stretching expanses. These horsemen of the plains and the canoemen of the Great Lakes and the Ohio were factors with which civilization had to reckon, for they constituted important portions of perhaps the fiercest native race with which the white man has ever battled for new lands.

The Frenchman had done but little fighting for this region. He swore brotherhood with its savages, traded with them, intermarried with them, and explored the Middle West; but he left the wilderness much as he found it. Some six or seven thousand French people in all, about Detroit and Vincennes, and in the Illinois country, and scattered among the Indian villages of the remote lakes and streams, held possession when George Washington reached the site of Pittsburgh, bearing Virginia's summons of eviction to France. In his person fate knocked at the portals of a "rising empire." France hurried her commanders and garrisons, with Indian allies, from the posts about the Great Lakes and the upper Mississippi; but it was in vain. In vain, too, the aftermath of Pontiac's widespread Indian uprising against the English occupation. When she came into possession of the lands between the Ohio, the Mississippi, and the Great Lakes, England organized them as a part of the Province of Quebec. The daring conquest of George Rogers Clark left Virginia in military possession of the Illinois country at the conclusion of the Revolutionary War; but over all the remainder of the Old Northwest, England was in control. Although she ceded the region by the treaty which closed the Revolution, she remained for many years the mistress of the Indians and the fur trade. When Lord Shelburne was upbraided in parliament for yielding the Northwest to the United States, the complaint was that he had clothed the Americans "in the warm covering of our fur trade," and his defense was that the peltry trade of the ceded tract was not sufficiently profitable to warrant further war. But the English government became convinced that the Indian trade demanded the retention of the Northwest, and she did in fact hold her posts there in spite of the treaty of peace. Dundas, the English secretary for the colonies, expressed the policy, when he declared, in 1792, that the object was to interpose an Indian barrier between Canada and the United States; and in pursuance of this policy of preserving the Northwest as an Indian buffer state, the Canadian authorities supported the Indians in their resistance to American settlement beyond the Ohio. The conception of the Northwest as an Indian reserve strikingly exhibits England's inability to foresee the future of the region, and to measure the forces of American expansion.

By the cessions of Virginia, New York, Massachusetts, and Connecticut, the Old Congress had come into nominal possession of an extensive public domain, and a field for the exercise of national authority. The significance of this fact in the development of national power is not likely to be overestimated. The first result was the completion of the Ordinance of 1787, which provided a territorial government for the Old Northwest, with provisions for the admission of states into the Union. This federal colonial system guaranteed that the new national possessions should not be governed as dependent provinces, but should enter as a group of sister states into the federation. While the importance of the article excluding slavery has often been pointed out, it is probable that the provisions for a federal colonial organization have been at least equally potent in our actual development. The full significance of this feature of the Ordinance is only appreciated when we consider its continuous influence upon the American territorial and state policy in the westward expansion to the Pacific, and the political preconceptions with which Americans approach the problems of government in the new insular possessions. The Land Ordinance of 1785 is also worthy of attention in this connection, for under its provisions almost all of the Middle West has been divided by the government surveyor into rectangles of sections and townships, by whose lines the settler has been able easily and certainly to locate his farm, and the forester his "forty." In the local organization of the Middle West these lines have played an important part.

It would be impossible within the limits of this paper to detail the history of the occupation of the Middle West; but the larger aspects of the flow of population into the region may be sketched. Massachusetts men had formed the Ohio Company, and had been influential in shaping the liberal provisions of the Ordinance. Their land purchase, paid for in soldiers' certificates, embraced an area larger than the state of Rhode Island. At Marietta in 1788, under the shelter of Fort Harmar, their bullet-proof barge landed the first New England colony. A New Jersey colony was planted soon after at Cincinnati in the Symmes Purchase. Thus American civilization crossed the Ohio. The French settlements at Detroit and in Indiana and Illinois belonged to other times and had their own ideals; but with the entrance of the American pioneer into the forest of the Middle West, a new era began. The Indians, with the moral support of England, resisted the invasion, and an Indian war followed. The conquest of Wayne, in 1795, pushed back the Indians to the Greenville line, extending irregularly across the state of Ohio from the site of Cleveland to Fort Recovery in the middle point of her present western boundary, and secured certain areas in Indiana. In the same period Jay's treaty provided for the withdrawal of the British posts. After this extension of the area open to the pioneer, new settlements were rapidly formed. Connecticut disposed of her reserved land about Lake Erie to companies, and in 1796 General Moses Cleaveland led the way to the site of the city that bears his name. This was the beginning of the occupation of the western Reserve, a district about as large as the parent state of Connecticut, a New England colony in the Middle West, which has maintained, even to the present time, the impress of New England traits. Virginia and Kentucky settlers sought the Virginia Military Bounty Lands, and the foundation of Chillicothe here, in 1796, afforded a center for southern settlement. The region is a modified extension of the limestone area of Kentucky, and naturally attracted the emigrants from the Bluegrass State. Ohio's history is deeply marked by the interaction of the New England, Middle, and southern colonies within her borders.

By the opening of the nineteenth century, when Napoleon's cession brought to the United States the vast spaces of the Louisiana Purchase beyond the Mississippi, the pioneers had hardly more than entered the outskirts of the forest along the Ohio and Lake Erie. But by 1810 the government had extinguished the Indian title to the unsecured portions of the western Reserve, and to great tracts of Indiana, along the Ohio and up the Wabash Valley; thus protecting the Ohio highway from the Indians, and opening new lands to settlement. The embargo had destroyed the trade of New England, and had weighted down her citizens with debt and taxation; caravans of Yankee emigrant wagons, precursors of the "prairie schooner," had already begun to cross Pennsylvania on their way to Ohio; and they now greatly increased in number. North Carolina back countrymen flocked to the Indiana settlements, giving the peculiar Hoosier flavor to the state, and other southerners followed, outnumbering the northern immigrants, who sought the eastern edge of Indiana.

Tecumthe, rendered desperate by the advance into his hunting grounds, took up the hatchet, made wide-reaching alliances among the Indians, and turned to England for protection. The Indian war merged into the War of 1812, and the settlers strove in vain to add Canadian lands to their empire. In the diplomatic negotiations that followed the war, England made another attempt to erect the Old Northwest beyond the Greenville line into a permanent Indian barrier between Canada and the United States; but the demand was refused, and by the treaties of 1818, the Indians were pressed still farther north. In the meantime, Indian treaties had released additional land in southern Illinois, and pioneers were widening the bounds of the old French settlements. Avoiding the rich savannas of the prairie regions, as devoid of wood, remote from transportation facilities, and suited only to grazing, they entered the hard woods—and in the early twenties they were advancing in a wedge-shaped column up the Illinois Valley.

The southern element constituted the main portion of this phalanx of ax-bearers. Abraham Lincoln's father joined the throng of Kentuckians that entered the Indiana woods in 1816, and the boy, when he had learned to hew out a forest home, betook himself, in 1830, to Sangamon county, Illinois. He represents the pioneer of the period; but his ax sank deeper than other men's, and the plaster cast of his great sinewy hand, at Washington, embodies the training of these frontier railsplitters, in the days when Fort Dearborn, on the site of Chicago, was but a military outpost in a desolate country. While the hard woods of Illinois were being entered, the pioneer movement passed also into the Missouri Valley. The French lead miners had already opened the southeastern section, and southern mountaineers had pushed up the Missouri; but now the planters from the Ohio Valley and the upper Tennessee followed, seeking the alluvial soils for slave labor. Moving across the southern border of free Illinois, they had awakened regrets in that state at the loss of so large a body of settlers.

Looking at the Middle West, as a whole, in the decade from 1810 to 1820, we perceive that settlement extended from the shores of Lake Erie in an arc, following the banks of the Ohio till it joined the Mississippi, and thence along that river and up the Missouri well into the center of the state. The next decade was marked by the increased use of the steamboat; pioneers pressed farther up the streams, etching out the hard wood forests well up to the prairie lands, and forming additional tracts of settlement in the region tributary to Detroit and in the southeastern part of Michigan. In the area of the Galena lead mines of northwestern Illinois, southwestern Wisconsin, and northeastern Iowa, southerners had already begun operations; and if we except Ohio and Michigan, the dominant element in all this overflow of settlement into the Middle West was southern, particularly from Kentucky, Virginia, and North Carolina. The settlements were still dependent on the rivers for transportation, and the areas between the rivers were but lightly occupied. The Mississippi constituted the principal outlet for the products of the Middle West; Pittsburgh furnished most of the supplies for the region, but New Orleans received its crops. The Old National road was built piecemeal, and too late, as a whole, to make a great artery of trade throughout the Middle West, in this early period; but it marked the northern borders of the southern stream of population, running, as this did, through Columbus, Indianapolis, and Vandalia.

The twenty years from 1830 to 1850 saw great changes in the composition of the population of the Middle West. The opening of the Erie Canal in 1825 was an epoch-making event. It furnished a new outlet and inlet for northwestern traffic; Buffalo began to grow, and New York City changed from a local market to a great commercial center. But even more important was the place which the canal occupied as the highway for a new migration.

In the march of the New England people from the coast, three movements are of especial importance: the advance from the seaboard up the Connecticut and Housatonic Valleys through Massachusetts and into Vermont; the advance thence to central and western New York; and the advance to the interior of the Old Northwest. The second of these stages occupied the generation from about 1790 to 1820; after that the second generation was ready to seek new lands; and these the Erie Canal and lake navigation opened to them, and to the Vermonters and other adventurous spirits of New England. It was this combined New York–New England stream that in the thirties poured in large volume into the zone north of the settlements which have been described. The newcomers filled in the southern counties of Michigan and Wisconsin, the northern countries of Illinois, and parts of the northern and central areas of Indiana. Pennsylvania and Ohio sent a similar type of people to the area adjacent to those states. In Iowa a stream combined of the southern element and of these settlers sought the wooded tributaries of the Mississippi in the southeastern part of the state. In default of legal authority, in this early period, they formed squatter governments and land associations, comparable to the action of the Massachusetts men who in the first third of the seventeenth century "squatted" in the Connecticut Valley.

A great forward movement had occurred, which took possession of oak openings and prairies, gave birth to the cities of Chicago, Milwaukee, St. Paul, and Minneapolis, as well as to a multitude of lesser cities, and replaced the dominance of the southern element by that of a modified Puritan stock. The railroad system of the early fifties bound the Mississippi to the North Atlantic seaboard; New Orleans gave way to New York as the outlet for the Middle West, and the day of river settlement was succeeded by the era of inter-river settlement and railway transportation. The change in the political and social ideals was at least equal to the change in economic connections, and together these forces made an intimate organic union between New England, New York, and the newly settled West. In estimating the New England influence in the Middle West, it must not be forgotten that the New York settlers were mainly New Englanders of a later generation.

Combined with the streams from the East came the German migration into the Middle West. Over half a million, mainly from the Palatinate, Würtemberg, and the adjacent regions, sought America between 1830 and 1850, and nearly a million more Germans came in the next decade. The larger portion of these went into the Middle West; they became pioneers in the newer parts of Ohio, especially along the central ridge, and in Cincinnati; they took up the hardwood lands of the Wisconsin counties along Lake Michigan; and they came in important numbers to Missouri, Illinois, Indiana, and Michigan, and to the river towns of Iowa. The migration in the thirties and forties contained an exceptionally large proportion of educated and forceful leaders, men who had struggled in vain for the ideal of a liberal German nation, and who contributed important intellectual forces to the communities in which they settled. The Germans, as a whole, furnished a conservative and thrifty agricultural element to the Middle West. In some of their social ideals they came into collision with the Puritan element from New England, and the outcome of the steady contest has been a compromise. Of all the states, Wisconsin has been most deeply influenced by the Germans.

By the later fifties, therefore, the control of the Middle West had passed to its northern zone of population, and this zone included representatives of the Middle states, New England, and Germany as its principal elements. The southern people, north of the Ohio, differed in important respects from the southerners across the river. They had sprung largely from the humbler classes of the South, although there were important exceptions. The early pioneer life, however, was ill-suited to the great plantations, and slavery was excluded under the Ordinance. Thus this southern zone of the Middle West, particularly in Indiana and Illinois, constituted a mediating section between the South and the North. The Mississippi still acted as a bond of union, and up to the close of the War of 1812 the Valley, north and south, had been fundamentally of the same social organization. In order to understand what follows, we must bear in mind the outlines of the occupation of the Gulf Plains. While settlement had been crossing the Ohio to the Northwest, the spread of cotton culture and Negro slavery into the Southwest had been equally significant. What the New England states and New York were in the occupation of the Middle West, Virginia, the Carolinas, and Georgia were in the occupation of the Gulf states. But, as in the case of the Northwest, a modification of the original stock occurred in the new environment. A greater energy and initiative appeared in the new southern lands; the pioneer's devotion to exploiting the territory in which he was placed transferred slavery from the patriarchal to the commercial basis. The same expansive tendency seen in the Northwest revealed itself, with a belligerent seasoning, in the Gulf states. They had a program of action. Abraham Lincoln migrated from Kentucky to Indiana and to Illinois. Jefferson Davis moved from Kentucky to Louisiana, and thence to Mississippi, in the same period. Starting from the same locality, each represented the divergent flow of streams of settlement into contrasted environments. The result of these antagonistic streams of migration to the West was a struggle between the Lake and Prairie plainsmen, on the one side, and the Gulf plainsmen, on the other, for the possession of the Mississippi Valley. It was the crucial part of the struggle between the northern and southern sections of the nation. What gave slavery and state sovereignty their power as issues was the fact that they involved the question of dominance over common territory in an expanding nation. The place of the Middle West in the origin and settlement of the great slavery struggle is of the highest significance.

In the early history of Ohio, Indiana, and Illinois, a modified form of slavery existed under a system of indenture of the colored servant; and the effort of southern settlers in Indiana and in Illinois to reintroduce slavery are indicative of the importance of the pro-slavery element in the Northwest. But the most significant early manifestation of the rival currents of migration with respect to slavery is seen in the contest which culminated in the Missouri Compromise. The historical obstacle of the Ordinance, as well as natural conditions, gave an advantage to the anti-slavery settlers northwest of the Ohio; but when the Mississippi was crossed, and the rival streams of settlement mingled in the area of the Louisiana Purchase, the struggle followed. It was an Illinois man, with constituents in both currents of settlement, who introduced the Missouri Compromise, which made a *modus vivendi* for the Middle West, until the Compromise of 1850 gave to Senator Douglas of Illinois, in 1854, the opportunity to reopen the issue by his Kansas-Nebraska bill. In his doctrine of "squatter-sovereignty," or the right of the territories to determine the question of slavery within their bounds, Douglas utilized a favorite western political idea, one which Cass of Michigan had promulgated before. Douglas set the love of the Middle West for local self-government against its preponderant antipathy to the spread of slavery. At the same time he brought to the support of the doctrine the Democratic party, which ever since the days of Andrew Jackson had voiced the love of the frontier for individualism and for popular power. In his "Young America" doctrines Douglas had also made himself the spokesman of western expansive tendencies. He thus found important sources of popular support when he invoked the localism of his section. Western appeals to Congress for aid in internal improvements, protective tariffs, and land grants had been indications of nationalism. The doctrine of squatter-sovereignty itself catered to the love of national union by presenting the appearance of a non-sectional compromise, which should allow the new areas of the Middle West to determine their own institutions. But the Free Soil Party, strongest in the regions occupied by the New York-New England colonists, and having for its program national prohibition of the spread of slavery into the territories, had already found in the Middle West an important center of power. The strength of the movement far surpassed the actual voting power of the Free Soil Party, for it compelled both Whigs and Democrats to propose fusion on the basis of concession to Free Soil doctrines. The New England settlers and the western New York settlers, the children of New England, were keenly alive to the importance of the issue. Indeed, Seward, in an address at Madison, Wisconsin, in 1860, declared that the Northwest, in reality, extended to the base of the Alleghanies, and that the new states had "matured just in the critical moment to rally the free states of the Atlantic coast, to call them back to their ancient principles."

These Free Soil forces and the nationalistic tendencies of the Middle West proved too strong for the opposing doctrines when the real struggle came. Calhoun and Taney shaped the issue so logically that the Middle West saw that the contest was not only a war for the preservation of the Union, but also a war for the possession of the unoccupied West, a struggle between the Middle West and the states of the Gulf Plains. The economic life of the Middle West had been bound by the railroad to the North Atlantic, and its interests, as well as its love of national unity, made it in every way hostile to secession. When Dr. Cutler had urged the desires of the Ohio Company upon Congress, in 1787, he had promised to plant in the Ohio Valley a colony that would stand for the Union. Vinton of Ohio, in arguing for the admission of Iowa, urged the position of the Middle West as the great unifying section of the country: "Disunion," he said, "is ruin to them. They have no alternative but to resist it whenever or wherever attempted.... Massachusetts and South Carolina might, for aught I know, find a dividing line that would be mutually satisfactory to them; but, Sir, they can find no such line to which the western country can assent." But it was Abraham Lincoln who stated the issue with the greatest precision, and who voiced most clearly the nationalism of the Middle West, when he declared, "A house divided against itself cannot stand. I believe this government cannot endure permanently half slave and half free."

So it was that when the civil war in Kansas grew into the Civil War in the Union, after Lincoln's election to the presidency, the Middle West, dominated by its combined Puritan and German population, ceased to compromise, and turned the scale in favor of the North. The Middle West furnished more than one-third of the Union troops. The names of Grant and Sherman are sufficient testimony to her leadership in the field. The names of Lincoln and Chase show that the presidential, the financial, and the war powers were in the hands of the Middle West. If we were to accept Seward's own classification, the conduct of foreign affairs as well belonged to the same section; it was, at least, in the hands of representatives of the dominant forces of the section. The Middle West, led by Grant and Sherman, hewed its way down the Mississippi and across the Gulf States, and

Lincoln could exult in 1863, "The Father of Waters again goes unvexed to the sea. Thanks to the great Northwest for it, nor yet wholly to them."

In thus outlining the relations of the Middle West to the slavery struggle, we have passed over important extensions of settlement in the decade before the war. In these years, not only did the density of settlement increase in the older portions of the region, but new waves of colonization passed into the remoter prairies. Iowa's pioneers, after Indian cessions had been secured, spread well toward her western limits. Minnesota, also, was recruited by a column of pioneers. The treaty of Traverse de Sioux, in 1851, opened over twenty million acres of arable land in that state, and Minnesota increased her population 2730.7 percent in the decade from 1850 to 1860.

Up to this decade the pine belt of the Middle West, in northern Michigan, Wisconsin, and Minnesota had been the field of operations of Indian traders. At first under English companies, and afterward under Astor's American Fur Company, the traders with their French and half-breed boatmen skirted the Great Lakes and followed the rivers into the forests, where they stationed their posts and spread goods and whiskey among the Indians. Their posts were centers of disintegration among the savages. The new wants and the demoralization which resulted from the Indian trade facilitated the purchases of their lands by the federal government. The trader was followed by the seeker for the best pine land "forties"; and by the time of the Civil War the exploitation of the pine belt had fairly begun. The Irish and Canadian choppers, followed by the Scandinavians, joined the forest men, and log drives succeeded the trading canoe. Men from the pine woods of Maine and Vermont directed the industry, and became magnates in the mill towns that grew up in the forests, millionaires, and afterwards political leaders. In the prairie country of the Middle West, the Indian trade that centered at St. Louis had been important ever since 1820, with an influence upon the Indians of the plains similar to the influence of the northern fur trade upon the Indians of the forest. By 1840 the removal policy had effected the transfer of most of the eastern tribes to lands across the Mississippi. Tribal names that formerly belonged to Ohio and the rest of the Old Northwest were found on the map of the Kansas Valley. The Platte country belonged to the Pawnee and their neighbors, and to the north along the Upper Missouri were the Sioux, or Dakota, Crow, Cheyenne, and other horse Indians, following the vast herds of buffalo that grazed on the Great Plains. The discovery of California gold and the opening of the Oregon country, in the middle of the century, made it necessary to secure a road through the Indian lands for the procession of pioneers that crossed the prairies to the Pacific. The organization of Kansas and Nebraska, in 1854, was the first step in the withdrawal of these territories from the Indians. A period of almost constant Indian hostility followed, for the savage lords of the boundless prairies instinctively felt the significance of the entrance of the farmer into their empire. In Minnesota the Sioux took advantage of the Civil War to rise; but the outcome was the destruction of their reservations in that state, and the opening of great tracts to the pioneers. When the Pacific railways were begun, Red Cloud, the astute Sioux chief, who, in some ways, stands as the successor of Pontiac and of Tecumthe, rallied the principal tribes of the Great Plains to resist the march of civilization. Their hostility resulted in the peace measure of 1867 and 1868, which assigned to the Sioux and their allies reservations embracing the major portion of Dakota territory, west of the Missouri River. The systematic slaughter of millions of buffalo, in the years between 1866 and 1873, for the sake of their hides, put an end to the vast herds of the Great Plains, and destroyed the economic foundation of the Indians. Henceforth they were dependent on the whites for their food supply, and the Great Plains were open to the cattle ranchers.

In a preface written in 1872 for a new edition of *The Oregon Trail*, which had appeared in 1847, Francis Parkman said, "The wild cavalcade that defiled with me down the gorges of the Black Hills, with its paint and war plumes, fluttering trophies and savage embroidery, bows, arrows, lances, and shields, will never be seen again." The prairies were ready for the final rush of occupation. The homestead law of 1862, passed in the midst of the war, did not reveal its full importance as an element in the settlement of the Middle West until after peace. It began to operate most actively, contemporaneously with the development of the several railways to the Pacific, in the two decades from 1870 to 1890, and in connection with the marketing of the railroad land grants. The outcome was an epoch-making extension of population.

Before 1870 the vast and fertile valley of the Red River, once the level bed of an ancient lake, occupying the region where North Dakota and Minnesota meet, was almost virgin soil. But in 1875 the great Dalrymple farm showed its advantages for wheat raising, and a tide of farm seekers turned to the region. The "Jim River" Valley of South Dakota attracted still other settlers. The northern Pacific and the Great northern Railway thrust out laterals into these Minnesota and Dakota wheat areas from which to draw the nourishment for their daring passage to the Pacific. The Chicago, Milwaukee and St. Paul, the Chicago and Northwestern Railway, Burlington, and other roads, gridironed the region; and the unoccupied lands of the Middle West were taken up by a migration that in its system and scale is unprecedented. The railroads sent their agents and their literature everywhere, "booming" the "Golden West"; the opportunity for economic and political fortunes in such rapidly growing communities attracted multitudes of Americans whom the cheap land alone would not have tempted. In 1870 the Dakotas had fourteen thousand settlers; in 1890 they had over five hundred ten thousand. Nebraska's population was twenty-eight thousand in 1860; one hundred twenty-three thousand in 1870; four hundred fifty-two thousand in 1880; and one million fifty-nine thousand in 1890. Kansas had one hundred seven thousand in 1860; three hundred sixty-four thousand in 1870; nine hundred ninety-six thousand in 1880; and one million four hundred twenty-seven thousand in 1890. Wisconsin and New York gave the largest fractions of the native element to Minnesota; Illinois and Ohio together sent perhaps one-third of the native element of Kansas and Nebraska, but the Missouri and southern settlers were strongly represented in Kansas; Wisconsin, New York, Minnesota, and Iowa gave North Dakota the most of her native settlers; and Wisconsin, Iowa, Illinois, and New York did the same for South Dakota.

Railroads and steamships organized foreign immigration on scale and system never before equaled; a high water mark of American immigration came in the early eighties. Germans and Scandinavians were rushed by emigrant trains out to the prairies, to fill the remaining spaces in the older states of the Middle West. The census of 1890 showed in Minnesota three hundred seventy-three thousand persons of Scandinavian parentage, and out of the total million and one-half persons of Scandinavian parentage in the United States, the Middle West received all but about three hundred thousand. The persons of German parentage in the Middle West numbered over four millions out of a total of less than seven millions in the whole country. The province had, in 1890, a smaller proportion of persons of foreign parentage than had the North Atlantic division, but the proportions varied greatly in the different states. Indiana had the lowest percentage, 20.38; and, rising in the scale, Missouri had 24.94; Kansas 26.75; Ohio 33.93; Nebraska 42.45; Iowa 43.57; Illinois 49.01; Michigan 54.58; Wisconsin 73.65; Minnesota 75.37; and North Dakota 78.87.

What these statistics of settlement mean when translated into the pioneer life of the prairie, cannot be told here. There were sharp contrasts with the pioneer life of the Old Northwest; for the forest shade, there was substituted the boundless prairie; the sod house for the log hut; the continental railway for the old National Turnpike and the Erie Canal. Life moved faster, in larger masses, and with greater momentum in this pioneer movement. The horizon line was more remote. Things were done in the gross. The transcontinental railroad, the bonanza farm, the steam plow, harvester, and thresher, the "league-long furrow," and the vast cattle ranches, all suggested spacious combination and systematization of industry. The largest hopes were excited by these conquests of the prairie. The occupation of western Kansas may illustrate the movement which went on also in the west of Nebraska and the Dakotas. The pioneer farmer tried to push into the region with the old methods of settlement. Deceived by rainy seasons and the railroad advertisements, and recklessly optimistic, hosts of settlers poured out into the plains beyond the region of sufficient rainfall for successful agriculture without irrigation. Dry seasons starved them back; but a repetition of good rainfalls again aroused the determination to occupy the western plains. Boom towns flourished like prairie weeds; eastern capital struggled for a chance to share in the venture, and the Kansas farmers eagerly mortgaged their possessions to secure the capital so freely offered for their attack on the arid lands. By 1887 the tide of the pioneer farmers had flowed across the semi-arid plains to the western boundary of the state. But it was a hopeless effort to conquer a new province by the forces that had won the prairies. The wave of settlement dashed itself in vain against the conditions of the Great Plains. The native American farmer had received his first defeat; farm products at the same period had depreciated, and he turned to the national government for reinforcements.

The Populistic movement of the western half of the Middle West is a complex of many forces. In some respects it is the latest manifestation of the same forces that brought on the crisis of 1837 in the earlier region of pioneer exploitation. That era of overconfidence, reckless internal improvements, and land purchases by borrowed capital, brought a reaction when it became apparent that the future had been over-discounted. But, in that time, there were the farther free lands to which the ruined pioneer could turn. The demand for an expansion of the currency has marked each area of Western advance. The greenback movement of Ohio and the eastern part of the Middle West grew into the fiat money, free silver, and land bank propositions of the Populists across the Mississippi. Efforts for cheaper transportation also appear in each stage of Western advance. When the pioneer left the rivers and had to haul his crops by wagon to a market, the transportation factor determined both his profits and the extension of settlement. Demands for national aid to roads and canals had marked the pioneer advance of the first third of the century. The "Granger" attacks upon the railway rates, and in favor of governmental regulation, marked a second advance of western settlement. The Farmers' Alliance and the Populist demand for government ownership of the railroad is a phase of the same effort of the pioneer farmer, on his latest frontier. The proposals have taken increasing proportions in each region of Western Advance. Taken as a whole, Populism is a manifestation of the old pioneer ideals of the native American, with the added element of increasing readiness to utilize the national government to effect its ends. This is not unnatural in a section whose lands were originally purchased by the government and given away to its settlers by the same authority, whose railroads were built largely by federal land grants, and whose settlements were protected by the United States army and governed by the national authority until they were carved into rectangular states and admitted into the Union. Its native settlers were drawn from many states, many of them former soldiers of the Civil War, who mingled in new lands with foreign immigrants accustomed to the vigorous authority of European national governments.

But these old ideals of the American pioneer, phrased in the new language of national power, did not meet with the assent of the East. Even in the Middle West a change of deepest import had been in progress during these years of prairie settlement. The agricultural preponderance of the country has passed to the prairies, and manufacturing has developed in the areas once devoted to pioneer farming. In the decade prior to the Civil War, the area of greatest wheat production passed from Ohio and the states to the east, into Illinois, Indiana, and Wisconsin; after 1880, the center of wheat growing moved across the Mississippi; and in 1890 the new settlements produced half the crop of the United States. The corn area shows a similar migration. In 1840 the southern states produced half the crop, and the Middle West one-fifth; by 1860 the situation was reversed and in 1890 nearly one-half the corn of the Union came from beyond the Mississippi. Thus the settlers of the Old Northwest and their crops have moved together across the Mississippi, and in the regions whence they migrated varied agriculture and manufacture have sprung up.

As these movements in population and products have passed across the Middle West, and as the economic life of the eastern border has been intensified, a huge industrial organism has been created in the province, an organism of tremendous power, activity, and unity. Fundamentally the Middle West is an agricultural area unequaled for its combination of space, variety, productiveness, and freedom from interruption by deserts or mountains. The huge water system of the Great Lakes has become the highway of a mighty commerce. The Sault Ste. Marie Canal, although open but two-thirds of the year, is the channel of a traffic of greater tonnage than that which passes through the Suez Canal, and nearly all this commerce moves almost the whole length of the Great Lakes system; the chief ports being Duluth, Chicago, Detroit, Cleveland, and Buffalo. The transportation facilities of the Great Lakes were revolutionized after 1886, to supply the needs of commerce between the East and the newly developed lands of the Middle West; the tonnage doubled; wooden ships gave way to steel; sailing vessels yielded to steam; and huge docks, derricks, and elevators, triumphs of mechanical skill, were constructed. A competent investigator has lately declared that "there is probably in the world today no place at tide water where ship plates can be laid down for a less price than they can be manufactured or purchased at the lake ports."

This rapid rise of the merchant marine of our inland seas has led to the demand for deep water canals to connect them with the ocean road to Europe. When the fleets of the Great Lakes plow the Atlantic, and when Duluth and Chicago become seaports, the water transportation of the Middle West will have completed its evolution. The significance of the development of the railway systems is not inferior to that of the great water way. Chicago has become the greatest railroad center of the world, nor is there another area of like size which equals this in its railroad facilities; all the forces of the nation intersect here. Improved terminals, steel rails, better rolling stock, and consolidation of railway systems have accompanied the advance of the people of the Middle West.

This unparalleled development of transportation facilities measures the magnitude of the material development of the province. Its wheat and corn surplus supplies the deficit of the rest of the United States and much of that of Europe. Such is the agricultural condition of the province of which Monroe wrote to Jefferson, in 1786, in these words: "A great part of the territory is miserably poor, especially that near Lakes Michigan and Erie, and that upon the Mississippi and the Illinois consists of extensive plains which have not had, from appearances, and will not have, a single bush on them for ages. The districts, therefore, within which these fall will never contain a sufficient number of inhabitants to entitle them to membership in the confederacy."

Minneapolis and Duluth receive the spring wheat of the northern prairies, and after manufacturing great portions of it into flour, transmit it to Buffalo, the eastern cities, and to Europe. Chicago is still the great city of the corn belt, but its power as a milling and wheat center has been passing to the cities that receive tribute from the northern prairies. It lies in the region of winter wheat, corn, oats, and live stock. Kansas City, St. Louis, and Cincinnati are the sister cities of this zone, which reaches into the grazing country of the Great Plains. The meeting point of corn and cattle has led to the development of the packing industries, large business systems that send the beef and pork of the region to supply the East and parts of Europe. The "feeding system" adopted in Kansas, Nebraska, and Iowa, whereby the stock is fattened from the surplus corn of the region, constitutes a species of varied farming that has saved these states from the disasters of the failure of a single industry, and has been one solution of the economic life of the transition belt between the prairies and the Great Plains. Under a more complex agriculture, better adapted to the various sections of the state, and with better crops, Kansas has become more prosperous and less a center of political discontent.

While this development of the agricultural interests of the Middle West has been in progress, the exploitation of the pine woods of the north has furnished another contribution to the commerce of the province. The center of activity has migrated from Michigan to Minnesota, and the lumber traffic furnishes one of the principal contributions to the vessels that ply the Great Lakes and supply the tributary mills. As the white pine vanishes before the organized forces of exploitation, the remaining hard woods serve to establish factories in the former mill towns. The more fertile denuded lands of the north are now receiving settlers who repeat the old pioneer life among the stumps.

But the most striking development in the industrial history of the Middle West in recent years has been due to the opening up of the iron mines of Lake Superior. Even in 1873 the Lake Superior ores furnished a quarter of the total production of American blast furnaces. The opening of the Gogebic mines in 1884, and the development of the Vermillion and Mesabi mines adjacent to the head of the lake, in the early nineties, completed the transfer of iron ore production to the Lake Superior region. Michigan, Minnesota, and Wisconsin together now produce the ore for eighty percent of the pig iron of the United States. Four-fifths of this great product moves to the ports on Lake Erie and the rest to the manufactories at Chicago and Milwaukee. The vast steel and iron industry that centers at

Pittsburgh and Cleveland, with important outposts like Chicago and Milwaukee, is the outcome of the meeting of the coal of the eastern and southern borders of the province and of Pennsylvania, with the iron ores of the north. The industry has been systematized and consolidated by a few captains of industry. Steam shovels dig the ore from many of the Mesabi mines; gravity roads carry it to the docks and to the ships, and huge hoisting and carrying devices, built especially for the traffic, unload it for the railroad and the furnace. Iron and coal mines, transportation fleets, railroad systems, and iron manufactories are concentrated in a few corporations, principally the United States Steel Corporation. The world has never seen such a consolidation of capital and so complete a systematization of economic processes.

Such is the economic appearance of the Middle West a century after the pioneers left the frontier village of Pittsburgh and crossed the Ohio into the forests. De Tocqueville exclaimed, with reason, in 1833: "This gradual and continuous progress of the European race toward the Rocky Mountains has the solemnity of a providential event. It is like a deluge of men, rising unabatedly, and driven daily onward by the hand of God."

The ideals of the Middle West began in the log huts set in the midst of the forest a century ago. While his horizon was still bounded by the clearing that his ax had made, the pioneer dreamed of continental conquests. The vastness of the wilderness kindled his imagination. His vision saw beyond the dank swamp at the edge of the great lake to the lofty buildings and the jostling multitudes of a mighty city; beyond the rank, grass-clad prairie to the seas of golden grain; beyond the harsh life of the log hut and the sod house to the home of his children, where should dwell comfort and the higher things of life, though they might not be for him. The men and women who made the Middle West were idealists, and they had the power of will to make their dreams come true. Here, also, were the pioneer's traits, individual activity, inventiveness, and competition for the prizes of the rich province that awaited exploitation under freedom and equality of opportunity. He honored the man whose eye was the quickest and whose grasp was the strongest in this contest: it was "every one for himself."

The early society of the Middle West was not a complex, highly differentiated and organized society. Almost every family was a self-sufficing unit, and liberty and equality flourished in the frontier periods of the Middle West as perhaps never before in history. American democracy came from the forest, and its destiny drove it to material conquests; but the materialism of the pioneer was not the dull contented materialism of an old and fixed society. Both native settler and European immigrant saw in this free and competitive movement of the frontier the chance to break the bondage of social rank, and to rise to a higher plane of existence. The pioneer was passionately desirous to secure for himself and for his family a favorable place in the midst of these large and free but vanishing opportunities. It took a century for this society to fit itself into the conditions of the whole province. Little by little, nature pressed into her mold the plastic pioneer life. The Middle West, yesterday a pioneer province, is today the field of industrial resources and systematization so vast that Europe, alarmed for her industries in competition with this new power, is discussing the policy of forming protective alliances among the nations of the continent. Into this region flowed the great forces of modern capitalism. Indeed, the region itself furnished favorable conditions for the creation of these forces, and trained many of the famous American industrial leaders. The Prairies, the Great Plains, and the Great Lakes furnished new standards of industrial measurement. From this society, seated amidst a wealth of material advantages, and breeding individualism, energetic competition, inventiveness, and spaciousness of design, came the triumph of the strongest. The captains of industry arose and seized on nature's gifts. Struggling with one another, increasing the scope of their ambitions as the largeness of the resources and the extent of the fields of activity revealed themselves, they were forced to accept the natural conditions of a province vast in area but simple in structure. Competition grew into consolidation. On the Pittsburgh border of the Middle West the completion of the process is most clearly seen. On the prairies of Kansas stands the Populist, a survival of the pioneer, striving to adjust present conditions to his old ideals.

The ideals of equality, freedom of opportunity, faith in the common man are deep rooted in all the Middle West. The frontier stage, through which each portion passed, left abiding traces on the older, as well as on the newer, areas of the province. Nor were these ideals limited to the native American settlers: Germans and Scandinavians who poured into the Middle West sought the country with like hopes and like faith. These facts must be remembered in estimating the effects of the economic transformation of the province upon its democracy. The peculiar democracy of the frontier has passed away with the conditions that produced it; but the democratic aspirations remain. They are held with passionate determination.

The task of the Middle West is that of adapting democracy to the vast economic organization of the present. This region which has so often needed the reminder that bigness is not greatness, may yet show that its training has produced the power to reconcile popular government and culture with the huge industrial society of the modern world. The democracies of the past have been small communities, under simple and primitive economic conditions. At bottom the problem is how to reconcile real greatness with bigness.

It is important that the Middle West should accomplish this; the future of the Republic is with her. Politically she is dominant, as is illustrated by the fact that six out of seven of the Presidents elected since 1860 have come from her borders. Twenty-six million people live in the Middle West as against twenty-one million in New England and the Middle states together, and the Middle West has indefinite capacity for growth. The educational forces are more democratic than in the East, and the Middle West has twice as many students (if we count together the common school, secondary, and collegiate attendance), as have New England and the Middle states combined. Nor is this educational system, as a whole, inferior to that of the eastern states. State universities crown the public school system in every one of these states of the Middle West, and rank with the universities of the seaboard, while private munificence has furnished others on an unexampled scale. The public and private art collections of Pittsburgh, Chicago, St. Paul, and other cities vie with those of the seaboard. "World's fairs," with their important popular educational influences, have been held at Chicago, Omaha, and Buffalo; and the next of these national gatherings is to be at St. Louis. There is throughout the Middle West a vigor and a mental activity among the common people that bode well for its future. If the task of reducing the Province of the Lake and Prairie Plains to the uses of civilization should for a time overweigh art and literature, and even high political and social ideals, it would not be surprising. But if the ideals of the pioneers shall survive the inundation of material success, we may expect to see in the Middle West the rise of a highly intelligent society where culture shall be reconciled with democracy in the large.

CHAPTER FIVE

THE OHIO VALLEY IN AMERICAN HISTORY

IN A NOTABLE ESSAY PROFESSOR JOSIAH ROYCE HAS ASSERTED THE salutary influence of a highly organized provincial life in order to counteract certain evils arising from the tremendous development of nationalism in our own day. Among these evils he enumerates: first, the frequent changes of dwelling place, whereby the community is in danger of losing the well-knit organization of a common life; second, the tendency to reduce variety in national civilization, to assimilate all to a common type and thus to discourage individuality, and produce a "remorseless mechanism—vast, irrational"; third, the evils arising from the fact that waves of emotion, the passion of the mob, tend in our day to sweep across the nation.

Against these surges of national feeling Professor Royce would erect dikes in the form of provincialism, the resistance of separate sections each with its own traditions, beliefs, and aspirations. "Our national unities have grown so vast, our forces of social consolidation so paramount, the resulting problems, conflicts, evils, have become so intensified," he says, that we must seek in the province renewed strength, usefulness, and beauty of American life.

Whatever may be thought of this philosopher's appeal for a revival of sectionalism, on a higher level, in order to check the tendencies to a deadening uniformity of national consolidation (and to me this appeal, under the limitations which he gives it, seems warranted by the conditions)—it is certainly true that in the history of the United States sectionalism holds a place too little recognized by the historians.

By sectionalism I do not mean the struggle between North and South which culminated in the Civil War. That extreme and tragic form of sectionalism indeed has almost engrossed the attention of historians, and it is, no doubt, the most striking and painful example of the phenomenon in our history. But there are older, and perhaps in the long run more enduring examples of the play of sectional forces than the slavery struggle, and there are various sections besides North and South.

Indeed, the United States is, in size and natural resources, an empire, a collection of potential nations, rather than a single nation. It is comparable in area to Europe. If the coast of California be placed along the coast of Spain, Charleston, South Carolina, would fall near Constantinople; the northern shores of Lake Superior would touch the Baltic, and New Orleans would lie in southern Italy. Within this vast empire there are geographic provinces, separate in physical conditions, into which American colonization has flowed, and in each of which a special society has developed, with an economic, political, and social life of its own. Each of these provinces, or sections, has developed its own leaders, who in the public life of the nation have voiced the needs of their section, contended with the representatives of other sections, and arranged compromises between sections in national legislation and policy, almost as ambassadors from separate countries in a European congress might make treaties.

Between these sections commercial relations have sprung up, and economic combinations and contests may be traced by the student who looks beneath the surface of our national life to the actual grouping of states in congressional votes on tariff, internal improvement, currency and banking, and all the varied legislation in the field of commerce. American industrial life is the outcome of the combinations and contests of groups of states in sections. And the intellectual, the spiritual life of the nation is the result of the interplay of the sectional ideals, fundamental assumptions, and emotions.

In short, the real federal aspect of the nation, if we penetrate beneath constitutional forms to the deeper currents of social, economic, and political life, will be found to lie in the relation of sections and nation, rather than in the relation of states and nation. Recently ex-secretary Root emphasized the danger that the states, by neglecting to fulfill their duties, might fall into decay, while the national government engrossed their former power. But even if the states disappeared altogether as effective factors in our national life, the sections might, in my opinion, gain from that very disappearance a strength and activity that would prove effective limitations upon the nationalizing process.

Without pursuing the interesting speculation, I may note as evidence of the development of sectionalism, the various gatherings of businessmen, religious denominations, and educational organizations in groups of states. Among the signs of growth of a healthy provincialism is the formation of sectional historical societies. While the American Historical Association has been growing vigorously and becoming a genuine gathering of historical students from all parts of the nation, there have also arisen societies in various sections to deal with the particular history of the groups of states. In part this is due to the great distances which render attendance difficult upon the meetings of the national body today, but we would be short-sighted, indeed, who failed to perceive in the formation of the Pacific Coast Historical Association, the Mississippi Valley Historical Association, and the Ohio Valley Historical Association, for example, genuine and spontaneous manifestations of a sectional consciousness.

These associations spring in large part from the recognition in each of a common past, a common body of experiences, traditions, institutions, and ideals. It is not necessary now to raise the question whether all of these associations are based on a real community of historical interest, whether there are overlapping areas, whether new combinations may not be made? They are at least substantial attempts to find a common sectional unity, and out of their interest in the past of the section, increasing tendencies to common sectional ideas and policies are certain to follow. I do not mean to prophesy any disruptive tendency in American life by the rejuvenation of sectional self-consciousness; but I do mean to assert that American life will be enriched and safe-guarded by the development of the greater variety of interest, purposes, and ideals which seem to be arising. A measure of local concentration seems necessary to produce healthy, intellectual, and moral life. The spread of social forces over too vast an area makes for monotony and stagnation.

Let us, then, raise the question of how far the Ohio Valley has had a part of its own in the making of the nation. I have not the temerity to attempt a history of the Valley in the brief compass of this address. Nor am I confident of my ability even to pick out the more important features of its history in our common national life. But I venture to put the problem, to state some familiar facts from the special point of view, with the hope of arousing interest in the theme among the many students who are advancing the science of history in this section.

To the physiographer the section is made up of the province of the Alleghany Plateaus and the southern portion of the Prairie Plains. In it are found rich mineral deposits which are changing the life of the section and of the nation. Although you reckon in your membership only the states that touch the Ohio River, parts of those states are, from the point of view of their social origins, more closely connected with the Northwest on the Lake Plains, than with the Ohio Valley; and, on the other hand, the Tennessee Valley, though it sweeps far toward the Lower South, and only joins the Ohio at the end of its course, has been through much of the history of the region an essential part of this society. Together these rivers made up the "Western World" of the pioneers of the Revolutionary era; the "Western Waters" of the backwoodsmen.

But, after all, the unity of the section and its place in history were determined by the "beautiful river," as the French explorers called it—the Ohio, which pours its flood for over a thousand miles, a great highway to the West; a historic artery of commerce, a wedge of advance between powerful Indian confederacies, and rival European nations, to the Mississippi Valley; a home for six mighty states, now in the heart of the nation, rich in material wealth, richer in the history of American democracy; a society that holds a place midway between the industrial sections of the seaboard and the plains and prairies of the agricultural West; between the society that formed later along the levels about the Great Lakes, and the society that arose in the Lower South on the plains of the Gulf of Mexico. The Alleghanies bound it on the east, the Mississippi on the west. At the forks of the great river lies Pittsburgh, the historic gateway to the West, the present symbol and embodiment of the age of steel, the type of modern industrialism. Near its western border is St. Louis, looking toward the Prairies, the Great Plains, and the Rocky Mountains, the land into which the tide of modern colonization turns.

Between these old cities, for whose sites European nations contended, stand the cities whose growth preëminently represents the Ohio Valley; Cincinnati, the historic queen of the river; Louisville, the warder of the falls; the cities of the "Old National Road," Columbus, Indianapolis; the cities of the Bluegrass lands, which made Kentucky the goal of the pioneers; and the cities of that young commonwealth, whom the Ohio River by force of its attraction tore away from an uncongenial control by the Old Dominion, and joined to the social section where it belonged.

The Ohio Valley is, therefore, not only a commercial highway, it is a middle kingdom between the East and the West, between the northern area, which was occupied by a greater New England and emigrants from northern Europe, and the southern area of the "Cotton Kingdom." As Pennsylvania and New York constituted the Middle Region in our earlier history, between New England and the seaboard South, so the Ohio Valley became the Middle Region of a later time. In its position as a highway and a Middle Region are found the keys to its place in American history.

From the beginning the Ohio Valley seems to have been a highway for migration, and the home of a culture of its own. The sciences of American archeology and ethnology are too new to enable us to speak with confidence upon the origins and earlier distribution of the aborigines, but it is at least clear that the Ohio River played an important part in the movements of the earlier men in America, and that the mounds of the valley indicate a special type of development intermediate between that of the northern hunter folk, and the pueblo building races of the south. This dim and yet fascinating introduction to the history of the Ohio will afford ample opportunity for later students of the relations between geography and population to make contributions to our history.

The French explorers saw the river, but failed to grasp its significance as a strategic line in the conquest of the West. Entangled in the water labyrinth of the vast interior, and kindled with aspirations to reach the "Sea of the West," their fur traders and explorers pushed their way through the forests of the North and across the plains of the South, from river to lake, from lake to river, until they met the mountains of the West. But while they were reaching the upper course of the Missouri and the Spanish outposts of Santa Fé, they missed the opportunity to hold the Ohio Valley, and before France could settle the Valley, the long and attenuated line of French posts in the West, reaching from Canada to Louisiana, was struck by the advancing column of the American backswoodsmen in the center by the way of the Ohio. Parkman, in whose golden pages is written the epic of the American wilderness, found his hero in the wandering Frenchman. Perhaps because he was a New Englander he missed a great opportunity and neglected to portray the formation and advance of the back-wood society which was finally to erase the traces of French control in the interior of North America.

It is not without significance in a consideration of the national aspects of the history of the Ohio Valley, that the messenger of English civilization, who summoned the French to evacuate the Valley and its approaches, and whose men near the forks of the Ohio fired the opening gun of the world-historic conflict that wrought the doom of New

France in America, was George Washington, the first American to win a national position in the United States. The father of his country was the prophet of the Ohio Valley.

Into this dominion, in the next scene of this drama, came the backwoodsmen, the men who began the formation of the society of the Valley. I wish to consider the effects of the formation of this society upon the nation. And first let us consider the stock itself.

The Ohio Valley was settled, for the most part (though with important exceptions, especially in Ohio), by men of the Upland South, and this determined a large part of its influence in the nation through a long period. As the Ohio Valley, as a whole, was an extension of the Upland South, so the Upland South was, broadly speaking, an extension from the old Middle Region, chiefly from Pennsylvania. The society of pioneers, English, Scotch-Irish, Germans, and other nationalities which formed in the beginning of the eighteenth century in the Great Valley of Pennsylvania and its lateral extensions was the nursery of the American backwoodsmen. Between about 1730 and the Revolution, successive tides of pioneers ascended the Shenandoah, occupied the Piedmont, or up-country of Virginia and the Carolinas, and received recruits from similar peoples who came by eastward advances from the coast toward this Old West.

Thus by the middle of the eighteenth century a new section had been created in America, a kind of peninsula thrust down from Pennsylvania between the falls of the rivers of the South Atlantic colonies on the one side and the Alleghany mountains on the other. Its population showed a mixture of nationalities and religions. Less English than the colonial coast, it was built on a basis of religious feeling different from that of Puritan New England, and still different from the conservative Anglicans of the southern seaboard. The Scotch-Irish Presbyterians with the glow of the covenanters; German sectaries with serious-minded devotion to one or another of a multiplicity of sects, but withal deeply responsive to the call of the religious spirit, and the English Quakers all furnish a foundation of emotional responsiveness to religion and a readiness to find a new heaven and a new earth in politics as well as in religion. In spite of the influence of the backwoods in hampering religious organization, this upland society was a fertile field for tillage by such democratic and emotional sects as the Baptists, Methodists and the later Campbellites, as well as by Presbyterians. Mr. Bryce has well characterized the South as a region of "high religious voltage," but this characterization is especially applicable to the Upland South, and its colonies in the Ohio Valley. It is not necessary to assert that this religious spirit resulted in the kind of conduct associated with the religious life of the Puritans. What I wish to point out is the responsiveness of the Upland South to emotional religious and political appeal.

Besides its variety of stocks and its religious sects responsive to emotion, the Upland South was intensely democratic and individualistic. It believed that government was based on a limited contract for the benefit of the individual, and it acted independently of governmental organs and restraints with such ease that in many regions this was the habitual mode of social procedure: voluntary coöperation was more natural to the southern Uplanders than action through the machinery of government, especially when government checked rather than aided their industrial and social tendencies and desires. It was a naturally radical society. It was moreover a rural section not of the planter or merchant type, but characterized by the small farmer, building his log cabin in the wilderness, raising a small crop and a few animals for family use. It was this stock which began to pass into the Ohio Valley when Daniel Boone, and the pioneers associated with his name, followed the "Wilderness Trace" from the Upland South to the Bluegrass lands in the midst of the Kentucky hills, on the Ohio River. In the opening years of the Revolution these pioneers were recruited by westward extensions from Pennsylvania and West Virginia. With this colonization of the Ohio Valley begins a chapter in American history.

This settlement contributed a new element to our national development and raised new national problems. It took a long time for the seaboard South to assimilate the Upland section. We cannot think of the South as a unit through much of its antebellum history without doing violence to the facts. The struggle between the men of the up-country and the men of the tidewater, made a large part of the domestic history of the "Old South." Nevertheless, the Upland South, as slavery and cotton cultivation extended westward from the coast, gradually merged in the East. On the other hand, its children, who placed the wall of the Alleghanies between them and the East, gave thereby a new life to the conditions and ideals which were lost in their former home. Nor was this all. Beyond the mountains new conditions, new problems, aroused new ambitions and new social ideals. Its entrance into the "Western World" was a tonic to this stock. Its crossing put new fire into its veins—fires of militant expansion, creative social energy, triumphant democracy. A new section was added to the

American nation, a new element was infused into the combination which we call the United States, a new flavor was given to the American spirit.

We may next rapidly note some of the results. First, let us consider the national effects of the settlement of this new social type in the Ohio Valley upon the expansion and diplomacy of the nation. Almost from the first the Ohio Valley had constituted the problem of westward expansion. It was the entering wedge to the possession of the Mississippi Valley, and, although reluctantly, the eastern colonies and then the eastern states were compelled to join in the struggle first to possess the Ohio, then to retain it, and finally to enforce its demand for the possession of the whole Mississippi Valley and the basin of the Great Lakes as a means of outlet for its crops and of defense for its settlements. The part played by the pioneers of the Ohio Valley as a flying column of the nation, sent across the mountains and making a line of advance between hostile Indians and English on the north, and hostile Indians and Spaniards on the south, is itself too extensive a theme to be more than mentioned.

Here in historic Kentucky, in the state which was the home of George Rogers Clark it is not necessary to dwell upon his clear insight and courage in carrying American arms into the Northwest. From the first, Washington also grasped the significance of the Ohio Valley as a "rising empire," whose population and trade were essential to the nation, but which found its natural outlet down the Mississippi, where Spain blocked the river, and which was in danger of withdrawing from the weak confederacy. The intrigues of England to attract the Valley to herself and those of Spain to add the setlements to the Spanish Empire, the use of the Indians by these rivals, and the efforts of France to use the pioneers of Kentucky to win New Orleans and the whole Valley between the Alleghanies and the Rocky Mountains for a revived French Empire in America, are among the fascinating chapters of American, as well as of Ohio Valley, history. This position of the Valley explains much of the Indian wars, the foreign relations, and, indirectly, the domestic politics of the period from the Revolution to the purchase of Louisiana. Indeed, the purchase was in large measure due to the pressure of the settlers of the Ohio Valley to secure this necessary outlet. It was the Ohio Valley which forced the nation away from a narrow colonial attitude into its career as a nation among other nations with an adequate physical basis for future growth.

In this development of a foreign policy in connection with the Ohio Valley, we find the germ of the Monroe Doctrine, and the beginnings of the definite independence of the United States from the state system of the Old World, the beginning, in fact, of its career as a world power. This expansive impulse went on into the War of 1812, a war which was in no inconsiderable degree, the result of the aggressive leadership of a group of men from Kentucky and Tennessee, and especially of the daring and lofty demands of Henry Clay, who even thus early voiced the spirit of the Ohio Valley. That in this war William Henry Harrison and the Kentucky troops achieved the real conquest of the northwest province and Andrew Jackson with his Tennesseeans achieved the real conquest of the Gulf Plains, is in itself abundant evidence of the part played in the expansion of the nation by the section which formed on the Ohio and its tributaries. Nor was this the end of the process, for the annexation of Texas and the Pacific Coast was in a very real sense only an aftermath of the same movement of expansion.

While the Ohio Valley was leading the way to the building of a greater nation, it was also the field wherein was formed an important contribution of the United States to political institutions. By this I mean what George Bancroft has well called "federal colonial system," that is, our system of territories and new states. It is a mistake to attribute this system to the Ordinance of 1787 and to the leadership of New England. It was in large measure the work of the communities of the Ohio Valley who wrought out the essentials of the system for themselves, and by their attitude imposed it, of necessity, upon the nation. The great Ordinance only perfected the system.

Under the belief that all men going into vacant lands have the right to shape their own political institutions, the riflemen of western Virginia, western Pennsylvania, Kentucky, and Tennessee, during the Revolution, protested against the rule of governments east of the mountains, and asserted with manly independence their right to self-government. But it is significant that in making this assertion, they at the same time petitioned congress to admit them to the sisterhood of states. Even when leaders like Wilkinson were attempting to induce Kentucky to act as an independent nation, the national spirit of the people as a whole led them to delay until at last they found themselves a state of the new Union. This recognition of the paramount authority of congress and this demand for self-government under that authority, constitute the foundations of the federal territorial system, as expressed in congressional resolutions, worked out tentatively in Jefferson's Ordinance of 1784, and finally shaped in the Ordinance of 1787.

Thus the Ohio Valley was not only the area to which this system was applied, but it was itself instrumental in shaping the system by its own demands and by the danger that too rigorous an assertion of either state or national power over these remote communities might result in their loss to the nation. The importance of the result can hardly be overestimated. It insured the peaceful and free development of the great West and gave it political organization not as the outcome of wars of hostile states, nor by arbitrary government by distant powers, but by territorial government combined with large local autonomy. These governments in turn were admitted as equal states of the Union. By this peaceful process of colonization a whole continent has been filled with free and orderly commonwealths so quietly, so naturally, that we can only appreciate the profound significance of the process by contrasting it with the spread of European nations through conquest and oppression.

Next let me invite your attention to the part played by the Ohio Valley in the economic legislation which shaped our history in the years of the making of the nation between the War of 1812 and the rise of the slavery struggle. It needs but slight reflection to discover that in the area in question, the men and measures of the Ohio Valley held the balance of power and set the course of our national progress. The problems before the country at that time were problems of internal development: the mode of dealing with the public domain; the building of roads and digging of canals for the internal improvement of a nation which was separated into East and West by the Alleghany Mountains; the formation of a tariff system for the protection of home industries and to supply a market for the surplus of the West which no longer found an outlet in warring Europe; the framing of a banking and currency system which should meet the needs of the new interstate commerce produced by the rise of the western surplus.

In the Ohio Valley, by the initiative of Ohio Valley men, and often against the protest of eastern sections, the public land policy was developed by laws which subordinated the revenue idea to the idea of the upbuilding of a democracy of small landholders. The squatters of the Ohio Valley forced the passage of preëmption laws and these laws in their turn led to the homestead agitation. There has been no single element more influential in shaping American democracy and its ideals than this land policy. And whether the system be regarded as harmful or helpful, there can be, I think, no doubt that it was the outcome of conditions imposed by the settlers of the Ohio Valley.

When one names the tariff, internal improvements, and the bank, he is bound to add the title "The American System," and to think of Henry Clay of Kentucky, the captivating young statesman, who fashioned a national policy, raised issues, and disciplined a party to support them and who finally imposed the system upon the nation. But, however clearly we recognize the genius and originality of Henry Clay as a political leader; however we recognize that he has a national standing as a constructive statesman, we must perceive, if we probe the matter deeply enough, that his policy and his power grew out of the economic and social conditions of the people who needs he voiced—the people of the Ohio Valley. It was the fact that in this period they had begun to create an agricultural surplus, which made the necessity for this legislation.

The nation has recently celebrated the one hundredth anniversary of Fulton's invention of the steamboat, and the Hudson River has been ablaze in his honor; but in truth it is on the Ohio and the Mississippi that the fires of celebration should really burn in honor of Fulton, for the historic significance to the United States of the invention of the steamboat does not lie in its use on eastern rivers; not even in its use on the ocean; for our own internal commerce carried in our own ships has had a vaster influence upon our national life than has our foreign commerce. And this internal commerce was at first, and for many years, the commerce of the Ohio Valley carried by way of the Mississippi. When Fulton's steamboat was applied in 1811 to the Western Waters, it became possible to develop agriculture and to get the western crops rapidly and cheaply to a market. The result was a tremendous growth in the entire Ohio Valley, but this invention did not solve the problem of cheap supplies of eastern manufactures, nor satisfy the desire of the West to build up its own factories in order to consume its own products. The Ohio Valley had seen the advantage of home markets, as her towns grew up with their commerce and manufacturers close to the rural regions. Lands had increased in value in proportion to their nearness to these cities, and crops were in higher demand near them. Thus Henry Clay found a whole section standing behind him when he demanded a protective tariff to create home markets on a national scale, and when he urged the breaking of the Alleghany barrier by a national system of roads and canals. If we analyze the congressional votes by which the tariff and internal improvement acts were passed, we shall find that there was an almost unbroken South against them, a Middle Region largely for them, a New England divided, and the Ohio Valley almost a unit, holding the balance of power and casting it in favor of the American system.

The next topic to which I ask your attention is the influence of the Ohio Valley in the promotion of democracy. On this I shall, by reason of lack of time, be obliged merely to point out that the powerful group of Ohio Valley states, which sprang out of the democracy of the backwoods, and which entered the Union one after the other with manhood suffrage, greatly recruited the effective forces of democracy in the Union. Not only did they add new recruits, but by their competitive pressure for population they forced the older states to break down their historic restraints upon the right of voting, unless they were to lose their people to the freer life of the West.

But in the era of Jacksonian democracy, Henry Clay and his followers engaged the great Tennesseean in a fierce political struggle out of which was born the rival Whig and Democratic parties. This struggle was in fact reflective of the conditions which had arisen in the Ohio Valley. As the section had grown in population and wealth, as the trails changed into roads, the cabins into well-built houses, the clearings into broad farms, the hamlets into towns; as barter became commerce and all the modern processes of industrial development began to operate in this rising region, the Ohio Valley broke apart into the rival interests of the industrial forces (the town-makers and the business builders), on the one side and the old rural democracy of the uplands on the other. This division was symbolical of national processes. In the contest between these forces, Andrew Jackson was the champion of the cause of the upland democracy. He denounced the money power, banks, and the whole credit system and sounded a fierce tocsin of danger against the increasing influence of wealth in politics. Henry Clay, on the other hand, represented the new industrial forces along the Ohio. It is certainly significant that in the rivalry between the great Whig of the Ohio Valley and the great Democrat of its Tennessee tributary lay the issues of American politics almost until the slavery struggle. The responsiveness of the Ohio Valley to leadership and its enthusiasm in action are illustrated by the Harrison campaign of 1840; in that "log cabin campaign" when the Whigs "stole the thunder" of pioneer Jacksonian democracy for another backwoods hero, the Ohio Valley carried its spirit as well as its political favorite throughout the nation.

Meanwhile, on each side of the Ohio Valley, other sections were forming. New England and the children of New England in western New York and an increasing flood of German immigrants were pouring into the Great Lake basin and the prairies, north of the upland peoples who had chopped out homes in the forests along the Ohio. This section was tied to the East by the Great Lake navigation and the Erie Canal, it became in fact an extension of New England and New York. Here the Free Soil Party found its strength and New York newspapers expressed the political ideas. Although this section tried to attach the Ohio River interests to itself by canals and later by railroads, it was in reality for a long time separate in its ideals and its interests and never succeeded in dominating the Ohio Valley.

On the south along the Gulf Plains there developed the "Cotton Kingdom," a Greater South with a radical program of slavery expansion mapped out by bold and aggressive leaders. Already this southern section had attempted to establish increasing commercial relations with the Ohio Valley. The staple-producing region was a principal consumer of its live stock and food products. South Carolina leaders like Calhoun tried to bind the Ohio to the chariot of the South by the Cincinnati and Charleston Railroad, designed to make an outlet for the Ohio Valley products to the southeast. Georgia in her turn was a rival of South Carolina in plans to drain this commerce itself. In all of these plans to connect the Ohio Valley commercially with the South, the political object was quite as prominent as the commercial.

In short, various areas were bidding for the support of the zone of population along the Ohio River. The Ohio Valley recognized its old relationship to the South, but its people were by no means champions of slavery. In the southern portion of the states north of the Ohio where indented servitude for many years opened a way to a system of semi-slavery, there were divided counsels. Kentucky also spoke with no certain voice. As a result, it is in these regions that we find the stronghold of the compromising movement in the slavery struggle. Kentucky furnished Abraham Lincoln to Illinois, and Jefferson Davis to Mississippi, and was in reality the very center of the region of adjustment between these rival interests. Senator Thomas, of southern Illinois, moved the Missouri Compromise, and Henry Clay was the most effective champion of that compromise, as he was the architect of the Compromise of 1850. The Crittenden compromise proposals on the eve of the Civil War came also from Kentucky and represent the persistence of the spirit of Henry Clay.

In a word, as I pointed out in the beginning, the Ohio Valley was a Middle Region with a strong national allegiance, striving to hold apart with either hand the sectional combatants in this struggle. In the cautious development of his policy of emancipation, we may see the profound influence of the Ohio Valley upon Abraham Lincoln—Kentucky's greatest son. No one can understand his presidency without proper appreciation of the deep influence of the Ohio Valley, its ideals and its prejudices upon America's original contribution to the great men of the world.

Enough has been said to make it clear, I trust, that the Ohio Valley has not only a local history worthy of study, a rich heritage to its people, but also that it has been an independent and powerful force in shaping the development of a nation. Of the late history of this Valley, the rise of its vast industrial power, its far-reaching commercial influence, it is not necessary that I should speak. You know its statesmen and their influence upon our own time; you know the relation of Ohio to the office of President of the United States! Nor is it necessary that I should attempt to prophesy concerning the future which the Ohio Valley will hold in the nation.

In that new age of inland water transportation, which is certain to supplement the age of the railroad, there can be no more important region than the Ohio Valley. Let us hope that its old love of democracy may endure, and that in this section, where the first trans-Alleghany pioneers struck blows at the forests, there may be brought to blossom and to fruit the ripe civilization of a people who know that whatever the glories of prosperity may be, there are greater glories of the spirit of man; who know that in the ultimate record of history, the place of the Ohio Valley will depend upon the contribution which her people and her leaders make to the cause of an enlightened, a cultivated, a God-fearing and a free, as well as a comfortable, democracy.

CHAPTER SIX

THE SIGNIFICANCE OF THE MISSISSIPPI VALLEY IN AMERICAN HISTORY

THE RISE OF A COMPANY OF SYMPATHETIC AND CRITICAL STUDENTS OF history in the South and in the West is bound to revolutionize the perspective of American history. Already our eastern colleagues are aware in general, if not in detail, of the importance of the work of this nation in dealing with the vast interior, and with the influence of the West upon the nation. Indeed, I might take as the text for this address the words of one of our eastern historians, Professor Albert Bushnell Hart, who, a decade ago, wrote:

> *The Mississippi Valley yields to no region in the world in interest, in romance, and in promise for the future. Here, if anywhere, is the real America—the field, the theater, and the basis of the civilization of the western World. The history of the Mississippi Valley is the history of the United States; its future is the future of one of the most powerful of modern nations.*

If those of us who have been insisting on the importance of our own region are led at times by the enthusiasm of the pioneer for the inviting historical domain that opens before us to overstate the importance of our subject, we may at least plead that we have gone no farther than some of our brethren of the East; and we may take comfort in this declaration of Theodore Roosevelt:

> The states that have grown up around the Great Lakes and in the Valley of the Upper Mississippi, [are] the states which are destined to be the greatest, the richest, the most prosperous of all the great, rich, and prosperous commonwealths which go to make up the mightiest republic the world has ever seen. These states . . . form the heart of the country geographically, and they will soon become the heart in population and in political and social importance. . . . I should be sorry to think that before these states there loomed a future of material prosperity merely. I regard this section of the country as the heart of true American sentiment.

In studying the history of the whole Mississippi Valley, therefore, the members of this Association are studying the origins of that portion of the nation which is admitted by competent eastern authorities to be the section potentially most influential in the future of America. They are also studying the region which has engaged the most vital activities of the whole nation; for the problems arising from the existence of the Mississippi Valley, whether of movement of population, diplomacy, politics, economic development, or social structure, have been fundamental problems in shaping the nation. It is not a narrow, not even a local, interest which determines the mission of this Association. It is nothing less than the study of the American people in the presence and under the influence of the vast spaces, the imperial resources of the great interior. The social destiny of this Valley will be the social destiny, and will mark the place in history, of the United States.

In a large sense, and in the one usually given to it by geographers and historians, the Mississippi Valley includes the whole interior basin, a province which drains into nearly two thousand miles of navigable waters of the Mississippi itself, two thousand miles of the tawny flood of the Missouri, and a thousand miles of the Ohio—five thousand miles of main water highways open to the steamboat, nearly two and a half million square miles of drainage basin, a land greater than all Europe except Russia, Norway, and Sweden, a land of levels, marked by essential geographic unity, a land estimated to be able to support a population of two or three hundred millions, three times the present population of the whole nation, an empire of natural resources in which to build a noble social structure worthy to hold its place as the heart of American industrial, political and spiritual life.

The significance of the Mississippi Valley in American history was first shown in the fact that it opened to various nations visions of power in the

New World—visions that sweep across the horizon of historical possibility like the luminous but unsubstantial aurora of a comet's train, portentous and fleeting.

Out of the darkness of the primitive history of the continent are being drawn the evidences of the rise and fall of Indian cultures, the migrations through and into the great Valley by men of the Stone Age, hinted at in legends and languages, dimly told in the records of mounds and artifacts, but waiting still for complete interpretation.

Into these spaces and among the savage peoples, came France and wrote a romantic page in our early history, a page that tells of unfulfilled empire. What is striking in the effect of the Mississippi Valley upon France is the pronounced influence of the unity of its great spaces. It is not without meaning that Radisson and Groseilliers not only reached the extreme of Lake Superior but also, in all probability, entered upon the waters of the Mississippi and learned of its western affluent; that Marquette not only received the Indians of the Illinois region in his post on the shores of Lake Superior, but traversed the length of the Mississippi almost to its mouth, and returning revealed the site of Chicago; that La Salle was inspired with the vision of a huge interior empire reaching from the Gulf to the Great Lakes. Before the close of the seventeenth century, Perrot's influence was supreme in the Upper Mississippi, while D'Iberville was laying the foundations of Louisiana toward the mouth of the river. Nor is it without significance that while the Verendryes were advancing toward the northwest (where they discovered the Big Horn Mountains and revealed the natural boundaries of the Valley) the Mallet brothers were ascending the Platte, crossing the Colorado plains to Santa Fé and so revealing the natural boundaries toward the southwest.

To the English the great Valley was a land beyond the Alleghanies. Spotswood, the farsighted governor of Virginia, predecessor of frontier builders, grasped the situation when he proposed western settlements to prevent the French from becoming a great people at the back of the colonies. He realized the importance of the Mississippi Valley as the field for expansion, and the necessity to the English empire of dominating it, if England would remain the great power of the New World.

In the war that followed between France and England, we now see what the men of the time could not have realized: that the main issue was neither the possession of the fisheries nor the approaches to the St. Lawrence on the one hemisphere, nor the possession of India on the other, but the mastery of the interior basin of North America.

How little the nations realized the true meaning of the final victory of England is shown in the fact that Spain reluctantly received from France the cession of the lands beyond the Mississippi, accepting it as a means of preventing the infringement of her colonial monopoly in Spanish America rather than as a field for imperial expansion.

But we know now that when George Washington came as a stripling to the camp of the French at the edge of the great Valley and demanded the relinquishment of the French posts in the name of Virginia, he was demanding in the name of the English speaking people the right to occupy and rule the real center of American resources and power. When Braddock's axmen cut their road from the Potomac toward the forks of the Ohio they were opening a channel through which the forces of civilization should flow with ever increasing momentum and "carving a cross on the wilderness rim" at the spot which is now the center of industrial power of the American nation.

England trembled on the brink of her great conquest, fearful of the effect of these far-stretching rivers upon her colonial system, timorous in the presence of the fierce peoples who held the vast domain beyond the Alleghanies. It seems clear, however, that the Proclamation of 1763, forbidding settlement and the patenting of lands beyond the Alleghanies, was not intended as a permanent creation of an Indian reservation out of this Valley, but was rather a temporary arrangement in order that British plans might mature and a system of gradual colonization be devised. Already our greatest leaders, men like Washington and Franklin, had been quick to see the importance of this new area for enlarged activities of the American people. A sudden revelation that it was the West, rather than the ocean, which was the real theater for the creative energy of America came with the triumph over France. The Ohio Company and the Loyal Land Company indicate the interest at the outbreak of the war, while the Mississippi Company, headed by the Washingtons and Lees, organized to occupy southern Illinois, Indiana, and western Kentucky, mark the Virginia interest in the Mississippi Valley, and Franklin's activity in promoting a colony in the Illinois country illustrates the interest of the Philadelphians. Indeed, Franklin saw clearly the possibilities of a settlement there as a means of breaking up Spanish America. Writing to his son in 1767 he declared that a "settlement should be made in the Illinois country . . . raising a strength there which on occasions of a future war might easily be poured down the Mississippi upon the lower country and into the Bay of Mexico to be used against Cuba, the French Islands, or Mexico itself."

The Mississippi Valley had been the despair of France in the matter of governmental control. The *coureurs de bois* escaping from restraints of law and order took their way through its extensive wilderness, exploring and trading as they listed. Similarly, when the English colonists crossed the Alleghanies they escaped from the control of mother colonies as well as of the mother country. If the Mississippi Valley revealed to the statesmen of the East, in the exultation of the war with France, an opportunity for new empire building, it revealed to the frontiersmen, who penetrated the passes of the Alleghanies, and entered into their new inheritance, the sharp distinctions between them and the eastern lands which they left behind. From the beginning it was clear that the lands beyond the Alleghanies furnished an opportunity and an incentive to develop American society on independent and unconventional lines. The "men of the Western Waters" broke with the old order of things, subordinated social restraint to the freedom of the individual, won their title to the rich lands which they entered by hard fighting against the Indians, hotly challenged the right of the East to rule them, demanded their own states, and would not be refused, spoke with contempt of the old social order of ranks and classes in the lands between the Alleghanies and the Atlantic, and proclaimed the ideal of democracy for the vast country which they had entered. Not with the mercurial facility of the French did they follow the river systems of the Great Valley. Like the advance of the glacier they changed the face of the country in their steady and inevitable progress, and they sought the sea. It was not long before the Spaniards at the mouth of the river realized the meaning of the new forces that had entered the Valley.

In 1794 the governor of Louisiana wrote:

This vast and restless population progressively driving the Indian tribes before them and upon us, seek to possess themselves of all the extensive regions which the Indians occupy between the Ohio and Mississippi rivers, the Gulf of Mexico, and the Appalachian Mountains, thus becoming our neighbors, at the same time that they menacingly ask for the free navigation of the Mississippi. If they achieve their object, their ambitions would not be confined to this side of the Mississippi. Their writings, public papers, and speeches, all turn on this point, the free navigation of the Gulf by the rivers . . . which empty into it, the rich fur trade of the Missouri, and in time the possession of the rich mines of the interior provinces of the very Kingdom of Mexico. Their mode of growth and their policy are as formidable for Spain as their armies. . . . Their roving spirit and the readiness with which they procure sustenance and shelter facilitate rapid settlement. A rifle and a little corn meal in a bag are enough for an American wandering alone in the woods for a month. . . . With logs crossed upon one another he makes a house, and even an impregnable fort against the Indians. . . . Cold does not terrify him, and when a family wearies of one place, it moves to another and settles there with the same ease.

If such men come to occupy the banks of the Mississippi and Missouri, or secure their navigation, doubtless nothing will prevent them from crossing and penetrating into our provinces on the other side, which, being to a great extent unoccupied, can oppose no resistance. . . . In my opinion, a general revolution in America threatens Spain unless the remedy be applied promptly.

In fact, the pioneers who had occupied the uplands of the South, the backwoods stock with its Scotch-Irish leaders which had formed on the eastern edge of the Alleghanies, separate and distinct from the type of tidewater and New England, had found in the Mississippi Valley a new field for expansion under conditions of free land and unrestraint. These conditions gave it promise of ample time to work out its own social type. But, first of all, these men who were occupying the Western Waters must find an outlet for their surplus products, if they were to become a powerful people. While the Alleghanies placed a veto toward the east, the Mississippi opened a broad highway to the south. Its swift current took their flat boats in its strong arms to bear them to the sea, but across the outlet of the great river Spain drew the barrier of her colonial monopoly and denied them exit.

The significance of the Mississippi Valley in American history at the opening of the new republic, therefore, lay in the fact that, beyond the area of the social and political control of the thirteen colonies, there had arisen a new and aggressive society which imperiously put the questions of the public lands, internal communication, local self-government, defense, and aggressive expansion, before the legislators of the old colonial régime. The men of the Mississippi Valley compelled the men of the East to think in American terms instead of European. They dragged a reluctant nation on in a new course.

From the Revolution to the end of the War of 1812 Europe regarded the destiny of the Mississippi Valley as undetermined. Spain desired to maintain her hold by means of the control given through the possession of the mouth of the river and the Gulf, by her influence upon the Indian tribes, and by intrigues with the settlers. Her object was primarily to safeguard the Spanish American monopoly which had made her a great nation in the world. Instinctively she seemed to surmise that out of this Valley were the issues of her future; here was the lever which might break successively, from her empire fragments about the Gulf—Louisiana, Florida and Texas, Cuba and Porto Rico—the Southwest and Pacific coast, and even the Philippines and the Isthmian Canal, while the American republic, building itself on the resources of the Valley, should become paramount over the independent republics into which her empire was to disintegrate.

France, seeking to regain her former colonial power, would use the Mississippi Valley as a means of provisioning her West Indian islands; of dominating Spanish America, and of subordinating to her purposes the feeble United States, which her policy assigned to the lands between the Atlantic and the Alleghanies. The ancient Bourbon monarchy, the revolutionary republic, and the Napoleonic empire—all contemplated the acquisition of the whole Valley of the Mississippi from the Alleghanies to the Rocky Mountains.

England holding the Great Lakes, dominating the northern Indian populations and threatening the Gulf and the mouth of the Mississippi by her fleet, watched during the Revolution, the Confederation, and the early republic for the breaking of the fragile bonds of the thirteen states, ready to extend her protection over the settlers in the Mississippi Valley.

Alarmed by the prospect of England's taking Louisiana and Florida from Spain, Jefferson wrote in 1790: "Embraced from St. Croix to St. Mary's on one side by their possessions, on the other by their fleet, we need not hesitate to say that they would soon find means to unite to them all the territory covered by the ramifications of the Mississippi." And that, he thought, must result in "bloody and eternal war or indissoluble confederacy" with England.

None of these nations deemed it impossible that American settlers in the Mississippi Valley might be won to accept another flag than that of the United States. Gardoqui had the effrontery in 1787 to suggest to Madison that the Kentuckians would make good Spanish subjects. France enlisted the support of frontiersmen led by George Rogers Clark for her attempted conquest of Louisiana in 1793. England tried to win support among the western settlers. Indeed, when we recall that George Rogers Clark accepted a commission as Major General from France in 1793 and again in 1798; that Wilkinson, afterwards commander-in-chief of the American army, secretly asked Spanish citizenship and promised renunciation of his

American allegiance; that Governor Sevier of Franklin, afterwards Senator from Tennessee and its first governor as a state, Robertson the founder of Cumberland, and Blount, governor of the Southwest Territory and afterwards Senator from Tennessee, were all willing to accept the rule of another nation sooner than see the navigation of the Mississippi yielded by the American government we can easily believe that it lay within the realm of possibility that another allegiance might have been accepted by the frontiersmen themselves. We may well trust Rufus Putnam, whose federalism and devotion to his country had been proved and whose work in founding New England's settlement at Marietta is well known, when he wrote in 1790 in answer to Fisher Ames' question whether the Mississippi Valley could be retained in the Union: "Should Congress give up her claim to the navigation of the Mississippi or cede it to the Spaniards, I believe the people in the western quarter would separate themselves from the United States very soon. Such a measure, I have no doubt, would excite so much rage and dissatisfaction that the people would sooner put themselves under the despotic government of Spain than remain the indented servants of Congress." He added that if Congress did not afford due protection also to these western settlers they might turn to England or Spain.

Prior to the railroad the Mississippi Valley was potentially the basis for an independent empire, in spite of the fact that its population would inevitably be drawn from the eastern states. Its natural outlet was down the current to the Gulf. New Orleans controlled the Valley, in the words of Wilkinson, "as the key the lock, or the citadel the outworks." So long as the Mississippi Valley was menaced, or in part controlled, by rival European states, just so long must the United States be a part of the state system of Europe, involved in its fortunes. And particularly was this the case in view of the fact that until the Union made internal commerce, based upon the Mississippi Valley, its dominant economic interest, the merchants and sailors of the northeastern states and the staple producers of the southern seaboard were a commercial appanage of Europe. The significance of the Mississippi Valley was clearly seen by Jefferson. Writing to Livingston in 1802 he declared:

> *There is on the globe one single spot, the possessor of which is our natural and habitual enemy. It is New Orleans, through which the produce of three-eights of our territory must pass to market, and from its fertility it will ere long yield more than half of our whole produce and contain more than half of our inhabitants. . . . The day that France takes possession of New*

Orleans fixes the sentence which is to restrain her within her low-water mark. It seals the union of two nations who in conjunction can maintain exclusive possession of the ocean. From that moment we must marry ourselves to the British fleet and nation . . . holding the two continents of America in sequestration for the common purposes of the united British and American nations.

The acquisition of Louisiana was a recognition of the essential unity of the Mississippi Valley. The French engineer Collot reported to his government after an investigation in 1796:

All the positions on the left [east] bank of the Mississippi . . . without the alliance of the western states are far from covering Louisiana. . . . When two nations possess, one the coasts and the other the plains, the former must inevitably embark or submit. From thence I conclude that the western states of the North American republic must unite themselves with Louisiana and form in the future one single compact nation; or else that colony to whatever power it shall belong will be conquered or devoured.

The effect of bringing political unity to the Mississippi Valley by the Louisiana Purchase was profound. It was the decisive step of the United States on an independent career as a world power, free from entangling foreign alliances. The victories of Harrison in the Northwest, in the War of 1812 that followed, ensured our expansion in the northern half of the Valley. Jackson's triumphal march to the Gulf and his defense of New Orleans in the same war won the basis for that Cotton Kingdom, so important in the economic life of the nation and so pregnant with the issue of slavery. The acquisition of Florida, Texas, and the Far West followed naturally. Not only was the nation set on an independent path in foreign relations; its political system was revolutionized, for the Mississippi Valley now opened the way for adding state after state, swamping the New England section and its Federalism. The doctrine of strict construction had received a fatal blow at the hands of its own prophet. The old conception of historic sovereign states, makers of a federation, was shattered by this vast addition of raw material for an indefinite number of parallelograms called states, nursed through a Territorial period by the federal government, admitted under conditions, and animated by national rather than by state patriotism.

The area of the nation had been so enlarged and the development of the internal resources so promoted, by the acquisition of the whole course of the mighty river, its tributaries and its outlet, that the Atlantic coast soon turned its economic energies from the sea to the interior. Cities and sections began to struggle for ascendancy over its industrial life. A real national activity, a genuine American culture began. The vast spaces, the huge natural resources, of the Valley demanded exploitation and population. Later there came the tide of foreign immigration which has risen so steadily that it has made a composite American people whose amalgamation is destined to produce a new national stock.

But without attempting to exhaust, or even to indicate, all the effects of the Louisiana Purchase, I wish next to ask your attention to the significance of the Mississippi Valley in the promotion of democracy and the transfer of the political center of gravity in the nation. The Mississippi Valley has been the especial home of democracy. Born of free land and the pioneer spirit, nurtured in the ideas of the Revolution and finding free play for these ideas in the freedom of the wilderness, democracy showed itself in the earliest utterances of the men of the western Waters and it has persisted there. The demand for local self-government, which was insistent on the frontier, and the endorsement given by the Alleghanies to these demands led to the creation of a system of independent western governments and to the Ordinance of 1787, an original contribution to colonial policy. This was framed in the period when any rigorous subjection of the West to eastern rule would have endangered the ties that bound them to the Union itself. In the Constitutional Convention prominent eastern statesmen expressed their fears of the western democracy and would have checked its ability to out-vote the regions of property by limiting its political power, so that it should never equal that of the Atlantic coast. But more liberal counsels prevailed. In the first debates upon the public lands, also, it was clearly stated that the social system of the nation was involved quite as much as the question of revenue. Eastern fears that cheap lands in abundance would depopulate the Atlantic states and check their industrial growth by a scarcity of labor supply were met by the answer of one of the representatives in 1796:

> I question if any man would be hardy enough to point out a class of citizens by name that ought to be the servants of the community; yet unless that is done to what class of the People could you direct such a law? But if you passed such an act [limiting the area offered

for sale in the Mississippi Valley], it would be tantamount to saying that there is some class which must remain here, and by law be obliged to serve the others for such wages as they please to give.

Gallatin showed his comprehension of the basis of the prosperous American democracy in the same debate when he said:

> If the cause of the happiness of this country was examined into, it would be found to arise as much from the great plenty of land in proportion to the inhabitants, which their citizens enjoyed as from the wisdom of their political institutions.

Out of this frontier democratic society where the freedom and abundance of land in the great Valley opened a refuge to the oppressed in all regions, came the Jacksonian democracy which governed the nation after the downfall of the party of John Quincy Adams. Its center rested in Tennessee, the region from which so large a portion of the Mississippi Valley was settled by descendants of the men of the Upland South. The rule of the Mississippi Valley is seen when we recall the place that Tennessee, Kentucky, and Missouri held in both parties. Besides Jackson, Clay, Harrison and Polk, we count such presidential candidates as Hugh White and John Bell, Vice President R. M. Johnson, Grundy, the chairman of the finance committee, and Benton, the champion of western radicalism.

It was in this same period, and largely by reason of the drainage of population to the West, and the stir in the air raised by the western winds of Jacksonian democracy, that most of the older states reconstructed their constitutions on a more democratic basis. From the Mississippi Valley where there were liberal suffrage provisions (based on population alone instead of property and population), disregard of vested interests, and insistence on the rights of man, came the inspiration for this era of change in the franchise and apportionment, of reform of laws for imprisonment for debt, of general attacks upon monopoly and privilege. "It is now plain," wrote Jackson in 1837, "that the war is to be carried on by the monied aristocracy of the few against the democracy of numbers; the [prosperous] to make the honest laborers hewers of wood and drawers of water . . . through the credit and paper system."

By this time the Mississippi Valley had grown in population and political power so that it ranked with the older sections. The next indication of its significance in American history which I shall mention is its position in shaping the economic and political course of the nation between the close of the War of 1812 and the slavery struggle. In 1790 the Mississippi Valley had a population of about a hundred thousand, or one-fortieth of that of the United States as a whole; by 1810 it had over a million, or one-seventh; by 1830 it had three and two-thirds millions, or over one-fourth; by 1840 over six millions, more than one-third. While the Atlantic coast increased only a million and a half souls between 1830 and 1840, the Mississippi Valley gained nearly three millions. Ohio (virgin wilderness in 1790) was, half a century later, nearly as populous as Pennsylvania and twice as populous as Massachusetts. While Virginia, North Carolina, and South Carolina were gaining sixty thousand souls between 1830 and 1840, Illinois gained three hundred eighteen thousand. Indeed, the growth of this state alone excelled that of the entire South Atlantic states.

These figures show the significance of the Mississippi Valley in its pressure upon the older section by the competition of its cheap lands, its abundant harvests, and its drainage of the labor supply. All of these things meant an upward lift to the eastern wage earner. But they meant also an increase of political power in the Valley. Before the War of 1812 the Mississippi Valley had six senators, New England ten, the Middle states ten, and the South eight. By 1840 the Mississippi Valley had twenty-two senators, double those of the Middle states and New England combined, and nearly three times as many as the Old South; while in the House of Representatives the Mississippi Valley outweighed any one of the old sections. In 1810 it had less than one-third the power of New England and the South together in the House. In 1840 it outweighed them both combined and because of its special circumstances it held the balance of power.

While the Mississippi Valley thus rose to superior political power as compared with any of the old sections, its economic development made it the inciting factor in the industrial life of the nation. After the War of 1812 the steamboat revolutionized the transportation facilities of the Mississippi Valley. In each economic area a surplus formed, demanding an outlet and demanding returns in manufactures. The spread of cotton into the lower Mississippi Valley and the Gulf Plains had a double significance. This transfer of the center of cotton production away from the Atlantic South not only brought increasing hardship and increasing unrest to the East as the competition of the virgin soils depressed Atlantic land values and made eastern labor increasingly dear, but the price of cotton fell also in due proportion to the increase in production by the Mississippi Valley. While the transfer of economic power from the Seaboard South to the Cotton Kingdom of the lower Mississippi Valley was in progress, the upper Mississippi Valley was leaping forward, partly under the stimulus of a market for its surplus in the plantations of the South, where almost exclusive cultivation of the great staples resulted in a lack of foodstuffs and livestock.

At the same time the great river and its affluents became the highway of a commerce that reached to the West Indies, the Atlantic Coast, Europe, and South America. The Mississippi Valley was an industrial entity, from Pittsburgh and Santa Fé to New Orleans. It became the most important influence in American politics and industry. Washington had declared in 1784 that it was the part of wisdom for Virginia to bind the West to the East by ties of interest through internal improvement thereby taking advantage of the extensive and valuable trade of a rising empire.

This realization of the fact that an economic empire was growing up beyond the mountains stimulated rival cities, New York, Philadelphia, and Baltimore, to engage in a struggle to supply the West with goods and receive its products. This resulted in an attempt to break down the barrier of the Alleghanies by internal improvements. The movement became especially active after the War of 1812, when New York carried out De Witt Clinton's vast conception of making by the Erie Canal a greater Hudson which should drain to the port of New York all the basin of the Great Lakes, and by means of other canals even divert the traffic from the tributaries of the Mississippi. New York City's commercial ascendancy dates from this connection with interior New York and the Mississippi Valley. A writer in Hunt's *Merchants' Magazine* in 1869 makes the significance of this clearer by these words:

> There was a period in the history of the seaboard cities when there was no West; and when the Alleghany Mountains formed the frontier of settlement and agricultural production. During that epoch the seaboard cities, North and South, grew in proportion to the extent and fertility of the country in their rear; and as Maryland, Virginia, the Carolinas and Georgia were more productive in staples valuable to commerce than the colonies north of them, the cities of Baltimore, Norfolk, Charleston, and Savannah enjoyed a greater trade and experienced a larger growth than those on the northern seaboard.

He, then, classifies the periods of city development into three: (1) the provincial, limited to the Atlantic seaboard; (2) that of canal and turnpike connected with the Mississippi Valley; and (3) that of railroad connection. Thus he was able to show how Norfolk, for example, was shut off from the enriching currents of interior trade and was outstripped by New York. The efforts of Philadelphia, Baltimore, Charleston, and Savannah to divert the trade of the Mississippi system to their own ports on the Atlantic, and the rise or fall of these cities in proportion as they succeeded are a sufficient indication of the meaning of the Mississippi Valley in American industrial life. What colonial empire has been for London that the Mississippi Valley is to the seaboard cities of the United States, awakening visions of industrial empire, systematic control of vast spaces, producing the American type of the captain of industry.

It was not alone city rivalry that converged upon the Mississippi Valley and sought its alliance. Sectional rivalry likewise saw that the balance of power possessed by the interior furnished an opportunity for combinations. This was a fundamental feature of Calhoun's policy when he urged the seaboard South to complete a railroad system to tap the Northwest. As Washington had hoped to make western trade seek its outlet in Virginia and build up the industrial power of the Old Dominion by enriching intercourse with the Mississippi Valley, as Monroe wished to bind the West to Virginia's political interests; and as De Witt Clinton wished to attach it to New York, so Calhoun and Hayne would make "Georgia and Carolina the commercial center of the Union, and the two most powerful and influential members of the confederacy," by draining the Mississippi Valley to their ports. "I believe," said Calhoun, "that the success of a connection of the West is of the last importance to us politically and commercially. . . . I do verily believe that Charleston has more advantages in her position for the western trade, than any city on the Atlantic, but to develop them we ought to look to the Tennessee instead of the Ohio, and much farther to the West than Cincinnati or Lexington."

This was the secret of Calhoun's advocacy in 1836 and 1837 both of the distribution of the surplus revenue and of the cession of the public lands to the states in which they lay, as an inducement to the West to ally itself with southern policies; and it is the key to the readiness of Calhoun, even after he lost his nationalism, to promote internal improvements which would foster the southward current of trade on the Mississippi.

Without going into details, I may simply call your attention to the fact that Clay's whole system of internal improvements and tariff was based upon the place of the Mississippi Valley in American life. It was the upper part of the Valley, and especially the Ohio Valley, that furnished the votes which carried the tariffs of 1816, 1824, and 1828. Its interests profoundly influenced the details of those tariffs and its need of internal improvement constituted a basis for sectional bargaining in all the constructive legislation after the War of 1812. New England, the Middle Region, and the South each sought alliance with the growing section beyond the mountains. American legislation bears the enduring evidence of these alliances. Even the National Bank found in this Valley the main sphere of its business. The nation had turned its energies to internal exploitation, and sections contended for the economic and political power derived from connection with the interior.

But already the Mississippi Valley was beginning to stratify, both socially and geographically. As the railroads pushed across the mountains, the tide of New England and New York colonists and German immigrants sought the basin of the Great Lakes and the Upper Mississippi. A distinct zone, industrially and socially connected with New England, was forming. The railroad reinforced the Erie Canal and, as De Bow put it, turned back the tide of the Father of Waters so that its outlet was in New York instead of New Orleans for a large part of the Valley. Below the northern zone was the border zone of the Upland South, the region of compromise, including both banks of the Ohio and the Missouri and reaching down to the hills on the north of the Gulf Plains. The Cotton Kingdom based on slavery found its center in the fertile soils along the Lower Mississippi and the black prairies of Georgia and Alabama, and was settled largely by planters from the old cotton lands of the Atlantic states. The Mississippi Valley had rejuvenated slavery, had given it an aggressive tone characteristic of western life.

Thus the Valley found itself in the midst of the slavery struggle at the very time when its own society had lost homogeneity. Let us allow two leaders, one of the South and one of the North, to describe the situation; and, first, let the South speak. Said Hammond, of South Carolina, in a speech in the Senate on March 4, 1858:

> I think it not improper that I should attempt to bring the North and South face-to-face, and see what resources each of us might have in the contingency of separate organizations.
>
> Through the heart of our country runs the great Mississippi, the father of waters, into whose bosom are poured thirty-six thousand miles of tributary streams; and beyond we have the desert prairie wastes to protect us in our rear. Can you hem in such a territory as

that? You talk of putting up a wall of fire around eight hundred and fifty thousand miles so situated! How absurd.

But in this territory lies the great valley of the Mississippi, now the real and soon to be the acknowledged seat of the empire of the world. The sway of that valley will be as great as ever the Nile knew in the earlier ages of mankind. We own the most of it. The most valuable part of it belongs to us now; and although those who have settled above us are now opposed to us, another generation will tell a different tale. They are ours by all the laws of nature; slave labor will go to every foot of this great valley where it will be found profitable to use it, and some of those who may not use it are soon to be united with us by such ties as will make us one and inseparable. The iron horse will soon be clattering over the sunny plains of the South to bear the products of its upper tributaries to our Atlantic ports, as it now does through the ice-bound North. There is the great Mississippi, bond of union made by nature herself. She will maintain it forever.

As the Seaboard South had transferred the mantle of leadership to Tennessee and then to the Cotton Kingdom of the Lower Mississippi, so New England and New York resigned their command to the northern half of the Mississippi Valley and the basin of the Great Lakes. Seward, the old-time leader of the eastern Whigs who had just lost the Republican nomination for the presidency to Lincoln, may rightfully speak for the Northeast. In the fall of 1860, addressing an audience at Madison, Wisconsin, he declared:

The empire established at Washington is of less than a hundred years' formation. It was the empire of thirteen Atlantic states. Still, practically, the mission of that empire is fulfilled. The power that directs it is ready to pass away from those thirteen states, and although held and exercised under the same constitution and national form of government, yet it is now in the very act of being transferred from the thirteen states east of the Alleghany mountains and on the coast of the Atlantic ocean, to the twenty states that lie west of the Alleghanies, and stretch away from their base to the base of the Rocky mountains on the West, and you are the heirs to it. When the next census shall reveal your power, you will be found to be the masters of the United States of America, and through them the dominating political power of the world.

Appealing to the Northwest on the slavery issue Seward declared:

> The whole responsibility rests henceforth directly or indirectly on the people of the Northwest. . . . There can be no virtue in commercial and manufacturing communities to maintain a democracy, when the democracy themselves do not want a democracy. There is no virtue in Pearl street, in Wall street, in Court street, in Chestnut street, in any other street of great commercial cities, that can save the great democratic government of ours, when you cease to uphold it with your intelligent votes, your strong and mighty hands. You must, therefore, lead us as we heretofore reserved and prepared the way for you. We resign to you the banner of human rights and human liberty, on this continent, and we bid you be firm, bold and onward and then you may hope that we will be able to follow you.

When we survey the course of the slavery struggle in the United States it is clear that the form the question took was due to the Mississippi Valley. The Ordinance of 1787, the Missouri Compromise, the Texas question, the Free Soil agitation, the Compromise of 1850, the Kansas-Nebraska bill, the Dred Scott decision, "bleeding Kansas"—these are all Mississippi Valley questions, and the mere enumeration makes it plain that it was the Mississippi Valley as an area for expansion which gave the slavery issue its significance in American history. But for this field of expansion, slavery might have fulfilled the expectation of the fathers and gradually died away.

Of the significance of the Mississippi Valley in the Civil War, it is unnecessary that I should speak. Illinois gave to the North its President; Mississippi gave to the South its President. Lincoln and Davis were both born in Kentucky. Grant and Sherman, the northern generals, came from the Mississippi Valley; and both of them believed that when Vicksburg fell the cause of the South was lost, and so it must have been if the Confederacy had been unable, after victories in the East, to regain the Father of Waters; for, as General Sherman said: "Whatever power holds that river can govern this continent."

With the close of the war political power passed for many years to the northern half of the Mississippi Valley, as the names of Grant, Hayes, Garfield, Harrison, and McKinley indicate. The population of the Valley grew from about fifteen millions in 1860 to over forty millions in 1900—over half the total population of the United States. The significance of its industrial growth is not likely to be overestimated or overlooked. On its northern border, from near Minnesota's boundary line, through the Great Lakes to Pittsburgh, on its eastern edge, runs a huge movement of iron from mine to factory. This industry is basal in American life, and it has revolutionized the industry of the world. The United States produces pig iron and steel in amount equal to her two greatest competitors combined, and the iron ores for this product are chiefly in the Mississippi Valley. It is the chief producer of coal, thereby enabling the United States almost to equal the combined production of Germany and Great Britain; and great oil fields of the nation are in its midst. Its huge crops of wheat and corn and its cattle are the main resources for the United States and are drawn upon by Europe. Its cotton furnishes two-thirds of the world's factory supply. Its railroad system constitutes the greatest transportation network in the world. Again it is seeking industrial consolidation by demanding improvement of its vast water system as a unit. If this design, favored by Roosevelt, shall at some time be accomplished, again the bulk of the commerce of the Valley may flow along the old routes to New Orleans; and to Galveston by the development of southern railroad outlets after the building of the Panama Canal. For the development and exploitation of these and of the transportation and trade interests of the Middle West, eastern capital has been consolidated into huge corporations, trusts, and combinations. With the influx of capital, and the rise of cities and manufactures, portions of the Mississippi Valley have become assimilated with the East. With the end of the era of free lands the basis of its democratic society is passing away.

The final topic on which I shall briefly comment in this discussion of the significance of the Mississippi Valley in American history is a corollary of this condition. Has the Mississippi Valley a permanent contribution to make to American society, or is it to be adjusted into a type characteristically eastern and European? In other words, has the United States itself an original contribution to make to the history of society? This is what it comes to. The most significant fact in the Mississippi Valley is its ideals. Here has been developed, not by revolutionary theory, but by growth among free opportunities, the conception of a vast democracy made up of mobile ascending individuals, conscious of their power and their responsibilities. Can these ideals of individualism and democracy be reconciled and applied to the twentieth century type of civilization?

Other nations have been rich and prosperous and powerful, art-loving and empire-building. No other nation on a vast scale has been controlled by a self-conscious, self-restrained democracy in the interests of progress and freedom, industrial as well as political. It is in the vast and level spaces of the Mississippi Valley, if anywhere, that the forces of social transformation and the modification of its democratic ideals may be arrested.

Beginning with competitive individualism, as well as with belief in equality, the farmers of the Mississippi Valley gradually learned that unrestrained competition and combination meant the triumph of the strongest, the seizure in the interest of a dominant class of the strategic points of the nation's life. They learned that between the ideal of individualism, unrestrained by society, and the ideal of democracy, was an innate conflict; that their very ambitions and forcefulness had endangered their democracy. The significance of the Mississippi Valley in American history has lain partly in the fact that it was a region of revolt. Here have arisen varied, sometimes ill-considered, but always devoted, movements for ameliorating the lot of the common man in the interests of democracy. Out of the Mississippi Valley have come successive and related tidal waves of popular demand for real or imagined legislative safeguards to their rights and their social ideals. The Granger movement, the Greenback movement, the Populist movement, Bryan Democracy, and Roosevelt Republicanism all found their greatest strength in the Mississippi Valley. They were Mississippi Valley ideals in action. Its people were learning by experiment and experience how to grapple with the fundamental problem of creating a just social order that shall sustain the free, progressive, individual in a real democracy. The Mississippi Valley is asking, "What shall it profit a man if he gain the whole world and lose his own soul?"

The Mississippi Valley has furnished a new social order to America. Its universities have set new types of institutions for social service and for the elevation of the plain people. Its historians should recount its old ambitions, and inventory its ideals, as well as its resources, for the information of the present age, to the end that building on its past, the mighty Valley may have a significance in the life of the nation even more profound than any which I have recounted.

→ CHAPTER SEVEN ←

The Problem of the West

The problem of the West is nothing less than the problem of American development. A glance at the map of the United States reveals the truth. To write of a "western sectionalism," bounded on the east by the Alleghanies, is, in itself, to proclaim the writer a provincial. What is the West? What has it been in American life? To have the answers to these questions, is to understand the most significant features of the United States of today.

The West, at bottom, is a form of society, rather than an area. It is the term applied to the region whose social conditions result from the application of older institutions and ideas to the transforming influences of free land. By this application, a new environment is suddenly entered, freedom of opportunity is opened, the cake of custom is broken, and new activities, new lines of growth, new institutions and new ideals, are brought into existence. The wilderness disappears, the "West" proper passes on to a new frontier, and in the former area, a new society has emerged from its contact with the backwoods. Gradually this society loses its primitive conditions, and assimilates itself to the type of the older social conditions of the East; but it bears within it enduring and distinguishing survivals of its frontier experience. Decade after decade, West after West, this rebirth of American society has gone on, has left its traces behind it, and has reacted on the East. The history of our political institutions, our democracy, is not a history of imitation, of simple borrowing; it is a history of the evolution and adaptation of organs in response to changed environment, a history of the origin of new political species. In this sense, therefore, the West has been a constructive force of the highest significance in our life. To use the words of that acute and widely informed observer, Mr. Bryce,

"The West is the most American part of America. . . . What Europe is to Asia, what America is to England, that the western states and territories are to the Atlantic states."

The West, as a phase of social organization, began with the Atlantic coast, and passed across the continent. But the colonial tidewater area was in close touch with the Old World, and soon lost its western aspects. In the middle of the eighteenth century, the newer social conditions appeared along the upper waters of the tributaries of the Atlantic. Here it was that the West took on its distinguishing features, and transmitted frontier traits and ideals to this area in later days. On the coast, were the fishermen and skippers, the merchants and planters, with eyes turned toward Europe. Beyond the falls of the rivers were the pioneer farmers, largely of non-English stock, Scotch-Irish and German. They constituted a distinct people, and may be regarded as an expansion of the social and economic life of the middle region into the back country of the South. These frontiersmen were the ancestors of Boone, Andrew Jackson, Calhoun, Clay, and Lincoln. Washington and Jefferson were profoundly affected by these frontier conditions. The forest clearings have been the seed plots of American character.

In the Revolutionary days, the settlers crossed the Alleghanies and put a barrier between them and the coast. They became, to use their phrases, "the men of the western waters," the heirs of the "western world." In this era, the backwoodsmen, all along the western slopes of the mountains, with a keen sense of the difference between them and the dwellers on the coast, demanded organization into independent states of the Union. Self-government was their ideal. Said one of their rude, but energetic petitions for statehood: "Some of our fellow citizens may think we are not able to conduct our affairs and consult our interests; but if our society is rude, much wisdom is not necessary to supply our wants, and a fool can sometimes put on his clothes better than a wise man can do it for him." This forest philosophy is the philosophy of American democracy. But the men of the coast were not ready to admit its implications. They apportioned the state legislatures so that the property-holding minority of the tidewater lands were able to outvote the more populous back countries. A similar system was proposed by Federalists in the constitutional convention of 1787. Gouverneur Morris, arguing in favor of basing representation on property as well as numbers, declared that "he looked forward, also, to that range of new states which would soon be formed in the West. He thought the rule of representation ought to be so fixed, as to secure to the Atlantic states a prevalence in the national councils." "The new states," said he, "will know less of the public interest than these; will have an interest in many respects different; in particular will be little scrupulous of involving the community in wars, the burdens and operations of which would fall chiefly on the maritime states. Provision ought, therefore, to be made to prevent the maritime states from being hereafter outvoted by them." He added that the western country "would not be able to furnish men equally enlightened to share in the administration of our common interests. The busy haunts of men, not the remote wilderness, was the proper school of political talents. If the western people get power into their hands, they will ruin the Atlantic interest. The back members are always most averse to the best measures." Add to these utterances of Gouverneur Morris the impassioned protest of Josiah Quincy, of Massachusetts, in the debates in the House of Representatives, on the admission of Louisiana. Referring to the discussion over the slave votes and the West in the constitutional convention, he declared,

> Suppose, then, that it had been distinctly foreseen that, in addition to the effect of this weight, the whole population of a world beyond the Mississippi was to be brought into this and the other branch of the legislature, to form our laws, control our rights, and decide our destiny. Sir, can it be pretended that the patriots of that day would for one moment have listened to it? . . . They had not taken degrees at the hospital of idiocy. . . . Why, sir, I have already heard of six states, and some say there will be, at no great distant time, more. I have also heard that the mouth of the Ohio will be far to the east of the center of the contemplated empire. . . . You have no authority to throw the rights and property of this people into "hotch-pot" with the wild men on the Missouri, nor with the mixed, though more respectable, race of Anglo-Hispano-Gallo-Americans who bask on the sands in the mouth of the Mississippi. . . . Do you suppose the people of the northern and Atlantic states will, or ought to, look on with patience and see Representatives and Senators from the Red River and Missouri, pouring themselves upon this and the other floor, managing the concerns of a seaboard fifteen hundred miles, at least, from their residence; and having a preponderancy in councils into which, constitutionally, they could never have been admitted?

Like an echo from the fears expressed by the East at the close of the eighteenth century come the words of an eminent eastern man of letters at the end of the nineteenth century, in warning against the West:

> Materialized in their temper; with few ideals of an ennobling sort; little instructed in the lessons of history; safe from exposure to the direct calamities and physical horrors of war; with undeveloped imaginations and sympathies—they form a community unfortunate and dangerous from the possession of power without a due sense of its corresponding responsibilities; a community in which the passion for war may easily be excited as the fancied means by which its greatness may be convincingly exhibited, and its ambitions gratified. . . . Some chance spark may fire the prairie.

Here, then, is the problem of the West, as it looked to New England leaders of thought in the beginning and at the end of this century. From the first, it was recognized that a new type was growing up beyond the seaboard, and that the time would come when the destiny of the nation would be in western hands. The divergence of these societies became clear in the struggle over the ratification of the federal constitution. The up-country agricultural regions, the communities that were in debt and desired paper money, with some western exceptions, opposed the instrument; but the areas of intercourse and property carried the day.

It is important to understand, therefore, what were some of the ideals of this early western democracy. How did the frontiersman differ from the man of the coast?

The most obvious fact regarding the man of the western Waters is that he had placed himself under influences destructive to many of the gains of civilization. Remote from the opportunity for systematic education, substituting a log hut in the forest-clearing for the social comforts of the town, he suffered hardships and privations, and reverted in many ways to primitive conditions of life. Engaged in a struggle to subdue the forest, working as an individual, and with little specie or capital, his interests were with the debtor class. At each stage of its advance, the West has favored an expansion of the currency. The pioneer had boundless confidence in the future of his own community, and when seasons of financial contraction and depression occurred, he, who had staked his all on confidence in western development, and had fought the savage for his home, was inclined to reproach the conservative sections and classes. To explain this antagonism requires more than denunciation of dishonesty, ignorance, and boorishness as fundamental western traits. Legislation in the United States has had to deal with two distinct social conditions. In some portions of the country there was, and is, an aggregation of property, and vested rights are in the foreground: in others, capital is lacking, more primitive conditions prevail, with different economic and social ideals, and the contentment of the average individual is placed in the foreground. That in the conflict between these two ideals an even hand has always been held by the government would be difficult to show.

The separation of the western man from the seaboard, and his environment, made him in a large degree free from European precedents and forces. He looked at things independently and with small regard or appreciation for the best Old World experience. He had no ideal of a philosophical, eclectic nation, that should advance civilization by "intercourse with foreigners and familiarity with their point of view, and readiness to adopt whatever is best and most suitable in their ideas, manners, and customs." His was rather the ideal of conserving and developing what was original and valuable in this new country. The entrance of old society upon free lands meant to him opportunity for a new type of democracy and new popular ideals. The West was not conservative: buoyant self-confidence and self-assertion were distinguishing traits in its composition. It saw in its growth nothing less than a new order of society and state. In this conception were elements of evil and elements of good.

But the fundamental fact in regard to this new society was its relation to land. Professor Boutmy has said of the United States, "Their one primary and predominant object is to cultivate and settle these prairies, forests, and vast waste lands. The striking and peculiar characteristic of American society is that it is not so much a democracy as a huge commercial company for the discovery, cultivation, and capitalization of its enormous territory. The United States are primarily a commercial society, and only secondarily a nation." Of course, this involves a serious misapprehension. By the very fact of the task here set forth, far-reaching ideals of the state and of society have been evolved in the West, accompanied by loyalty to the nation representative of these ideals. But M. Boutmy's description hits the substantial fact, that the fundamental traits of the man of the interior were due to the free lands of the West. These turned his attention to the great task of subduing them to the purposes of civilization, and to the task of advancing his economic and social status in the new democracy which he was helping to create. Art, literature, refinement, scientific administration, all had to give way to this Titanic labor. Energy, incessant activity, became the lot of this new American. Says a traveler of the time of Andrew Jackson, "America is like a vast workshop, over the door of which is printed in blazing characters, 'No admittance here, except on business.'" The West of our own day reminds Mr. Bryce "of the crowd which Vathek found in the hall of Eblis, each darting hither and thither with swift steps and unquiet mien, driven to and fro by a fire in the heart. Time seems too short for what they have to do, and the result always to come short of their desire."

But free lands and the consciousness of working out their social destiny did more than turn the westerner to material interests and devote him to a restless existence. They promoted equality among the western settlers, and reacted as a check on the aristocratic influences of the East. Where everybody could have a farm, almost for taking it, economic equality easily resulted, and this involved political equality. Not without a struggle would the western man abandon this ideal, and it goes far to explain the unrest in the remote West today.

Western democracy included individual liberty, as well as equality. The frontiersman was impatient of restraints. He knew how to preserve order, even in the absence of legal authority. If there were cattle thieves, lynch law was sudden and effective: the regulators of the Carolinas were the predecessors of the claims associations of Iowa and the vigilance committees of California. But the individual was not ready to submit to complex regulations. Population was sparse, there was no multitude of jostling interests, as in older settlements, demanding an elaborate system of personal restraints. Society became atomic. There was a reproduction of the primitive idea of the personality of the law, a crime was more an offense against the victim than a violation of the law of the land. Substantial justice, secured in the most direct way, was the ideal of the backwoodsman. He had little patience with finely drawn distinctions or scruples of method. If the thing was one proper to be done, then the most immediate, rough and ready, effective way was the best way.

It followed from the lack of organized political life, from the atomic conditions of the backwoods society, that the individual was exalted and given free play. The West was another name for opportunity. Here were mines to be seized, fertile valleys to be preëmpted, all the natural resources open to the shrewdest and the boldest. The United States is unique in the extent to which the individual has been given an open field, unchecked by restraints of an old social order, or of scientific administration of government. The self-made man was the western man's ideal, was the kind of man that all men might become. Out of his wilderness experience, out of the freedom of his opportunities, he fashioned a formula for social regeneration, the freedom of the individual to seek his own. He did not consider that his conditions were exceptional and temporary.

Under such conditions, leadership easily develops, a leadership based on the possession of the qualities most serviceable to the young society. In the history of western settlement, we see each forted village following its local hero. Clay, Jackson, Harrison, Lincoln, were illustrations of this tendency in periods when the western hero rose to the dignity of national hero.

The western man believed in the manifest destiny of his country. On his border, and checking his advance, were the Indian, the Spaniard, and the Englishman. He was indignant at eastern indifference and lack of sympathy with his view of his relations to these peoples; at the shortsightedness of eastern policy. The closure of the Mississippi by Spain, and the proposal to exchange our claim of freedom of navigating the river, in return for commercial advantages to New England, nearly led to the withdrawal of the West from the Union. It was the western demands that brought about the purchase of Louisiana, and turned the scale in favor of declaring the War of 1812. Militant qualities were favored by the annual expansion of the settled area in the face of hostile Indians and the stubborn wilderness. The West caught the vision of the nation's continental destiny. Henry Adams, in his *History of the United States,* makes the American of 1800 exclaim to the foreign visitor,

> Look at my wealth! See these solid mountains of salt and iron, of lead, copper, silver, and gold. See these magnificent cities scattered broadcast to the Pacific! See my cornfields rustling and waving in the summer breeze from ocean to ocean, so far that the sun itself is not high enough to mark where the distant mountains bound my golden seas. Look at this continent of mine, fairest of created worlds, as she lies turning up to the sun's never failing caress her broad and exuberant breasts, overflowing with milk for her hundred million children.

And the foreigner saw only dreary deserts, tenanted by sparse, aguestricken pioneers and savages. The cities were log huts and gambling dens. But the frontiersman's dream was prophetic. In spite of his rude, gross nature, this early western man was an idealist withal. He dreamed dreams and beheld visions. He had faith in man, hope for democracy, belief in America's destiny, unbounded confidence in his ability to make his dreams come true. Said Harriet Martineau in 1834,

> I regard the American people as a great embryo poet, now moody, now wild, but bringing out results of absolute good sense: restless and wayward in action, but with deep peace at his heart; exulting that he has caught the true aspect of things past, and the depth of futurity which lies before him, wherein to create something so magnificent as the world has scarcely begun to dream of. There is the strongest hope of a nation that is capable of being possessed with an idea.

It is important to bear this idealism of the West in mind. The very materialism that has been urged against the West was accompanied by ideals of equality, of the exaltation of the common man, of national expansion, that makes it a profound mistake to write of the West as though it were engrossed in mere material ends. It has been, and is, preëminently a region of ideals, mistaken or not.

It is obvious that these economic and social conditions were so fundamental in western life that they might well dominate whatever accessions came to the West by immigration from the coast sections or from Europe. Nevertheless, the West cannot be understood without bearing in mind the fact that it has received the great streams from the North and from the South, and that the Mississippi compelled these currents to intermingle. Here it was that sectionalism first gave way under the pressure of unification. Ultimately the conflicting ideas and institutions of the old sections struggled for dominance in this area under the influence of the forces that made for uniformity, but this is merely another phase of the truth that the West must become unified, that it could not rest in sectional groupings. For precisely this reason the struggle occurred. In the period from the Revolution to the close of the War of 1812, the democracy of the southern and Middle states contributed the main streams of settlement and social influence to the West. Even in Ohio political power was soon lost by the New England leaders. The democratic spirit of the Middle region left an indelible impress on the West in this its formative period. After the War of 1812, New England, its supremacy in the carrying trade of the world having vanished, became a hive from which swarms of settlers went out to western New York and the remoter regions.

These settlers spread New England ideals of education and character and political institutions, and acted as a leaven of great significance in the Northwest. But it would be a mistake to believe that an unmixed New England influence took possession of the Northwest. These pioneers did not come from the class that conserved the type of New England civilization pure and undefiled. They represented a less contented, less conservative influence. Moreover, by their sojourn in the Middle Region, on their westward march, they underwent modification, and when the farther West received them, they suffered a forest-change, indeed. The westernized New England man was no longer the representative of the section that he left. He was less conservative, less provincial, more adaptable and approachable, less rigorous in his Puritan ideals, less a man of culture, more a man of action.

As might have been expected, therefore, the western men, in the "era of good feeling," had much homogeneity throughout the Mississippi Valley, and began to stand as a new national type. Under the lead of Henry Clay they invoked the national government to break down the mountain barrier by internal improvements, and thus to give their crops an outlet to the coast. Under him they appealed to the national government for a protective tariff to create a home market. A group of frontier states entered the Union with democratic provisions respecting the suffrage, and with devotion to the nation that had given them their lands, built their roads and canals, regulated their territorial life, and made them equals in the sisterhood of states. At last these western forces of aggressive nationalism and democracy took possession of the government in the person of the man who best embodied them, Andrew Jackson. This new democracy that captured the country and destroyed the ideals of statesmanship came from no theorist's dreams of the German forest. It came, stark and strong and full of life, from the American forest. But the triumph of this western democracy revealed also the fact that it could rally to its aid the laboring classes of the coast, then just beginning to acquire self-consciousness and organization.

The next phase of western development revealed forces of division between the northern and southern portions of the West. With the spread of the cotton culture went the slave system and the great plantation. The small farmer in his log cabin, raising varied crops, was displaced by the planter raising cotton. In all except the mountainous areas the industrial organization of the tidewater took possession of the Southwest, the unity of the back country was broken, and the solid South was formed.

In the Northwest this was the era of railroads and canals, opening the region to the increasing stream of Middle state and New England settlement, and strengthening the opposition to slavery. A map showing the location of the men of New England ancestry in the Northwest would represent also the counties in which the Free Soil Party cast its heaviest votes. The commercial connections of the Northwest likewise were reversed by the railroad. The result is stated by a writer in *De Bow's Review* in 1852 in these words:

> What is New Orleans now? Where are her dreams of greatness and glory? . . . Whilst she slept, an enemy has sowed tares in her most prolific fields. Armed with energy, enterprise, and an indomitable spirit, that enemy, by a system of bold, vigorous, and sustained efforts, has succeeded in reversing the very laws of nature and of nature's God, rolled back the mighty tide of the Mississippi and its thousand tributary streams, until their mouth, practically and commercially, is more at New York or Boston than at New Orleans.

The West broke asunder, and the great struggle over the social system to be given to the lands beyond the Mississippi followed. In the Civil War the Northwest furnished the national hero, Lincoln was the very flower of frontier training and ideals, and it also took into its hands the whole power of the government. Before the war closed, the West could claim the President, Vice-President, Chief Justice, Speaker of the House, Secretary of the Treasury, Postmaster-General, Attorney-General, General of the army, and Admiral of the navy. The leading generals of the war had been furnished by the West. It was the region of action, and in the crisis it took the reins.

The triumph of the nation was followed by a new era of western development. The national forces projected themselves across the prairies and plains. Railroads, fostered by government loans and land grants, opened the way for settlement and poured a flood of European immigrants and restless pioneers from all sections of the Union into the government lands. The army of the United States pushed back the Indian, rectangular Territories were carved into checkerboard states, creations of the federal government, without a history, without physiographical unity, without particularistic ideas. The later frontiersman leaned on the strong arm of national power.

At the same time the South underwent a revolution. The plantation, based on slavery, gave place to the farm, the gentry to the democratic elements. As in the West, new industries, of mining and of manufacture, sprang up as by magic. The New South, like the New West, was an area of construction, a debtor area, an area of unrest; and it, too, had learned the uses to which federal legislation might be put.

In the meantime the Old Northwest passed through an economic and social transformation. The whole West furnished an area over which successive waves of economic development have passed. The state of Wisconsin, now much like parts of the state of New York, was at an earlier period like the state of Nebraska of today; the Granger movement and Greenback party had for a time the ascendancy; and in the northern counties of the state, where there is a sparser population, and the country is being settled, its sympathies are still with the debtor class. Thus the Old Northwest is a region where the older frontier conditions survive in parts, and where the inherited ways of looking at things are largely to be traced to its frontier days. At the same time it is a region in many ways assimilated to the East. It understands both sections. It is not entirely content with the existing structure of economic society in the sections where wealth has accumulated and corporate organizations are powerful; but neither has it seemed to feel that its interests lie in supporting the program of the prairies and the South. In the Fifty-third Congress it voted for the income tax, but it rejected free coinage. It is still affected by the ideal of the self-made man, rather than by the ideal of industrial nationalism. It is more American, but less cosmopolitan than the seaboard.

We are now in a position to see clearly some of the factors involved in the western problem. For nearly three centuries the dominant fact in American life has been expansion. With the settlement of the Pacific coast and the occupation of the free lands, this movement has come to a check. That these energies of expansion will no longer operate would be a rash prediction; and the demands for a vigorous foreign policy, for an interoceanic canal, for a revival of our power upon the seas, and for the extension of American influence to outlying islands and adjoining countries, are indications that the movement will continue. The stronghold of these demands lies west of the Alleghanies.

In the remoter West, the restless, rushing wave of settlement has broken with a shock against the arid plains. The free lands are gone, the continent is crossed, and all this push and energy is turning into channels of agitation. Failures in one area can no longer be made good by taking up land on a new frontier; the conditions of a settled society are being reached with suddenness and with confusion. The West has been built up with borrowed capital, and the question of the stability of gold, as a standard of deferred payments, is eagerly agitated by the debtor West, profoundly dissatisfied with the industrial conditions that confront it, and actuated by frontier directness and rigor in its remedies. For the most part, the men who built up the West beyond the Mississippi, and who are now leading the agitation, came as pioneers from the old Northwest, in the days when it was just passing from the stage of a frontier section. For example, Senator Allen of Nebraska, president of the recent national Populist Convention, and a type of the political leaders of his section, was born in Ohio in the middle of the century, went in his youth to Iowa, and not long after the Civil War made his home in Nebraska. As a boy, he saw the buffalo driven out by the settlers; he saw the Indian retreat as the pioneer advanced. His training is that of the old West, in its frontier days. And now the frontier opportunities are gone. Discontent is demanding an extension of governmental activity in its behalf. In these demands, it finds itself in touch with the depressed agricultural classes and the workingmen of the South and East. The western problem is no longer a sectional problem: it is a social problem on a national scale. The greater West, extending from the Alleghanies to the Pacific, cannot be regarded as a unit; it requires analysis into regions and classes. But its area, its population, and its material resources would give force to its assertion that if there is a sectionalism in the country, the sectionalism is eastern. The old West, united to the new South, would produce, not a new sectionalism, but a new Americanism. It would not mean sectional disunion, as some have speculated, but it might mean a drastic assertion of national government and imperial expansion under a popular hero.

This, then, is the real situation: a people composed of heterogeneous materials, with diverse and conflicting ideals and social interests, having passed from the task of filling up the vacant spaces of the continent, is now thrown back upon itself, and is seeking an equilibrium. The diverse elements are being fused into national unity. The forces of reorganization are turbulent and the nation seems like a witches' kettle.

But the West has its own centers of industrial life and culture not unlike those of the East. It has state universities, rivaling in conservative and scientific economic instruction those of any other part of the Union, and its citizens more often visit the East, than do eastern men the West. As time goes on, its industrial development will bring it more into harmony with the East.

Moreover, the Old Northwest holds the balance of power, and is the battlefield on which these issues of American development are to be settled. It has more in common with all parts of the nation than has any other region. It understands the East, as the East does not understand the West. The White City which recently rose on the shores of Lake Michigan fitly typified its growing culture as well as its capacity for great achievement. Its complex and representative industrial organization and business ties, its determination to hold fast to what is original and good in its western experience, and its readiness to learn and receive the results of the experience of other sections and nations, make it an open-minded and safe arbiter of the American destiny.

In the long run the "Center of the Republic" may be trusted to strike a wise balance between the contending ideals. But she does not deceive herself; she knows that the problem of the West means nothing less than the problem of working out original social ideals and social adjustments for the American nation.

→ CHAPTER EIGHT ←

DOMINANT FORCES IN WESTERN LIFE

THE OLD NORTHWEST IS A NAME WHICH TELLS OF THE VESTIGES WHICH THE march of settlement across the American continent has left behind it. The New Northwest fronts the watery labyrinth of Puget Sound and awaits its destiny upon the Pacific. The Old Northwest, the historic Northwest Territory, is now the new Middle Region of the United States. A century ago it was a wilderness, broken only by a few French settlements and the straggling American hamlets along the Ohio and its tributaries, while, on the shore of Lake Erie, Moses Cleaveland had just led a handful of men to the Connecticut Reserve. Today it is the keystone of the American Commonwealth. Since 1860 the center of population of the United States has rested within its limits, and the center of manufacturing in the nation lies eight miles from President McKinley's Ohio home. Of the seven men who have been elected to the presidency of the United States since 1860, six have come from the Old Northwest, and the seventh came from the kindred region of western New York. The congressional Representatives from these five states of the Old Northwest already outnumber those from the old Middle states, and are three times as numerous as those from New England.

The elements that have contributed to the civilization of this region are therefore well worth consideration. To know the states that make up the Old Northwest—Ohio, Indiana, Illinois, Michigan and Wisconsin—one must understand their social origins.

Eldest in this sisterhood was Ohio. New England gave the formative impulses to this state by the part which the Ohio Company played in securing the Ordinance of 1787, and at Marietta and Cleveland Massachusetts and Connecticut planted enduring centers of Puritan influence. During the same period New Jersey and Pennsylvania sent their colonists to the Symmes Purchase, in which Cincinnati was the rallying-point, while Virginians sought the Military Bounty Lands in the region of Chillicothe. The Middle states and the South, with their democratic ideas, constituted the dominant element in Ohio politics in the early part of her history. This dominance is shown by the nativity of the members of the Ohio legislature elected in 1820: New England furnished nine Senators and sixteen Representatives, chiefly from Connecticut; New York, New Jersey, and Pennsylvania, seventeen Senators and twenty-one Representatives, mostly from Pennsylvania; while the South furnished nine Senators and twenty-seven Representatives, of whom the majority came from Virginia. Five of the Representatives were native of Ireland, presumably Scotch-Irishmen. In the Ohio Senate, therefore, the Middle states had as many representatives as had New England and the South together, while the southern men slightly outnumbered the Middle states men in the Assembly. Together, the emigrants from the Democratic South and Middle Region outnumbered the Federalist New Englanders three to one. Although Ohio is popularly considered a child of New England, it is clear that in these formative years of her statehood the commonwealth was dominated by other forces.

By the close of this early period, in 1820, the settlement in Ohio had covered more or less fully all except the northwest corner of the state, and Indiana's formative period was well started. Here, as in Ohio, there was a large southern element. But while the southern stream that flowed into Ohio had its sources in Virginia, the main current that sought Indiana came from North Carolina; and these settlers were for the most part from the humbler classes. In the settlement of Indiana from the South two separate elements are distinguishable: the Quaker migration from North Carolina, moving chiefly because of antislavery convictions; the "poor white" stream, made up in part of restless hunters and thriftless pioneers moving without definite ambitions, and in part of other classes, such as former overseers, migrating to the new country with definite purpose of improving their fortunes.

These elements constituted well-marked features in the southern contribution to Indiana, and they explain why she has been named the Hoosier State; but it should by no means be thought that all of the southern immigrants came under these classes, nor that these have been the normal elements in the development of the Indiana of today. In the Northwest, where interstate migration has been so continuous and widespread, the lack of typical state peculiarities is obvious, and the student of society, like the traveler, is tempted, in his effort to distinguish the community from its neighbors, to exaggerate the odd and exceptional elements which give a particular flavor to the state. Indiana has suffered somewhat from this tendency; but it is undoubted that these peculiarities of origin left deep and abiding influences upon the state. In 1820 her settlement was chiefly in the southern counties, where southern and Middle states influence was dominant. Her two United States Senators were Virginians by birth, while her Representative was from Pennsylvania. The southern element continued so powerful that one student of Indiana origins has estimated that in 1850 one-third of the population of the state were native Carolinians and their children in the first generation. Not until a few years before the Civil War did the northern current exert a decisive influence upon Indiana. She had no such lake ports as had her sister states, and extension of settlement into the state from ports like Chicago was interrupted by the less attractive area of the northwestern part of Indiana. Add to this the geological fact that the limestone ridges and the best soils ran in nearly perpendicular belts northward from the Ohio, and it will be seen how circumstances combined to diminish northern and to facilitate southern influences in the state prior to the railroad development.

In Illinois, also, the current of migration was at first preponderantly southern, but the settlers were less often from the Atlantic coast. Kentucky and Tennessee were generous contributors, but many of the distinguished leaders came from Virginia, and it is worthy of note that in 1820 the two United States Senators of Illinois were of Maryland ancestry, while her Representative was of Kentucky origin. The swarms of land-seekers between 1820 and 1830 ascended the Illinois river, and spread out between that river and the Mississippi. It was in this period that Abraham Lincoln's father, who had come from Kentucky to Indiana, again left his log cabin and traveled by ox-team with his family to the popular Illinois county of Sangamon. Here Lincoln split his famous rails to fence their land, and grew up under the influences of this migration of the southern pioneers to the prairies. They were not predominantly of the planter class; but the fierce contest in 1824 over the proposition to open Illinois to slavery was won for freedom by a narrow majority.

Looking at the three states, Ohio, Indiana, and Illinois, prior to 1850, we perceive how important was the voice of the South here, and we can the more easily understand the early affiliation of the Northwest with her sister states to the south on the western waters. It was not without reason that the proposal of the Missouri Compromise came from Illinois, and it was a natural enthusiasm with which these states followed Henry Clay in the war policy of 1812. The combination of the South, the western portion of the Middle states, and the Mississippi Valley gave the ascendancy to the democratic ideals of the followers of Jefferson, and left New England a weakened and isolated section for nearly half a century. Many of the most characteristic elements in American life in the first part of the century were due to this relationship between the South and the trans-Alleghany region. But even thus early the Northwest had revealed strong predilections for the northern economic ideals as against the peculiar institution of the South, and this tendency grew with the increase of New England immigration.

The northern two in this sisterhood of northwestern states were the first to be entered by the French, but latest by the English settlers. Why Michigan was not occupied by New York men at an earlier period is at first sight not easy to understand. Perhaps the adverse reports of surveyors who visited the interior of the state, the partial geographical isolation, and the unprogressive character of the French settlers account for the tardy occupation of the area. Certain it is that while the southern tier of states was sought by swarms of settlers, Wisconsin and Michigan still echoed to Canadian boating-songs, and voyageurs paddled their birch canoes along the streams of the wilderness to traffic with the savages. Great Britain maintained the dominant position until after the War of 1812, and the real center of authority was in Canada.

But after the digging of the Erie Canal, settlement began to turn into Michigan. Between 1830 and 1840 the population of the state leaped from thirty-one thousand to two hundred twelve thousand, in the face of the fact that the heavy debt of the state and the crisis of 1837 turned from her borders many of the thrifty, debt-hating Germans. The vast majority of the settlers were New Yorkers. Michigan is distinctly a child of the Empire State. Canadians, both French and English, continued to come as the lumber interests of the region increased. By 1850 Michigan contained nearly four hundred thousand inhabitants, who occupied the southern half of the state.

But she now found an active competitor for settlement in Wisconsin. In this region two forces had attracted the earlier inhabitants. The fur-trading posts of Green Bay, Prairie du Chien, and Milwaukee constituted one element, in which the French influence was continued. The lead region of the southwest corner of the state formed the center of attraction for Illinois and southern pioneers. The soldiers who followed Black Hawk's trail in 1832 reported the richness of the soil, and an era of immigration followed. To the port of Milwaukee came a combined migration from western New York and New England, and spread along the southern tier of prairie counties until it met the southern settlers in the lead region. Many of the early political contests in the state were connected, as in Ohio and Illinois, with the antagonisms between the sections thus brought together in a limited area.

The other element in the formation of Wisconsin was that of the Germans, then just entering upon their vast immigration to the United States. Wisconsin was free from debt; she made a constitution of exceptional liberality to foreigners, and instead of treasuring her school lands or using them for internal improvements, she sold them for almost nothing to attract immigration. The result was that the prudent Germans, who loved light taxes and cheap hard wood lands, turned toward Wisconsin, another *Völkerwanderung*. From Milwaukee as a center they spread north along the shore of Lake Michigan, and later into northern central Wisconsin, following the belt of the hardwood forests. So considerable were their numbers that such an economist as Roscher wrote of the feasibility of making Wisconsin a German state. "They can plant the vine on the hills," cried Franz Löher in 1847, "and drink with happy song and dance; they can have German schools and universities, German literature and art, German science and philosophy, German courts and assemblies; in short, they can form a German State, in which the German language shall be as much the popular and official language as the English is now, and in which the German spirit shall rule." By 1860 the German-born were sixteen percent of the population of the state. But the New York and New England stream proved even more broad and steady in its flow in these years before the war. Wisconsin's population rose from thirty thousand in 1840 to three hundred thousand in 1850.

The New England element that entered this state is probably typical of the same element in Wisconsin's neighboring states, and demands notice. It came for the most part, not from the seaboard of Massachusetts, which has so frequently represented New England to the popular apprehension. A large element in this stock was the product of the migration that ascended the valleys of Connecticut and central Massachusetts through the hills into Vermont and New York, a pioneer folk almost from the time of their origin. The Vermont colonists decidedly outnumbered those of

Massachusetts in both Michigan and Wisconsin, and were far more numerous in other northwestern states than the population of Vermont warranted. Together with this current came the settlers from western New York. These were generally descendants of this same pioneer New England stock, continuing into a remoter West the movement that had brought their parents to New York. The combined current from New England and New York thus constituted a distinctly modified New England stock, and was clearly the dominant native element in Michigan and Wisconsin.

The decade of the forties was also the period of Iowa's rapid increase. Although not politically a part of the Old Northwest, in history she is closely related to that region. Her growth was by no means so rapid as was Wisconsin's, for the proportion of foreign immigration was less. Whereas in 1850 more than one-third of Wisconsin's population was foreign-born, the proportion for Iowa was not much over one-tenth. The main body of her people finally came from the Middle states, and Illinois and Ohio; but southern elements were well represented, particularly among her political leaders.

The middle of the century was the turning-point in the transfer of control in the Northwest. Below the line of the old national turnpike, marked by the cities of Columbus, Indianapolis, Vandalia, and St. Louis, the counties had acquired a stability of settlement; and partly because of the southern element, partly because of a natural tendency of new communities toward Jacksonian ideals, these counties were preponderantly Democratic. But the southern migration had turned to the cotton areas of the Southwest, and the development of railroads and canals had broken the historic commercial ascendancy of the Mississippi River; New Orleans was yielding the scepter to New York. The tide of migration from the North poured along these newly opened channels, and occupied the less settled counties above the national turnpike. In cities like Columbus and Indianapolis, where the two currents had run side by side, the combined elements were most clearly marked, but in the Northwest as a whole a varied population had been formed. This region seemed to represent and understand the various parts of the Union. It was this aspect which Mr. Vinton, of Ohio, urged in Congress when he made his notable speech in favor of the admission of Iowa. He pleaded the mission of the Northwest as the mediator between the sections and the unifying agency in the nation, with such power and pathos as to thrill even John Quincy Adams.

But there are some issues which cannot be settled by compromise, tendencies one of which must conquer the other. Such an issue the slave power raised, and raised too late for support in the upper half of the

Mississippi Basin. The northern and the southern elements found themselves in opposition to each other. "A house divided against itself cannot stand," said Abraham Lincoln, a northern leader of southern origin. Douglas, a leader of the southern forces, though coming from New England, declared his indifference whether slavery were voted up or down in the western Territories. The historic debates between these two champions reveal the complex conditions in the Northwest, and take on a new meaning when considered in the light of this contest between the northern and the southern elements. The state that had been so potent for compromise was at last the battle-ground itself, and the places selected for the various debates of Lincoln and Douglas marked the strongholds and the outposts of the antagonistic forces.

At this time the kinship of western New York and the dominant element in the Northwest was clearly revealed. Speaking for the anti-slavery forces at Madison, Wisconsin, in 1860, Seward said:

> The Northwest is by no means so small as you may think it. I speak to you because I feel that I am, and during all my mature life have been, one of you. Although of New York, I am still a citizen of the Northwest. The Northwest extends eastward to the base of the Alleghany Mountains, and does not all of western New York lie westward of the Alleghany Mountains? Whence comes all the inspiration of free soil which spreads itself with such cheerful voices over all these plains? Why, from New York westward of the Alleghany Mountains. The people before me, who are you but New York men, while you are men of the Northwest?

In the Civil War, western New York and the Northwest were powerful in the forum and in the field. A million soldiers came from the states that the Ordinance, passed by southern votes, had devoted to freedom.

This was the first grave time of trial for the Northwest, and it did much eventually to give to the region a homogeneity and self-consciousness. But at the close of the war the region was still agricultural, only half-developed; still breaking ground in northern forests; still receiving contributions of peoples which radically modified the social organism, and undergoing economic changes almost revolutionary in their rapidity and extent. The changes since the war are of more social importance, in many respects, than those in the years commonly referred to as the formative period. As a result, the Northwest finds herself again between contending forces, sharing the interests of East and West, as once before those of North and South, and forced to give her voice on issues of equal significance for the destiny of the republic.

In these transforming years since 1860, Ohio, finding the magician's talisman that revealed the treasury of mineral wealth, gas, and petroleum beneath her fields, has leaped to a front rank among the manufacturing states of the Union. Potential on the Great Lakes by reason of her ports of Toledo and Cleveland, tapping the Ohio River artery of trade at Cincinnati, and closely connected with all the vast material development of the upper waters of this river in western Pennsylvania and West Virginia, Ohio has become distinctly a part of the eastern social organism, much like the state of Pennsylvania. The complexity of her origin still persists. Ohio has no preponderant social center; her multiplicity of colleges and universities bears tribute to the diversity of the elements that have made the state. One-third of her people are of foreign parentage (one or both parents foreign-born), and the city of Cincinnati has been deeply affected by the German stock, while Cleveland strongly reflects the influence of the New England element. That influence is still very palpable, but it is New England in the presence of natural gas, iron, and coal, New England shaped by blast and forge. The Middle state ideals will dominate Ohio's future.

Bucolic Indiana, too, within the last decade has come into the possession of gas-fields and has increased the exploitation of her coals until she seems destined to share in the industrial type represented by Ohio. Cities have arisen, like a dream, on the sites of country villages. But Indiana has a much smaller proportion of foreign elements than any other state of the Old Northwest, and it is the southern element that still differentiates her from her sisters. While Ohio's political leaders still attest the Puritan migration, Indiana's clasp hands with the leaders from the South.

The southern elements continue also to reveal themselves in the Democratic southwestern counties of Illinois, grouped like a broad delta of the Illinois River, while northern Illinois holds a larger proportion of descendants of the Middle states and New England. About one-half her population is of foreign parentage, in which the German, Irish, and Scandinavians furnish the largest elements. She is a great agricultural state and a great manufacturing state, the connecting link between the Mississippi and the Great Lakes. Her metropolis, Chicago, is the very type of Northwestern development for good and for evil. It is an epitome of her composite nationality. A recent writer, analyzing the school census of Chicago, points out that "only two cities in the German Empire, Berlin and

Hamburg, have a greater German population than Chicago; only two in Sweden, Stockholm and Göteborg, have more Swedes; and only two in Norway, Christiana and Bergen, have more Norwegians"; while the Irish, Polish, Bohemians, and Dutch elements are also largely represented. But in spite of her rapidity of growth and her complex elements, Chicago stands as the representative of the will-power and genius for action of the Middle West, and the state of Illinois will be the battleground for social and economic ideals for the next generation.

Michigan is two states. The northern peninsula is cut off from the southern physically, industrially, and in the history of settlement. It would seem that her natural destiny was with Wisconsin, or some possible new state embracing the iron and copper, forest and shipping areas of Michigan, Wisconsin, and Minnesota on Lake Superior. The lower peninsula of Michigan is the daughter of New York and over twelve percent of Michigan's present population were born in that state, and her traits are those of the parent state. Over half her population is of foreign parentage, of which Canada and England together have furnished one-half, while the Germans outnumber any other single foreign element. The state has undergone a steady industrial development, exploiting her northern mines and forests, developing her lumber interests with Saginaw as the center, raising fruits along the lake shore counties, and producing grain in the middle trough of counties running from Saginaw Bay to the south of Lake Michigan. Her state university has been her peculiar glory, furnishing the first model for the state university, and it is the educational contribution of the Northwest to the nation.

Wisconsin's future is dependent upon the influence of the large proportion of her population of foreign parentage, for nearly three-fourths of her inhabitants are of that class. She thus has a smaller percentage of native population than any other of the states formed from the Old Northwest. Of this foreign element the Germans constitute by far the largest part, with the Scandinavians second. Her American population born outside of Wisconsin comes chiefly from New York. In contrast with the Ohio River states, she lacks the southern element. Her greater foreign population and her dairy interests contrast with Michigan's Canadian and English elements and fruit culture. Her relations are more western than Michigan's by reason of her connection with the Mississippi and the prairie states. Her foreign element is slightly less than Minnesota's, and in the latter state the Scandinavians take the place held by the Germans in Wisconsin. The facility with which the Scandinavians catch the spirit of western America and assimilate with their neighbors is much greater than is the case with the Germans, so that Wisconsin seems to offer opportunity for non-English influence in a greater degree than her sister on the west. While Minnesota's economic development has heretofore been closely dependent on the wheat-producing prairies, the opening of the iron fields of the Mesabi and Vermilion ranges, together with the development of St. Paul and Minneapolis, Duluth and West Superior, and the prospective achievement of a deep-water communication with the Atlantic, seem to offer to that state a new and imperial industrial destiny. Between this stupendous economic future to the northwest and the colossal growth of Chicago on the southeast Wisconsin seems likely to become a middle agricultural area, developing particularly into a dairy state. She is powerfully affected by the conservative tendencies of her German element in times of political agitation and of proposals of social change.

Some of the social modifications in this state are more or less typical of important processes at work among the neighboring states of the Old Northwest. In the north, the men who built up the lumber interests of the state, who founded a mill town surrounded by the stumps of the pine forests which they exploited for the prairie markets, have acquired wealth and political power. The spacious and well-appointed home of the town-builder may now be seen in many a northern community, in a group of less pretentious homes of operatives and tradesmen, the social distinctions between them emphasized by the difference in nationality. A few years before, this captain of industry was perhaps actively engaged in the task of seeking the best "forties" or directing the operations of his log-drivers. His wife and daughters make extensive visits to Europe, his sons go to some university, and he himself is likely to acquire political position, or to devote his energies to saving the town from industrial decline, as the timber is cut away, by transforming it into a manufacturing center for more finished products. Still others continue their activity among the forests of the South. This social history of the timber areas of Wisconsin has left clear indications in the development of the peculiar political leadership in the northern portion of the state.

In the southern and middle counties of the state, the original settlement of the native American pioneer farmer, a tendency is showing itself to divide the farms and to sell to thrifty Germans, or to cultivate the soil by tenants, while the farmer retires to live in the neighboring village, and perhaps to organize creameries and develop a dairy business. The result is that a replacement of nationalities is in progress. Townships and even counties once dominated by the native American farmers of New York extraction are now possessed by Germans or other European nationalities. Large portions of the retail trades of the towns are also passing into German hands, while the native element seeks the cities, the professions, or mercantile enterprises of larger character. The non-native element shows distinct tendencies to dwell in groups. One of the most striking illustrations of this fact is the community of New Glarus, in Wisconsin, formed by a carefully organized migration from Glarus in Switzerland, aided by the canton itself. For some years this community was a miniature Swiss canton in social organization and customs, but of late it has become increasingly assimilated to the American type, and has left an impress by transforming the county in which it is from a grain-raising to a dairy region.

From Milwaukee as a center, the influence of the Germans upon the social customs and ideals of Wisconsin has been marked. Milwaukee has many of the aspects of a German city, and has furnished a stronghold of resistance to native American efforts to enact rigid temperance legislation, laws regulative of parochial schools, and similar attempts to bend the German type to the social ideas of the pioneer American stock. In the last presidential election, the German area of the state deserted the Democratic party, and its opposition to free silver was a decisive factor in the overwhelming victory of the Republicans in Wisconsin. With all the evidence of the persistence of the influence of this nationality, it is nevertheless clear that each decade marks an increased assimilation and homogeneity in the state; but the result is a compromise, and not a conquest by either element.

The states of the Old Northwest gave to McKinley a plurality of over 367,000 out of a total vote of about 3,734,000. New England and the Middle states together gave him a plurality of 979,000 in about the same vote, while the farther West gave to Bryan a decisive net plurality. It thus appears that the Old Northwest occupied the position of a political middle region between East and West. The significance of this position is manifest when it is recalled that this section is the child of the East and the mother of the Populistic West.

The occupation of the western prairies was determined by forces similar to those which settled the Old Northwest. In the decade before the war, Minnesota succeeded to the place held by Wisconsin as the Mecca of settlers in the prior decade. To Wisconsin and New York she owes the largest proportion of her native settlers born outside of the state. Kansas and Nebraska were settled most rapidly in the decade following the war, and had a large proportion of soldiers in their American immigrants. Illinois and Ohio together furnished about one-third of the native settlers of these states, but the element coming from southern states was stronger in Kansas than in Nebraska. Both these states have an exceptionally large proportion of native whites as compared with their neighbors among the prairie states. Kansas, for example, has about twenty-six percent of persons of foreign parentage, while Nebraska has about forty-two, Iowa forty-three, South Dakota sixty, Wisconsin seventy-three, Minnesota seventy-five, and North Dakota seventy-nine. North Dakota's development was greatest in the decade prior to 1890. Her native stock came in largest numbers from Wisconsin, with New York, Minnesota, and Iowa next in order. The growth of South Dakota occupied the two decades prior to the census of 1890, and she has recruited her native element from Wisconsin, Iowa, Illinois, and New York.

In consequence of the large migration from the states of the Old Northwest to the virgin soils of these prairie states many counties in the parent states show a considerable decline in growth in the decade before 1890. There is significance in the fact that, with the exception of Iowa, these prairie states, the colonies of the Old Northwest, gave Bryan votes in the election of 1896 in the ratio of their proportion of persons of native parentage. North Dakota, with the heaviest foreign element, was carried for McKinley, while South Dakota, with a much smaller foreign vote, went for Bryan. Kansas and Nebraska rank with Ohio in their native percentage, and they were the center of prairie Populism. Of course, there were other important local economic and political explanations for this ratio, but it seems to have a basis of real meaning. Certain it is that the leaders of the silver movement came from the native element furnished by the Old Northwest. The original Populists in the Kansas legislature of 1891 were born in different states as follows: in Ohio, twelve; Indiana, six; Illinois, five; New York, four; Pennsylvania, two; Connecticut, Vermont, and Maine, one each, making a total, for the northern current, of thirty-two. Of the remaining eighteen, thirteen were from the South, and one each from Kansas, Missouri, California, England and Ireland. Nearly all were Methodists and former Republicans.

Looking at the silver movement more largely, we find that of the Kansas delegation in the Fifty-fourth Congress, one was born in Kansas, and the rest in Indiana, Illinois, Ohio, Pennsylvania, West Virginia, and Maine. All of the Nebraska delegation in the House came from the Old Northwest or from Iowa. The biographies of the two Representatives from the state of Washington tell an interesting story. These men came as children to the pine woods of Wisconsin, took up public lands, and worked on the farm and in the pineries. One passed on to a homestead in Nebraska before settling in Washington. Thus they kept one stage ahead of the social transformations of the West. This is the usual training of the western politicians. If the reader would see a picture of the representative Kansas Populist, let him examine the family portraits of the Ohio farmer in the middle of this century.

In a word, the Populist is the American farmer who has kept in advance of the economic and social transformations that have overtaken those who remained behind. While, doubtless, investigation into the ancestry of the Populists and "silver men" who came to the prairies from the Old Northwest would show a large proportion of southern origin, yet the center of discontent seems to have been among the men of the New England and New York current. If New England looks with care at these men, she may recognize in them the familiar lineaments of the embattled farmers who fired the shot heard round the world. The continuous advance of this pioneer stock from New England has preserved for us the older type of the pioneer of frontier New England.

I do not overlook the transforming influences of the wilderness on this stock ever since it left the earlier frontier to follow up the valleys of western Connecticut, Massachusetts, and Vermont, into western New York, into Ohio, into Iowa, and out to the arid plains of western Kansas and Nebraska; nor do I overlook the peculiar industrial conditions of the prairie states. But I desire to insist upon the other truth, also, that these westward immigrants, keeping for generations in advance of the transforming industrial and social forces that have wrought so vast a revolution in the older regions of the East which they left, could not but preserve important aspects of the older farmer type. In the arid West these pioneers have halted and have turned to perceive an altered nation and changed social ideals. They see the sharp contrast between their traditional idea of America, as the land of opportunity, the land of the self-made man, free from class distinctions and from the power of wealth, and the existing America, so unlike the earlier ideal. If we follow back the line of march of the Puritan farmer, we shall see how responsive he has always been to *isms,* and how persistently he has resisted encroachments on his ideals of individual opportunity and democracy. He is the prophet of the "higher law" in Kansas before the Civil War. He is the Prohibitionist of Iowa and Wisconsin, crying out against German customs as an invasion of his traditional ideals. He is the Granger of Wisconsin, passing restrictive railroad legislation. He is the Abolitionist, the Anti-mason, the Millerite, the Woman Suffragist, the Spiritualist, the Mormon, of western New York. Follow him to his New England home in the turbulent days of Shays' rebellion, paper money, stay and tender laws, and land banks. The radicals among these New England farmers hated lawyers and capitalists. "I would not trust them," said Abraham White, in the ratification convention of Massachusetts, in 1788, "though every one of them should be a Moses." "These lawyers," cried Amos Singletary, "and men of learning and moneyed men that talk so finely and gloss over matters so smoothly to make us poor illiterate people swallow the pill, expect to get into Congress themselves! They mean to get all the money into their hands, and then they will swallow up all us little folk, like the Leviathan, Mr. President; yea, just as the whale swallowed up Jonah."

If the voice of Mary Ellen Lease sounds raucous to the New England man today, while it is sweet music in the ears of the Kansas farmer, let him ponder the utterances of these frontier farmers in the days of the Revolution; and if he is still doubtful of this spiritual kinship, let him read the words of the levelers and sectaries of Cromwell's army.

The story of the political leaders who remained in the place of their birth and shared its economic changes differs from the story of those who by moving to the West continued on a new area the old social type. In the throng of Scotch-Irish pioneers that entered the uplands of the Carolinas in the second quarter of the eighteenth century were the ancestors of Calhoun and of Andrew Jackson. Remaining in this region, Calhoun shared the transformations of the South Carolina interior. He saw it change from the area of the pioneer farmers to an area of great planters raising cotton by slave labor. This explains the transformation of the nationalist and protectionist Calhoun of 1816 into the state-sovereignty and free-trade Calhoun. Jackson, on the other hand, left the region while it was still a frontier, shared the frontier life of Tennessee, and reflected the democracy and nationalism of his people. Henry Clay lived long enough in the kindred state of Kentucky to see it pass from a frontier to a settled community, and his views on slavery reflected the transitional history of that state. Lincoln, on the other hand, born in Kentucky in 1809, while the state was still under frontier conditions, migrated in 1816 to Indiana, and in 1830 to Illinois. The pioneer influences of his community did much to shape his life, and the development of the raw frontiersman into the statesman was not unlike the development of his own state. Political leaders who experienced the later growth of the Northwest, like Garfield, Hayes, Harrison, and McKinley, show clearly the continued transformations of the section. But in the days when the Northwest was still in the gristle, she sent her sons into the newer West to continue the views of life and the policies of the half-frontier region they had left.

Today, the Northwest, standing between her ancestral connections in the East and her children in the West, partly like the East, partly like the West, finds herself in a position strangely like that in the days of the slavery struggle, when her origins presented to her a "divided duty." But these issues are not with the same imperious "Which?" as was the issue of freedom or slavery.

Looking at the Northwest as a whole, one sees, in the character of its industries and in the elements of its population, it is identified on the east with the zone of states including the middle region and New England. Cotton culture and the Negro make a clear line of division between the Old Northwest and the South. And yet in important historical ideals—in the process of expansion, in the persistence of agricultural interests, in impulsiveness, in imperialistic ways of looking at the American destiny, in hero-worship, in the newness of its present social structure—the Old Northwest has much in common with the South and the Far West.

Behind her is the old pioneer past of simple democratic conditions, and freedom of opportunity for all men. Before her is a superb industrial development, the brilliancy of success as evinced in a vast population, aggregate wealth, and sectional power.

→ CHAPTER NINE ←

Contributions of the West to American Democracy

Political thought in the period of the French Revolution tended to treat democracy as an absolute system applicable to all times and to all peoples, a system that was to be created by the act of the people themselves on philosophical principles. Ever since that era there has been an inclination on the part of writers on democracy to emphasize the analytical and theoretical treatment to the neglect of the underlying factors of historical development.

If, however, we consider the underlying conditions and forces that create the democratic type of government, and at times contradict the external forms to which the name democracy is applied, we shall find that under this name there have appeared a multitude of political types radically unlike in fact.

The careful student of history must, therefore, seek the explanation of the forms and changes of political institutions in the social and economic forces that determine them. To know that at any one time a nation may be called a democracy, an aristocracy, or a monarchy, is not so important as to know what are the social and economic tendencies of the state. These are the vital forces that work beneath the surface and dominate the external form. It is to changes in the economic and social life of a people that we must look for the forces that ultimately create and modify organs of political action. For the time, adaptation of political structure may be incomplete or concealed. Old organs will be utilized to express new forces, and so gradual and subtle will be the change that it may hardly be recognized. The pseudo-democracies under the Medici at Florence and under Augustus at Rome are familiar examples of this type. Or again, if the political structure be rigid, incapable of responding to the changes demanded by growth, the expansive forces of social and economic transformation may rend it in some catastrophe like that of the French Revolution. In all these changes both conscious ideals and unconscious social reorganization are at work.

These facts are familiar to the student, and yet it is doubtful if they have been fully considered in connection with American democracy. For a century at least, in conventional expression, Americans have referred to a "glorious Constitution" in explaining the stability and prosperity of their democracy. We have believed as a nation that other peoples had only to will our democratic institutions in order to repeat our own career.

In dealing with western contributions to democracy, it is essential that the considerations which have just been mentioned shall be kept in mind. Whatever these contributions may have been, we find ourselves at the present time in an era of such profound economic and social transformation as to raise the question of the effect of these changes upon the democratic institutions of the United States. Within a decade four marked changes have occurred in our national development; taken together they constitute a revolution.

First, there is the exhaustion of the supply of free land and the closing of the movement of Western advance as an effective factor in American development. The first rough conquest of the wilderness is accomplished, and that great supply of free lands which year after year has served to reinforce the democratic influences in the United States is exhausted. It is true that vast tracts of government land are still untaken, but they constitute the mountain and arid regions, only a small fraction of them capable of conquest, and then only by the application of capital and combined effort. The free lands that made the American pioneer have gone.

In the second place, contemporaneously with this there has been such a concentration of capital in the control of fundamental industries as to make a new epoch in the economic development of the United States. The iron, the coal, and the cattle of the country have all fallen under the domination of a few great corporations with allied interests, and by the rapid combination of the important railroad systems and steamship lines, in concert with these same forces, even the breadstuffs and the manufactures of the nation are to some degree controlled in a similar way. This is largely the work of the last decade. The development of the greatest iron mines of Lake Superior occurred in the early nineties, and in the same decade came the combination by which the coal and the coke of the country, and the transportation systems that connect them with the iron mines, have been brought under a few concentrated managements. Side by side with this concentration of capital has gone the combination of labor in the same vast industries. The one is in a certain sense the concomitant of the other, but the movement acquires an additional significance because of the fact that during the past fifteen years the labor class has been so recruited by a tide of foreign immigration that this class is now largely made up of persons of foreign parentage, and the lines of cleavage which begin to appear in this country between capital and labor have been accentuated by distinctions of nationality.

A third phenomenon connected with the two just mentioned is the expansion of the United States politically and commercially into lands beyond the seas. A cycle of American development has been completed. Up to the close of the War of 1812, this country was involved in the fortunes of the European state system. The first quarter of a century of our national existence was almost a continual struggle to prevent ourselves being drawn into the European wars. At the close of that era of conflict, the United States set its face toward the West. It began the settlement and improvement of the vast interior of the country. Here was the field of our colonization, here the field of our political activity. This process being completed, it is not strange that we find the United States again involved in world-politics. The revolution that occurred four years ago, when the United States struck down that ancient nation under whose auspices the New World was discovered, is hardly yet more than dimly understood. The insular wreckage of the Spanish War, Porto Rico and the Philippines, with the problems presented by the Hawaiian Islands, Cuba, the Isthmian Canal, and China, all are indications of the new direction of the ship of state, and while we thus turn our attention overseas, our concentrated industrial strength has given us a striking power against the commerce of Europe that is already producing consternation in the Old World. Having completed the conquest of the wilderness, and having consolidated our interests, we are beginning to consider the relations of democracy and empire.

And fourth, the political parties of the United States now tend to divide on issues that involve the question of Socialism. The rise of the Populist party in the last decade, and the acceptance of so many of its principles by the Democratic party under the leadership of Mr. Bryan, show in striking manner the birth of new political ideas, the reformation of the lines of political conflict.

It is doubtful if in any ten years of American history more significant factors in our growth have revealed themselves. The struggle of the pioneer farmers to subdue the arid lands of the Great Plains in the eighties was followed by the official announcement of the extinction of the frontier line in 1890. The dramatic outcome of the Chicago Convention of 1896 marked the rise into power of the representatives of Populistic change. Two years later came the battle of Manila, which broke down the old isolation of the nation, and started it on a path the goal of which no man can foretell; and finally, but two years ago came that concentration of which the billion and a half dollar steel trust and the union of the northern continental railways are stupendous examples. Is it not obvious, then, that the student who seeks for the explanation of democracy in the social and economic forces that underlie political forms must make inquiry into the conditions that have produced our democratic institutions, if he would estimate the effect of these vast changes? As a contribution to this inquiry, let us now turn to an examination of the part that the West has played in shaping our democracy.

From the beginning of the settlement of America, the frontier regions have exercised a steady influence toward democracy. In Virginia, to take an example, it can be traced as early as the period of Bacon's Rebellion, a hundred years before our Declaration of Independence. The small landholders, seeing that their powers were steadily passing into the hands of the wealthy planters who controlled church and state and lands, rose in revolt. A generation later, in the governorship of Alexander Spotswood, we find a contest between the frontier settlers and the property-holding classes of the coast. The democracy with which Spotswood had to struggle, and of which he so bitterly complained, was a democracy made up of small landholders, of the newer immigrants, and of indented servants, who at the expiration of their time of servitude passed into the interior to take up lands and engage in pioneer farming. The "War of the Regulation," just on the eve of the American Revolution, shows the steady persistence of this struggle between the classes of the interior and those of the coast. The Declaration of Grievances which the back counties of the Carolinas then drew up against the aristocracy that dominated the politics of those colonies exhibits the contest between the democracy of the frontier and the established classes who apportioned the legislature in such fashion as to secure effective control of government. Indeed, in a period before the outbreak of the American Revolution, one can trace a distinct belt of democratic territory extending from the back country of New England down through western New York, Pennsylvania, and the South.

In each colony this region was in conflict with the dominant classes of the coast. It constituted a quasi-revolutionary area before the days of the Revolution, and it formed the basis on which the Democratic party was afterwards established. It was, therefore, in the West, as it was in the period before the Declaration of Independence, that the struggle for democratic development first revealed itself, and in that area the essential ideas of American democracy had already appeared. Through the period of the Revolution and of the Confederation a similar contest can be noted. On the frontier of New England, along the western border of Pennsylvania, Virginia, and the Carolinas, and in the communities beyond the Alleghany Mountains, there arose a demand of the frontier settlers for independent statehood based on democratic provisions. There is a strain of fierceness in their energetic petitions demanding self-government under the theory that every people have the right to establish their own political institutions in an area which they have won from the wilderness. Those revolutionary principles based on natural rights, for which the seaboard colonies were contending, were taken up with frontier energy in an attempt to apply them to the lands of the West. No one can read their petitions denouncing the control exercised by the wealthy landholders of the coast, appealing to the record of their conquest of the wilderness, and demanding the possession of the lands for which they have fought the Indians, and which they had reduced by their ax to civilization, without recognizing in these frontier communities the cradle of a belligerent western democracy. "A fool can sometimes put on his coat better than a wise man can do it for him"—such is the philosophy of its petitioners. In this period also came the contests of the interior agricultural portion of New England against the coast-wise merchants and property-holders, of which Shays' Rebellion is the best known, although by no means an isolated instance.

By the time of the constitutional convention, this struggle for democracy had effected, a fairly well-defined division into parties. Although these parties did not at first recognize their interstate connections, there were similar issues on which they split in almost all the states. The demands for an issue of paper money, the stay of execution against debtors, and the relief against excessive taxation were found in every colony in the interior agricultural regions. The rise of this significant movement wakened the apprehensions of the men of means, and in the debates over the basis of suffrage for the House of Representatives in the constitutional convention of 1787 leaders of the conservative party did not hesitate to demand that safeguards to the property should be furnished the coast against the interior. The outcome of the debate left the question of suffrage for the House of Representatives dependent upon the policy of the separate states. This was in effect imposing a property qualification throughout the nation as a whole, and it was only as the interior of the country developed that these restrictions gradually gave way in the direction of manhood suffrage.

All of these scattered democratic tendencies Jefferson combined, in the period of Washington's presidency, into the Democratic-Republican party. Jefferson was the first prophet of American democracy, and when we analyze the essential features of his gospel, it is clear that the western influence was the dominant element. Jefferson himself was born in the frontier region of Virginia, on the edge of the Blue Ridge, in the middle of the eighteenth century. His father was a pioneer. Jefferson's *Notes on Virginia* reveal clearly his conception that democracy should have an agricultural basis, and that manufacturing development and city life were dangerous to the purity of the body politic. Simplicity and economy in government, the right of revolution, the freedom of the individual, the belief that those who win the vacant lands are entitled to shape their own government in their own way, these are all parts of the platform of political principles to which he gave his adhesion, and they are all elements eminently characteristic of the western democracy into which he was born.

In the period of the Revolution he had brought in a series of measures which tended to throw the power of Virginia into the hands of the settlers in the interior rather than of the coastwise aristocracy. The repeal of the laws of entail and primogeniture would have destroyed the great estates on which the planting aristocracy based its power. The abolition of the Established Church would still further have diminished the influence of the coastwise party in favor of the dissenting sects of the interior. His scheme of general public education reflected the same tendency, and his demand for the abolition of slavery was characteristic of a representative of the West rather than of the old-time aristocracy of the coast. His sympathy with the western expansion culminated in the Louisiana Purchase. In short, the tendencies of Jefferson's legislation were to replace the dominance of the planting aristocracy by the dominance of the interior class, which had sought in vain to achieve its liberties in the period of Bacon's Rebellion.

Nevertheless, Thomas Jefferson was the John the Baptist of democracy, not its Moses. Only with the slow setting of the tide of settlement farther and farther toward the interior did the democratic influence grow strong enough to take actual possession of the government. The period from 1800 to 1820 saw a steady increase in these tendencies. The established classes in New England and the South began to take alarm. Perhaps no better illustration of the apprehensions of the old-time federal conservative can be given than these utterances of President Dwight, of Yale College, in the book of travels which he published in that period:

> The class of pioneers cannot live in regular society. They are too idle, too talkative, too passionate, too prodigal, and too shiftless to acquire either property or character. They are impatient of the restraints of law, religion, and morality, and grumble about the taxes by which the Rulers, Ministers, and Schoolmasters are supported. . . . After exposing the injustice of the community in neglecting to invest persons of such superior merit in public offices, in many an eloquent harangue uttered by many a kitchen fire, in every blacksmith shop, in every corner of the streets, and finding all their efforts vain, they become at length discouraged, and under the pressure of poverty, the fear of the gaol, and consciousness of public contempt, leave their native places and betake themselves to the wilderness.

Such was a conservative's impression of that pioneer movement of New England colonists who had spread up the valley of the Connecticut into New Hampshire, Vermont, and western New York in the period of which he wrote, and who afterwards went on to possess the Northwest. New England Federalism looked with a shudder at the democratic ideas of those who refused to recognize the established order. But in that period there came into the Union a sisterhood of frontier states—Ohio, Indiana, Illinois, Missouri—with provisions for the franchise that brought in complete democracy.

Even the newly created states of the Southwest showed the tendency. The wind of democracy blew so strongly from the West, that even in the older states of New York, Massachusetts, Connecticut, and Virginia, conventions were called, which liberalized their constitutions by strengthening the democratic basis of the state. In the same time the labor population of the cities began to assert its power and its determination to share in government. Of this frontier democracy which now took possession of the nation, Andrew Jackson was the very personification. He was born in the backwoods of the Carolinas in the midst of the turbulent democracy that preceded the Revolution, and he grew up in the frontier state of Tennessee. In the midst of this region of personal feuds and frontier ideals of law, he quickly rose to leadership. The appearance of this frontiersman on the floor of Congress was an omen full of significance. He reached Philadelphia at the close of Washington's administration, having ridden on horseback nearly eight hundred miles to his destination. Gallatin, himself a western man, describes Jackson as he entered the halls of Congress: "A tall, lank, uncouth-looking personage, with long locks of hair hanging over his face and a cue down his back tied in an eel-skin; his dress singular; his manners those of a rough backwoodsman." And Jefferson testified: "When I was President of the Senate he was a Senator, and he could never speak on account of the rashness of his feelings. I have seen him attempt it repeatedly and as often choke with rage." At last the frontier in the person of its typical man had found a place in the government. This six-foot backwoodsman, with blue eyes that could blaze on occasion, this choleric, impetuous, self-willed Scotch-Irish leader of men, this expert duelist, and ready fighter, this embodiment of the tenacious, vehement, personal West, was in politics to stay. The frontier democracy of that time had the instincts of the clansman in the days of Scotch border warfare. Vehement and tenacious as the democracy was, strenuously as each man contended with his neighbor for the spoils of the new country that opened before them, they all had respect for the man who best expressed their aspirations and their ideas. Every community had its hero. In the War of 1812 and the subsequent Indian fighting Jackson made good his claim, not only to the loyalty of the people of Tennessee, but of the whole West, and even of the nation. He had the essential traits of the Kentucky and Tennessee frontier. It was a frontier free from the influence of European ideas and institutions. The men of the "Western World" turned their backs upon the Atlantic Ocean, and with a grim energy and self-reliance began to build up a society free from the dominance of ancient forms.

 The westerner defended himself and resented governmental restrictions. The duel and the blood-feud found congenial soil in Kentucky and Tennessee. The idea of the personality of law was often dominant over the organized machinery of justice. That method was best which was most direct and effective. The backwoodsman was intolerant of men who split hairs, or scrupled over the method of reaching the right. In a word, the unchecked development of the individual was the significant product of this frontier democracy. It sought rather to express itself by choosing a man of the people, than by the formation of elaborate governmental institutions.

It was because Andrew Jackson personified these essential western traits that in his presidency he became the idol and the mouthpiece of the popular will. In his assault upon the Bank as an engine of aristocracy, and in his denunciation of nullification, he went directly to his object with the ruthless energy of a frontiersman. For formal law and the subtleties of state sovereignty he had the contempt of a backwoodsman. Nor is it without significance that this typical man of the new democracy will always be associated with the triumph of the spoils system in national politics. To the new democracy of the West, office was an opportunity to exercise natural rights as an equal citizen of the community. Rotation in office served not simply to allow the successful man to punish his enemies and reward his friends, but it also furnished the training in the actual conduct of political affairs which every American claimed as his birthright. Only in a primitive democracy of the type of the United States in 1830 could such a system have existed without the ruin of the state. National government in that period was no complex and nicely adjusted machine, and the evils of the system were long in making themselves fully apparent.

The triumph of Andrew Jackson marked the end of the old era of trained statesmen for the presidency. With him began the era of the popular hero. Even Martin Van Buren, whom we think of in connection with the East, was born in a log house under conditions that were not unlike parts of the older West. Harrison was the hero of the Northwest, as Jackson had been of the Southwest. Polk was a typical Tennesseean, eager to expand the nation, and Zachary Taylor was what Webster called a "frontier colonel." During the period that followed Jackson, power passed from the region of Kentucky and Tennessee to the border of the Mississippi. The natural democratic tendencies that had earlier shown themselves in the Gulf States were destroyed, however, by the spread of cotton culture, and the development of great plantations in that region. What had been typical of the democracy of the Revolutionary frontier and of the frontier of Andrew Jackson was now to be seen in the states between the Ohio and the Mississippi. As Andrew Jackson is the typical democrat of the former region, so Abraham Lincoln is the very embodiment of the pioneer period of the Old Northwest. Indeed, he is the embodiment of the democracy of the West. How can one speak of him except in the words of Lowell's great "Commemoration Ode":

For him her Old-World molds aside she threw,
And, choosing sweet clay from the breast
   Of the unexhausted West,
With stuff untainted shaped a hero new,
Wise, steadfast in the strength of God, and true.
 .   .   .   .
His was no lonely mountain-peak of mind,
Thrusting to thin air o'er our cloudy bars,
A sea-mark now, now lost in vapors blind;
Broad prairie rather, genial, level-lined,
Fruitful and friendly for all human kind,
Yet also nigh to heaven and loved of loftiest stars.
   Nothing of Europe here,
Or, then, of Europe fronting mornward still,
Ere any names of Serf and Peer,
Could Nature's equal scheme deface;
New birth of our new soil, the first American.

The pioneer life from which Lincoln came differed in important respects from the frontier democracy typified by Andrew Jackson. Jackson's democracy was contentious, individualistic, and it sought the ideal of local self-government and expansion. Lincoln represents rather the pioneer folk who entered the forest of the great Northwest to chop out a home, to build up their fortunes in the midst of a continually ascending industrial movement. In the democracy of the Southwest, industrial development and city life were only minor factors, but to the democracy of the Northwest they were its very life. To widen the area of the clearing, to contend with one another for the mastery of the industrial resources of the rich provinces, to struggle for a place in the ascending movement of society, to transmit to one's offspring the chance for education, for industrial betterment, for the rise in life which the hardships of the pioneer existence denied to the pioneer himself, these were some of the ideals of the region to which Lincoln came. The men were commonwealth builders, industry builders. Whereas the type of hero in the Southwest was militant, in the Northwest he was industrial. It was in the midst of these "plain people," as he loved to call them, that Lincoln grew to manhood. As Emerson says: "He is the true history of the American people in his time." The years of his early life were the years when the democracy of the Northwest came into struggle with the institution of slavery which threatened to forbid the expansion of the democratic pioneer life in the West. In President Eliot's essay on *Five American Contributions to Civilization,* he instances as one of the supreme tests of American democracy its attitude upon the question of slavery. But if democracy chose wisely and worked effectively toward the solution of this problem, it must be remembered that western democracy took the lead. The rail-splitter himself became the nation's President in that fierce time of struggle, and armies of the woodsmen and pioneer farmers recruited in the Old Northwest made free the Father of Waters, marched through Georgia, and helped to force the struggle to a conclusion at Appomattox. The free pioneer democracy struck down the slave-holding aristocracy on its march to the West.

The last chapter in the development of western democracy is the one that deals with its conquest over the vast spaces of the new West. At each new stage of western development, the people have had to grapple with larger areas, with bigger combinations. The little colony of Massachusetts veterans that settled at Marietta received a land grant as large as the state of Rhode Island. The band of Connecticut pioneers that followed Moses Cleaveland to the Connecticut Reserve occupied a region as large as the parent state. The area which settlers of New England stock occupied on the prairies of northern Illinois surpassed the combined area of Massachusetts, Connecticut, and Rhode Island. Men who had become accustomed to the narrow valleys and the little towns of the East found themselves out on the boundless spaces of the West dealing with units of such magnitude as dwarfed their former experience. The Great Lakes, the Prairies, the Great Plains, the Rocky Mountains, the Mississippi and the Missouri, furnished new standards of measurement for the achievement of this industrial democracy. Individualism began to give way to coöperation and to governmental activity. Even in the earlier days of the democratic conquest of the wilderness, demands had been made upon the government for support in internal improvements, but this new West showed a growing tendency to call to its assistance the powerful arm of national authority. In the period since the Civil War, the vast public domain has been donated to the individual farmer, to states for education, to railroads for the construction of transportation lines.

Moreover, with the advent of democracy in the last fifteen years upon the Great Plains, new physical conditions have presented themselves which have accelerated the social tendency of western democracy. The pioneer farmer of the days of Lincoln could place his family on a flatboat, strike into the wilderness, cut out his clearing, and with little or no capital go on to the achievement of industrial independence. Even the homesteader on the western prairies found it possible to work out a similar independent destiny, although the factor of transportation made a serious and increasing impediment to the free working-out of his individual career. But when the arid lands and the mineral resources of the Far West were reached, no conquest was possible by the old individual pioneer methods. Here expensive irrigation works must be constructed, coöperative activity was demanded in utilization of the water supply, capital beyond the reach of the small farmer was required. In a word, the physiographic province itself decreed that the destiny of this new frontier should be social rather than individual.

Magnitude of social achievement is the watchword of the democracy since the Civil War. From petty towns built in the marshes, cities arose whose greatness and industrial power are the wonder of our time. The conditions were ideal for the production of captains of industry. The old democratic admiration for the self-made man, its old deference to the rights of competitive individual development, together with the stupendous natural resources that opened to the conquest of the keenest and the strongest, gave such conditions of mobility as enabled the development of the large corporate industries which in our own decade have marked the West.

Thus, in brief, have been outlined the chief phases of the development of western democracy in the different areas which it has conquered. There has been a steady development of the industrial ideal, and a steady increase of the social tendency, in this later movement of western democracy. While the individualism of the frontier, so prominent in the earliest days of the Western advance, has been preserved as an ideal, more and more these individuals struggling each with the other, dealing with vaster and vaster areas, with larger and larger problems, have found it necessary to combine under the leadership of the strongest. This is the explanation of the rise of those preëminent captains of industry whose genius has concentrated capital to control the fundamental resources of the nation. If now in the way of recapitulation, we try to pick out from the influences that have gone to the making of western democracy the factors which constitute the net result of this movement, we shall have to mention at least the following:

Most important of all has been the fact that an area of free land has continually lain on the western border of the settled area of the United States. Whenever social conditions tended to crystallize in the East, whenever capital tended to press upon labor or political restraints to impede the freedom of the mass, there was this gate of escape to the free conditions of the frontier. These free lands promoted individualism, economic equality, freedom to rise, democracy. Men would not accept inferior wages and a permanent position of social subordination when this promised land of freedom and equality was theirs for the taking. Who would rest content under oppressive legislative conditions when with a slight effort he might reach a land wherein to become a co-worker in the building of free cities and free states on the lines of his own ideal? In a word, then, free lands meant free opportunities. Their existence has differentiated the American democracy from the democracies which have preceded it, because ever, as democracy in the East took the form of highly specialized and complicated industrial society, in the West it kept in touch with primitive conditions, and by action and reaction these two forces have shaped our history.

In the next place, these free lands and this treasury of industrial resources have existed over such vast spaces that they have demanded of democracy increasing spaciousness of design and power of execution. western democracy is contrasted with the democracy of all other times in the largeness of the tasks to which it has set its hand, and in the vast achievements which it has wrought out in the control of nature and of politics. It would be difficult to over-emphasize the importance of this training upon democracy. Never before in the history of the world has a democracy existed on so vast an area and handled things in the gross with such success, with such largeness of design, and such grasp upon the means of execution. In short, democracy has learned in the West of the United States how to deal with the problem of magnitude. The old historic democracies were but little states with primitive economic conditions.

But the very task of dealing with vast resources, over vast areas, under the conditions of free competition furnished by the West, has produced the rise of those captains of industry whose success in consolidating economic power now raises the question as to whether democracy under such conditions can survive. For the old military type of western leaders like George Rogers Clark, Andrew Jackson, and William Henry Harrison have been substituted such industrial leaders as James J. Hill, John D. Rockefeller, and Andrew Carnegie.

The question is imperative, then, What ideals persist from this democratic experience of the West; and have they acquired sufficient momentum to sustain themselves under conditions so radically unlike those in the days of their origin? In other words, the question put at the beginning of this discussion becomes pertinent. Under the forms of the American democracy is there in reality evolving such a concentration of economic and social power in the hands of a comparatively few men as may make political democracy an appearance rather than a reality? The free lands are gone. The material forces that gave vitality to western democracy are passing away. It is to the realm of the spirit, to the domain of ideals and legislation, that we must look for western influence upon democracy in our own days.

Western democracy has been from the time of its birth idealistic. The very fact of the wilderness appealed to men as a fair, blank page on which to write a new chapter in the story of man's struggle for a higher type of society. The western wilds, from the Alleghanies to the Pacific, constituted the richest free gift that was ever spread out before civilized man. To the peasant and artisan of the Old World, bound by the chains of social class, as old as custom and as inevitable as fate, the West offered an exit into a free life and greater well-being among the bounties of nature, into the midst of resources that demanded manly exertion, and that gave in return the chance for indefinite ascent in the scale of social advance. "To each she offered gifts after his will." Never again can such an opportunity come to the sons of men. It was unique, and the thing is so near us, so much a part of our lives, that we do not even yet comprehend its full significance. The existence of this land of opportunity has made America the goal of idealists from the days of the Pilgrim Fathers. With all the materialism of the pioneer movements, this idealistic conception of the vacant lands as an opportunity for a new order of things is unmistakably present. Kipling's *Song of the English* has given it expression:

> We were dreamers, dreaming greatly, in the man-stifled town;
> We yearned beyond the sky-line where the strange roads go down.
> Came the Whisper, came the Vision, came the Power with the Need,
> Till the Soul that is not man's soul was lent us to lead.
> As the deer breaks—as the steer breaks—from the herd where they graze,
> In the faith of little children we went on our ways.
> Then the wood failed—then the food failed—then the last water dried—
> In the faith of little children we lay down and died.
>
> On the sand-drift—on the veldt-side—in the fern-scrub we lay,
> That our sons might follow after by the bones on the way.
> Follow after—follow after! We have watered the root

And the bud has come to blossom that ripens for fruit!
Follow after—we are waiting by the trails that we lost
For the sound of many footsteps, for the tread of a host.

Follow after—follow after—for the harvest is sown:
By the bones about the wayside ye shall come to your own!

This was the vision that called to Roger Williams, that "prophetic soul ravished of truth disembodied," "unable to enter into treaty with its environment," and forced to seek the wilderness. "Oh, how sweet," wrote William Penn, from his forest refuge, "is the quiet of these parts, freed from the troubles and perplexities of woeful Europe." And here he projected what he called his *Holy Experiment in government.*

If the later West offers few such striking illustrations of the relation of the wilderness to idealistic schemes, and if some of the designs were fantastic and abortive, none the less the influence is a fact. Hardly a western state but has been the Mecca of some sect or band of social reformers, anxious to put into practice their ideals, in vacant land, far removed from the checks of a settled form of social organization. Consider the Dunkards, the Icarians, the Fourierists, the Mormons, and similar idealists who sought our western wilds. But the idealistic influence is not limited to the dreamers' conception of a new state. It gave to the pioneer farmer and city builder a restless energy, a quick capacity for judgment and action, a belief in liberty, freedom of opportunity, and a resistance to the domination of class which infused a vitality and power into the individual atoms of this democratic mass. Even as he dwelt among the stumps of his newly cut clearing, the pioneer had the creative vision of a new order of society. In imagination he pushed back the forest boundary to the confines of a mighty Commonwealth; he willed that log cabins should become the lofty buildings of great cities. He decreed that his children should enter into a heritage of education, comfort, and social welfare, and for this ideal he bore the scars of the wilderness. Possessed with this idea he ennobled his task and laid deep foundations for a democratic state. Nor was this idealism by any means limited to the American pioneer.

To the old native democratic stock has been added a vast army of recruits from the Old World. There are in the Middle West alone four million persons of German parentage out of a total of seven millions in the country. Over a million persons of Scandinavian parentage live in the same region. The democracy of the newer West is deeply affected by the ideals brought by these immigrants from the Old World. To them America was not simply a new home; it was a land of opportunity, of freedom, of democracy. It meant to them, as to the American pioneer that preceded them, the opportunity to destroy the bonds of social caste that bound them in their older home, to hew out for themselves in a new country a destiny proportioned to the powers that God had given them, a chance to place their families under better conditions and to win a larger life than the life that they had left behind. He who believes that even the hordes of recent immigrants from southern Italy are drawn to these shores by nothing more than a dull and blind materialism has not penetrated into the heart of the problem. The idealism and expectation of these children of the Old World, the hopes which they have formed for a newer and freer life across the seas, are almost pathetic when one considers how far they are from the possibility of fruition. He who would take stock of American democracy must not forget the accumulation of human purposes and ideals which immigration has added to the American populace.

In this connection it must also be remembered that these democratic ideals have existed at each stage of the advance of the frontier, and have left behind them deep and enduring effects on the thinking of the whole country. Long after the frontier period of a particular region of the United States has passed away, the conception of society, the ideals and aspirations which it produced, persist in the minds of the people. So recent has been the transition of the greater portion of the United States from frontier conditions to condi-ditions of settled life, that we are, over the large portion of the United States, hardly a generation removed from the primitive conditions of the West. If, indeed, we ourselves were not pioneers, our fathers were, and the inherited ways of looking at things, the fundamental assumptions of the American people, have all been shaped by this experience of democracy on its westward march. This experience has been wrought into the very warp and woof of American thought.

Even those masters of industry and capital who have risen to power by the conquest of western resources came from the midst of this society and still profess its principles. John D. Rockefeller was born on a New York farm, and began his career as a young business man in St. Louis. Marcus Hanna was a Cleveland grocer's clerk at the age of twenty. Claus Spreckles, the sugar king, came from Germany as a steerage passenger to the United States in 1848. Marshall Field was a farmer boy in Conway, Massachusetts, until he left to grow up with the young Chicago. Andrew Carnegie came as a ten-year-old boy from Scotland to Pittsburgh, then a distinctively western town. He built up his fortunes through successive grades until he became the dominating factor in the great iron industries, and paved the way for that colossal achievement, the Steel Trust. Whatever may be the tendencies of this corporation, there can be little doubt of the democratic ideals of Mr. Carnegie himself. With lavish hand he has strewn millions through the United States for the promotion of libraries. The effect of this library movement in perpetuating the democracy that comes from an intelligent and self-respecting people can hardly be measured. In his *Triumphant Democracy*, published in 1886, Mr. Carnegie, the ironmaster, said, in reference to the mineral wealth of the United States: "Thank God, these treasures are in the hands of an intelligent people, the Democracy, to be used for the general good of the masses, and not made the spoils of monarchs, courts, and aristocracy, to be turned to the base and selfish ends of a privileged hereditary class." It would be hard to find a more rigorous assertion of democratic doctrine than the celebrated utterance, attributed to the same man, that he should feel it a disgrace to die rich.

In enumerating the services of American democracy, President Eliot included the corporation as one of its achievements, declaring that "freedom of incorporation, though no longer exclusively a democratic agency, has given a strong support to democratic institutions." In one sense this is doubtless true, since the corporation has been one of the means by which small properties can be aggregated into an effective working body. Socialistic writers have long been fond of pointing out also that these various concentrations pave the way for and make possible social control. From this point of view it is possible that the masters of industry may prove to be not so much an incipient aristocracy as the pathfinders for democracy in reducing the industrial world to systematic consolidation suited to democratic control. The great geniuses that have built up the modern industrial concentration were trained in the midst of democratic society. They were the product of these democratic conditions. Freedom to rise was the very condition of their existence. Whether they will be followed by successors who will adopt the exploitation of the masses, and who will be capable of retaining under efficient control these vast resources, is one of the questions which we shall have to face.

This, at least, is clear: American democracy is fundamentally the outcome of the experiences of the American people in dealing with the West. western democracy through the whole of its earlier period tended to the production of a society of which the most distinctive fact was the freedom of the individual to rise under conditions of social mobility, and whose ambition was the liberty and well-being of the masses. This conception has vitalized all American democracy, and has brought it into sharp contrasts with the democracies of history, and with those modern efforts of Europe to create an artificial democratic order by legislation. The problem of the United States is not to create democracy, but to conserve democratic institutions and ideals. In the later period of its development, western democracy has been gaining experience in the problem of social control. It has steadily enlarged the sphere of its action and the instruments for its perpetuation. By its system of public schools, from the grades to the graduate work of the great universities, the West has created a larger single body of intelligent plain people than can be found elsewhere in the world. Its political tendencies, whether we consider Democracy, Populism, or Republicanism, are distinctly in the direction of greater social control and the conservation of the old democratic ideals.

To these ideals the West adheres with even a passionate determination. If, in working out its mastery of the resources of the interior, it has produced a type of industrial leader so powerful as to be the wonder of the world, nevertheless, it is still to be determined whether these men constitute a menace to democratic institutions, or the most efficient factor for adjusting democratic control to the new conditions.

Whatever shall be the outcome of the rush of this huge industrial modern United States to its place among the nations of the earth, the formation of its western democracy will always remain one of the wonderful chapters in the history of the human race. Into this vast shaggy continent of ours poured the first feeble tide of European settlement. European men, institutions, and ideas were lodged in the American wilderness, and this great American West took them to her bosom, taught them a new way of looking upon the destiny of the common man, trained them in adaptation to the conditions of the New World, to the creation of new institutions to meet new needs; and ever as society on her eastern border grew to resemble the Old World in its social forms and its industry, ever, as it began to lose faith in the ideals of democracy, she opened new provinces, and dowered new democracies in her most distant domains with her material treasures and with the ennobling influence that the fierce love of freedom, the strength that came from hewing out a home, making a school and a church, and creating a higher future for his family, furnished to the pioneer.

She gave to the world such types as the farmer Thomas Jefferson, with his Declaration of Independence, his statute for religious toleration, and his purchase of Louisiana. She gave us Andrew Jackson, that fierce Tennessee spirit who broke down the traditions of conservative rule, swept away the privacies and privileges of officialdom, and, like a Gothic leader, opened the temple of the nation to the populace. She gave us Abraham Lincoln, whose gaunt frontier form and gnarled, massive hand told of the conflict with the forest, whose grasp of the ax-handle of the pioneer was no firmer than his grasp of the helm of the ship of state as it breasted the seas of civil war. She has furnished to this new democracy her stores of mineral wealth, that dwarf of those of the Old World, and her provinces that in themselves are vaster and more productive than most of the nations of Europe. Out of her bounty has come a nation whose industrial competition alarms the Old World, and the masters of whose resources wield wealth and power vaster than the wealth and power of kings. Best of all, the West gave, not only to the American, but to the unhappy and oppressed of all lands, a vision of hope, and assurance that the world held a place where were to be found high faith in man and the will and power to furnish him the opportunity to grow to the full measure of his own capacity. Great and powerful as are the new sons of her loins, the Republic is greater than they. The paths of the pioneer have widened into broad highways. The forest clearing has expanded into affluent commonwealths. Let us see to it that the ideals of the pioneer in his log cabin shall enlarge into the spiritual life of a democracy where civic power shall dominate and utilize individual achievement for the common good.

→ CHAPTER TEN ←

PIONEER IDEALS AND THE STATE UNIVERSITY

THE IDEALS OF A PEOPLE, THEIR ASPIRATIONS AND CONVICTIONS, THEIR hopes and ambitions, their dreams and determinations, are assets in their civilization as real and important as per capita wealth or industrial skill.

This nation was formed under pioneer ideals. During three centuries after Captain John Smith struck the first blow at the American forest on the eastern edge of the continent, the pioneers were abandoning settled society for the wilderness, seeking, for generation after generation, new frontiers. Their experiences left abiding influences upon the ideas and purposes of the nation. Indeed the older settled regions themselves were shaped profoundly by the very fact that the whole nation was pioneering and that in the development of the West the East had its own part.

The first ideal of the pioneer was that of conquest. It was his task to fight with nature for the chance to exist. Not as in older countries did this contest take place in a mythical past, told in folk lore and epic. It has been continuous to our own day. Facing each generation of pioneers was the unmastered continent. Vast forests blocked the way; mountainous ramparts interposed; desolate, grass-clad prairies, barren oceans of rolling plains, arid deserts, and a fierce race of savages, all had to be met and defeated. The rifle and the ax are the symbols of the backwoods pioneer. They meant a training in aggressive courage, in domination, in directness of action, in destructiveness.

To the pioneer the forest was no friendly resource for posterity, no object of careful economy. He must wage a hand-to-hand war upon it, cutting and burning a little space to let in the light upon a dozen acres of hard-won soil, and year after year expanding the clearing into new woodlands against the stubborn resistance of primeval trunks and matted roots. He made war against the rank fertility of the soil. While new worlds of virgin land lay ever just beyond, it was idle to expect the pioneer to stay his hand and turn to scientific farming. Indeed, as Secretary Wilson has said, the pioneer would, in that case, have raised wheat that no one wanted to eat, corn to store on the farm, and cotton not worth the picking.

Thus, fired with the ideal of subduing the wilderness, the destroying pioneer fought his way across the continent, masterful and wasteful, preparing the way by seeking the immediate thing, rejoicing in rude strength and wilful achievement.

But even this backwoodsman was more than a mere destroyer. He had visions. He was finder as well as fighter—the trail-maker for civilization, the inventor of new ways. Although Rudyard Kipling's *Foreloper* deals with the English pioneer in lands beneath the southern Cross, yet the poem portrays American traits as well:

> The gull shall whistle in his wake, the blind wave break in fire,
> He shall fulfill God's utmost will, unknowing his desire;
> And he shall see old planets pass and alien stars arise,
> And give the gale his reckless sail in shadow of new skies.
>
> Strong lust of gear shall drive him out and hunger arm his hand
> To wring food from desert nude, his foothold from the sand.
> His neighbors' smoke shall vex his eyes, their voices break his rest;
> He shall go forth till south is north, sullen and dispossessed;
> He shall desire loneliness and his desire shall bring
> Hard on his heels, a thousand wheels, a people and a king.
>
> He shall come back on his own track, and by his scarce cool camp,
> There shall he meet the roaring street, the derrick and the stamp;
> For he must blaze a nation's way with hatchet and with brand,
> Till on his last won wilderness an empire's bulwarks stand.

This quest after the unknown, this yearning "beyond the sky line, where the strange roads go down," is of the very essence of the backwoods pioneer, even though he was unconscious of its spiritual significance.

The pioneer was taught in the school of experience that the crops of one area would not do for a new frontier; that the scythe of the clearing must be replaced by the reaper of the prairies. He was forced to make old tools serve new uses; to shape former habits, institutions and ideas to changed conditions; and to find new means when the old proved inapplicable. He was building a new society as well as breaking new soil; he had the ideal of nonconformity and of change. He rebelled against the conventional.

Besides the ideals of conquest and of discovery, the pioneer had the ideal of personal development, free from social and governmental constraint. He came from a civilization based on individual competition, and he brought the conception with him to the wilderness where a wealth of resources, and innumerable opportunities gave it a new scope. The prizes were for the keenest and the strongest; for them were the best bottom lands, the finest timber tracts, the best salt-springs, the richest ore beds; and not only these natural gifts, but also the opportunities afforded in the midst of a forming society. Here were mill sites, town sites, transportation lines, banking centers, openings in the law, in politics—all the varied chances for advancement afforded in a rapidly developing society where everything was open to him who knew how to seize the opportunity.

The squatter enforced his claim to lands even against the government's title by the use of extra-legal combinations and force. He appealed to lynch law with little hesitation. He was impatient of any governmental restriction upon his individual right to deal with the wilderness.

In our own day we sometimes hear of congressmen sent to jail for violating land laws; but the different spirit in the pioneer days may be illustrated by a speech of Delegate Sibley of Minnesota in Congress in 1852. In view of the fact that he became the state's first governor, a regent of its university, president of its historical society, and a doctor of laws of Princeton, we may assume that he was a pillar of society. He said:

> The government has watched its public domain with jealous eye, and there are now enactments upon your statute books, aimed at the trespassers upon it, which should be expunged as a disgrace to the country and to the nineteenth century. Especially is he pursued with unrelenting severity, who has dared to break the silence of the primeval forest by the blows of the American ax. The hardy lumberman who has penetrated to the remotest wilds of the Northwest, to drag from their recesses the materials for building up towns and cities in the great valley of the Mississippi, has been particularly marked out as a victim. After enduring all the privations and subjecting himself to all the perils incident to

his vocation—when he has toiled for months to add by his honest labor to the comfort of his fellow men, and to the aggregate wealth of the nation, he finds himself suddenly in the clutches of the law for trespassing on the public domain. The proceeds of his long winter's work are reft from him, and exposed to public sale for the benefit of his paternal government . . . and the object of this oppression and wrong is further harassed by vexatious law proceedings against him.

Sibley's protest in congress against these "outrages" by which the northern lumbermen were "harassed" in their work of what would now be called stealing government timber, aroused no protest from his colleagues. No president called this congressman an undesirable citizen or gave him over to the courts.

Thus many of the pioneers, following the ideal of the right of the individual to rise, subordinated the rights of the nation and posterity to the desire that the country should be "developed" and that the individual should advance with as little interference as possible. Squatter doctrines and individualism have left deep traces upon American conceptions.

But quite as deeply fixed in the pioneer's mind as the ideal of individualism was the ideal of democracy. He had a passionate hatred for aristocracy, monopoly and special privilege; he believed in simplicity, economy and in the rule of the people. It is true that he honored the successful man, and that he strove in all ways to advance himself. But the West was so free and so vast, the barriers to individual achievement were so remote, that the pioneer was hardly conscious that any danger to equality could come from his competition for natural resources. He thought of democracy as in some way the result of our political institutions, and he failed to see that it was primarily the result of the free lands and immense opportunities which surrounded him. Occasional statesmen voiced the idea that American democracy was based on the abundance of unoccupied land, even in the first debates on the public domain.

This early recognition of the influence of abundance of land in shaping the economic conditions of American democracy is peculiarly significant today in view of the practical exhaustion of the supply of cheap arable public lands open to the poor man, and the coincident development of labor unions to keep up wages.

Certain it is that the strength of democratic movements has chiefly lain in the regions of the pioneer. "Our governments tend too much to democracy," wrote Izard, of South Carolina, to Jefferson, in 1785. "A handicraftsman thinks an apprenticeship necessary to make him acquainted with his business. But our backcountrymen are of the opinion that a politician may be born just as well as a poet."

The Revolutionary ideas, of course, gave a great impetus to democracy, and in substantially every colony there was a double revolution, one for independence and the other for the overthrow of aristocratic control. But in the long run the effective force behind American democracy was the presence of the practically free land into which men might escape from oppression or inequalities which burdened them in the older settlements. This possibility compelled the coastwise states to liberalize the franchise; and it prevented the formation of a dominant class, whether based on property or on custom. Among the pioneers one man was as good as his neighbor. He had the same chance; conditions were simple and free. Economic equality fostered political equality. An optimistic and buoyant belief in the worth of the plain people, a devout faith in man prevailed in the West. Democracy became almost the religion of the pioneer. He held with passionate devotion the idea that he was building under freedom a new society, based on self government, and for the welfare of the average man.

And yet even as he proclaimed the gospel of democracy the pioneer showed a vague apprehension lest the time be short—lest equality should not endure—lest he might fall behind in the ascending movement of western society. This led him on in feverish haste to acquire advantages as though he only half believed his dream. "Before him lies a boundless continent," wrote De Tocqueville, in the days when pioneer democracy was triumphant under Jackson, "and he urges forward as if time pressed and he was afraid of finding no room for his exertions."

Even while Jackson lived, labor leaders and speculative thinkers were demanding legislation to place a limit on the amount of land which one person might acquire and to provide free farms. De Tocqueville saw the signs of change. "Between the workman and the master," he said, "there are frequent relations but no real association. . . . I am of the opinion, upon the whole, that the manufacturing aristocracy which is growing up under our eyes is one of the harshest which ever existed in the world; . . . if ever a permanent inequality, of conditions and aristocracy again penetrate into the world, it may be predicted that this is the gate by which they will enter." But the sanative influences of the free spaces of the West were destined to ameliorate labor's condition, to afford new hopes and new faith to pioneer democracy, and to postpone the problem.

As the settlers advanced into provinces whose area dwarfed that of the older sections, pioneer democracy itself began to undergo changes, both in its composition and in its processes of expansion. At the close of the Civil War, when settlement was spreading with greatest vigor across the Mississippi, the railways began their work as colonists. Their land grants from the government, amounting altogether by 1871 to an area five times that of the state of Pennsylvania, demanded purchasers, and so the railroads pioneered the way for the pioneer.

The homestead law increased the tide of settlers. The improved farm machinery made it possible for him to go boldly out on to the prairie and to deal effectively with virgin soil in farms whose cultivated area made the old clearings of the backwoodsman seem mere garden plots. Two things resulted from these conditions, which profoundly modified pioneer ideals. In the first place the new form of colonization demanded an increasing use of capital; and the rapidity of the formation of towns, the speed with which society developed, made men the more eager to secure bank credit to deal with the new West. This made the pioneer more dependent on the eastern economic forces. In the second place the farmer became dependent as never before on transportation companies. In this speculative movement the railroads, finding that they had pressed too far in advance and had issued stock to freely for their earnings to justify the face of the investment, came into collision with the pioneer on the question of rates and of discriminations. The Greenback movement and the Granger movements were appeals to government to prevent what the pioneer thought to be invasions of pioneer democracy.

As the western settler began to face the problem of magnitude in the areas he was occupying; as he began to adjust his life to the modern forces of capital and to complex productive processes; as he began to see that, go where he would, the question of credit and currency, of transportation and distribution in general conditioned his success, he sought relief by legislation. He began to lose his primitive attitude of individualism, government began to look less like a necessary evil and more like an instrument for the perpetuation of his democratic ideals. In brief, the defenses of the pioneer democrat began to shift from free land to legislation, from the ideal of individualism to the ideal of social control through regulation by law. He had no sympathy with a radical reconstruction of society by the revolution of socialism; even his alliances with the movement of organized labor, which paralleled that of organized capital in the East, were only half-hearted. But he was becoming alarmed over the future of the free democratic ideal. The wisdom of his legislation it is not necessary to discuss here. The essential point is that his conception of the right of government to control social process had undergone a change. He was coming to regard legislation as an instrument of social construction. The individualism of the Kentucky pioneer of 1796 was giving way to the Populism of the Kansas pioneer of 1896.

The later days of pioneer democracy are too familiar to require much exposition. But they are profoundly significant. As the pioneer doctrine of free competition for the resources of the nation revealed its tendencies; as individual, corporation and trust, like the pioneer, turned increasingly to legal devices to promote their contrasting ideals, the natural resources were falling into private possession. Tides of alien immigrants were surging into the country to replace the old American stock in the labor market, to lower the standard of living and to increase the pressure of population upon the land. These recent foreigners have lodged almost exclusively in the dozen great centers of industrial life, and there they have accented the antagonisms between capital and labor by the fact that the labor supply has become increasingly foreign born, and recruited from nationalities who arouse no sympathy on the part of capital and little on the part of the general public. Class distinctions are accented by national prejudices, and democracy is thereby invaded. But even in the dull brains of great masses of these unfortunates from southern and eastern Europe the idea of America as the land of freedom and of opportunity to rise, the land of pioneer democratic ideals, has found lodgment, and if it is given time and is not turned into revolutionary lines it will fructify.

As the American pioneer passed on in advance of this new tide of European immigration, he found lands increasingly limited. In place of the old lavish opportunity for the settler to set his stakes where he would, there were frantic rushes of thousands of eager pioneers across the line of newly opened Indian reservations. Even in 1889, when Oklahoma was opened to settlement, twenty thousand settlers crowded at the boundaries, like straining athletes, waiting the bugle note that should start the race across the line. Today great crowds gather at the land lotteries of the government as the remaining fragments of the public domain are flung to hungry settlers.

Hundreds of thousands of pioneers from the Middle West have crossed the national boundary into Canadian wheat fields eager to find farms for their children, although under an alien flag. And finally the government has taken to itself great areas of arid land for reclamation by costly irrigation projects whereby to furnish twenty-acre tracts in the desert to settlers under careful regulation of water rights. The government supplies the capital for huge irrigation dams and reservoirs and builds them itself. It owns and operates quarries, coal mines and timber to facilitate this work. It seeks the remotest regions of the earth for crops suitable for these areas. It analyzes the soils and tells the farmer what and when and how to plant. It has even considered the rental to manufacturers of the surplus water, electrical and steam power generated in its irrigation works and the utilization of this power to extract nitrates from the air to replenish worn-out soils. The pioneer of the arid regions must be both a capitalist and the protégé of the government.

Consider the contrast between the conditions of the pioneers at the beginning and at the end of this period of development. Three hundred years ago adventurous Englishmen on the coast of Virginia began the attack on the wilderness. Three years ago the President of the United States summoned the governors of forty-six states to deliberate upon the danger of the exhaustion of the natural resources of the nation.

The pressure of population upon the food supply is already felt and we are at the beginning only of this transformation. It is profoundly significant that at the very time when American democracy is becoming conscious that its pioneer basis of free land and sparse population is giving way, it is also brought face-to-face with the startling outcome of its old ideals of individualism and exploitation under competition uncontrolled by government. Pioneer society itself was not sufficiently sophisticated to work out to its logical result the conception of the self-made man. But the captains of industry by applying squatter doctrines to the evolution of American industrial society, have made the process so clear that he who runs may read. Contests imply alliances as well as rivalries. The increasing magnitude of the areas to be dealt with and the occurrences of times of industrial stress furnished occasion for such unions. The panic of 1873 was followed by an unprecedented combination of individual businesses and partnerships into corporations. The panic of 1893 marked the beginning of an extraordinary development of corporate combinations into pools and trusts, agreements and absorptions, until, by the time of the panic of 1907, it seemed not impossible that the outcome of free competition under individualism was to be monopoly of the most important natural resources and processes by a limited group of men whose vast fortunes were so invested in allied and dependent industries that they constituted the dominating force in the industrial life of the nation. The development of large scale factory production, the benefit of combination in the competitive struggle, and the tremendous advantage of concentration in securing possession of the unoccupied opportunities, were so great that vast accumulations of capital became the normal agency of the industrial world. In almost exact ratio to the diminution of the supply of unpossessed resources, combinations of capital have increased in magnitude and in efficiency of conquest. The solitary backwoodsman wielding his ax at the edge of a measureless forest is replaced by companies capitalized at millions, operating railroads, sawmills, and all the enginery of modern machinery to harvest the remaining trees.

A new national development is before us without the former safety valve of abundant resources open to him who would take. Classes are becoming alarmingly distinct: There is the demand on the one side voiced by Mr. Harriman so well and by others since, that nothing must be done to interfere with the early pioneer ideals of the exploitation and the development of the country's wealth; that restrictive and reforming legislation must on no account threaten prosperity even for a moment. In fact, we sometimes hear in these days, from men of influence, serious doubts of democracy, and intimations that the country would be better off if it freely resigned itself to guidance by the geniuses who are mastering the economic forces of the nation, and who, it is alleged, would work out the prosperity of the United States more effectively, if unvexed by politicians and people.

On the other hand, an inharmonious group of reformers are sounding the warning that American democratic ideals and society are menaced and already invaded by the very conditions that make this apparent prosperity; that the economic resources are no longer limitless and free; that the aggregate national wealth is increasing at the cost of present social justice and moral health, and the future well-being of the American people. The Granger and the Populist were prophets of this reform movement. Mr. Bryan's Democracy, Mr. Debs' Socialism, and Mr. Roosevelt's Republicanism all had in common the emphasis upon the need of governmental regulation of industrial tendencies in the interest of the common man; the checking of the power of those business Titans who emerged successful out of the competitive individualism of pioneer America. As land values rise, as meat and bread grow dearer, as the process of industrial consolidation goes on, and as eastern industrial conditions spread across the West, the problems of traditional American democracy will become increasingly grave.

The time has come when University men may well consider pioneer ideals, for American society has reached the end of the first great period in its formation. It must survey itself, reflect upon its origins, consider what freightage of purposes it carried in its long march across the continent, what ambitions it had for the man, what rôle it would play in the world. How shall we conserve what was best in pioneer ideals? How adjust the old conceptions to the changed conditions of modern life?

Other nations have been rich and prosperous and powerful. But the United States has believed that it had an original contribution to make to the history of society by the production of a self-determining, self-restrained, intelligent democracy. It is in the Middle West that society has formed on lines least like those of Europe. It is here, if anywhere, that American democracy will make its stand against the tendency to adjust to a European type.

This consideration gives importance to my final topic, the relation of the university to pioneer ideals and to the changing conditions of American democracy. President Pritchett of the Carnegie Foundation has recently declared that in no other form of popular activity does a nation or state so clearly reveal its ideals or the quality of its civilization as in its system of education; and he finds, especially in the state university, "a conception of education from the standpoint of the whole people." "If our American democracy were today called to give proof of its constructive ability," he says, "the state university and the public school system which it crowns would be the strongest evidence of its fitness which it could offer."

It may at least be conceded that an essential characteristic of the state university is its democracy in the largest sense. The provision in the Constitution of Indiana of 1816, so familiar to you all, for a "general system of education ascending in regular gradations from township schools to a state university, wherein tuition shall be gratis and equally open to all," expresses the Middle Western conception born in the days of pioneer society and doubtless deeply influenced by Jeffersonian democracy.

The most obvious fact about these universities, perhaps, lies in their integral relation with the public schools, whereby the pupil has pressed upon him the question whether he shall go to college, and whereby the road is made open and direct to the highest training. By this means the state offers to every class the means of education, and even engages in propaganda to induce students to continue. It sinks deep shafts through the social strata to find the gold of real ability in the underlying rock of the masses. It fosters that due degree of individualism which is implied in the right of every human being to have opportunity to rise in whatever directions his peculiar abilities entitle him to go, subordinate to the welfare of the state. It keeps the avenues of promotion to the highest offices, the highest honors, open to the humblest and most obscure lad who has the natural gifts, at the same time that it aids in the improvement of the masses.

Nothing in our educational history is more striking than the steady pressure of democracy upon its universities to adapt them to the requirements of all the people. From the state universities of the Middle West, shaped under pioneer ideals, have come the fuller recognition of scientific studies, and especially those of applied science devoted to the conquest of nature; the breaking down of the traditional required curriculum; the union of vocational and college work in the same institution; the development of agricultural and engineering colleges and business courses; the training of lawyers, administrators, public men, and journalists—all under the ideal of service to democracy rather than of individual advancement alone. Other universities do the same thing; but the head springs and the main current of this great stream of tendency come from the land of the pioneers, the democratic states of the Middle West. And the people themselves, through their boards of trustees and the legislature, are in the last resort the court of appeal as to the directions and conditions of growth, as well as have the fountain of income from which these universities derive their existence.

The state university has thus both a peculiar power in the directness of its influence upon the whole people and a peculiar limitation in its dependence upon the people. The ideals of the people constitute the atmosphere in which it moves, though it can itself affect this atmosphere. Herein is the source of its strength and the direction of its difficulties. For to fulfill its mission of uplifting the state to continuously higher levels the University must, in the words of Mr. Bryce, "serve the time without yielding to it"; it must recognize new needs without becoming subordinate to the immediately practical, to the short-sightedly expedient. It must not sacrifice the higher efficiency for the more obvious but lower efficiency. It must have the wisdom to make expenditures for results which pay manifold in the enrichment of civilization, but which are not immediate and palpable.

In the transitional condition of American democracy which I have tried to indicate, the mission of the university is most important. The times call for educated leaders. General experience and rule-of-thumb information are inadequate for the solution of the problems of a democracy which no longer owns the safety fund of an unlimited quantity of untouched resources. Scientific farming must increase the yield of the field, scientific forestry must economize the woodlands, scientific experiment and construction by chemist, physicist, biologist and engineer must be applied to all of nature's forces in our complex modern society. The test tube and the microscope are needed rather than ax and rifle in this new ideal of conquest. The very discoveries of science in such fields as public health and manufacturing processes have made it necessary to depend upon the expert, and if the ranks of experts are to be recruited broadly from the democratic masses as well as from those of larger means, the state universities must furnish at least as liberal opportunities for research and training as the universities based on private endowments furnish. It needs no argument to show that it is not to the advantage of democracy to give over the training of the expert exclusively to privately endowed institutions.

But quite as much in the field of legislation and of public life in general as in the industrial world is the expert needed. The industrial conditions which shape society are too complex, problems of labor, finance, social reform too difficult to be dealt with intelligently and wisely without the leadership of highly educated men familiar with the legislation and literature on social questions in other states and nations.

By training in science, in law, politics, economics and history the universities may supply from the ranks of democracy administrators, legislators, judges and experts for commissions who shall disinterestedly and intelligently mediate between contending interests. When the words "capitalistic classes" and "the proletariate" can be used and understood in America it is surely time to develop such men, with the ideal of service to the state, who may help to break the force of these collisions, to find common grounds between the contestants and to possess the respect and confidence of all parties which are genuinely loyal to the best American ideals.

The signs of such a development are already plain in the expert commissions of some states; in the increasing proportion of university men in legislatures; in the university men's influence in federal departments and commissions. It is hardly too much to say that the best hope of intelligent and principled progress in economic and social legislation and administration lies in the increasing influence of American universities. By sending out these open-minded experts, by furnishing well-fitted legislators, public leaders and teachers, by graduating successive armies of enlightened citizens accustomed to deal dispassionately with the problems of modern life, able to think for themselves, governed not by ignorance, by prejudice or by impulse, but by knowledge and reason and high-mindedness, the state universities will safeguard democracy. Without such leaders and followers democratic reactions may create revolutions, but they will not be able to produce industrial and social progress. America's problem is not violently to introduce democratic ideals, but to preserve and entrench them by courageous adaptation to new conditions. Educated leadership sets bulwarks against both the passionate impulses of the mob and the sinister designs of those who would subordinate public welfare to private greed. Lord Bacon's splendid utterance still rings true: "The learning of the few is despotism; the learning of the many is liberty. And intelligent and principled liberty is fame, wisdom and power."

There is a danger to the universities in this very opportunity. At first pioneer democracy had scant respect for the expert. He believed that "a fool can put on his coat better than a wise man can do it for him." There is much truth in the belief; and the educated leader, even he who has been trained under present university conditions, in direct contact with the world about him, will still have to contend with this inherited suspicion of the expert. But if he be well trained and worthy of his training, if he be endowed with creative imagination and personality, he will make good his leadership.

A more serious danger will come when the universities are fully recognized as powerful factors in shaping the life of the state—not mere cloisters, remote from its life, but an influential element in its life. Then it may easily happen that the smoke of the battle-field of political and social controversy will obscure their pure air, that efforts will be made to stamp out the exceptional doctrine and the exceptional man. Those who investigate and teach within the university walls must respond to the injunction of the church, "*Sursum corda*"—lift up the heart to high thinking and impartial search for the unsullied truth in the interests of all the people; this is the holy grail of the universities.

That they may perform their work they must be left free, as the pioneer was free, to explore new regions and to report what they find; for like the pioneers they have the ideal of investigation, they seek new horizons. They are not tied to past knowledge; they recognize the fact that the universe still abounds in mystery, that science and society have not crystallized, but are still growing and need their pioneer trail-makers. New and beneficent discoveries in nature, new and beneficial discoveries in the processes and directions of the growth of society, substitutes for the vanishing material basis of pioneer democracy may be expected if the university pioneers are left free to seek the trail.

In conclusion, the university has a duty in adjusting pioneer ideals to the new requirements of American democracy, even more important than those which I have named. The early pioneer was an individualist and a seeker after the undiscovered; but he did not understand the richness and complexity of life as a whole; he did not fully realize his opportunities of individualism and discovery. He stood in his somber forest as the traveler sometimes stands in a village on the Alps when the mist has shrouded everything, and only the squalid hut, the stony field, the muddy pathway are in view. But suddenly a wind sweeps the fog away. Vast fields of radiant snow and sparkling ice lie before him; profound abysses open at his feet; and as he lifts his eyes the unimaginable peak of the Matterhorn cleaves the thin air, far, far above. A new and unsuspected world is revealed all about him. Thus it is the function of the university to reveal to the individual the mystery and the glory of life as a whole—to open all the realms of rational human enjoyment and achievement; to preserve the consciousness of the past; to spread before the eye the beauty of the universe; and to throw wide its portals of duty and of power to the human soul. It must honor the poet and painter, the writer and the teacher, the scientist and the inventor, the musician and the prophet of righteousness—the men of genius in all fields who make life nobler. It must call forth anew, and for finer uses, the pioneer's love of creative individualism and provide for it a spiritual atmosphere friendly to the development of personality in all uplifting ways. It must check the tendency to act in mediocre social masses with undue emphasis upon the ideals of prosperity and politics. In short, it must summon ability of all kinds to joyous and earnest effort for the welfare and the spiritual enrichment of society. It must awaken new tastes and ambitions among the people.

The light of these university watch towers should flash from state to state until American democracy itself is illuminated with higher and broader ideals of what constitutes service to the state and to mankind; of what are prizes; of what is worthy of praise and reward. So long as success in amassing great wealth for the aggrandizement of the individual is the exclusive or the dominant standard of success, so long as material prosperity, regardless of the conditions of its cost, or the civilization which results, is the shibboleth, American democracy, that faith in the common man which the pioneer cherishes, is in danger. For the strongest will make their way unerringly to whatever goal society sets up as the mark of conceded preëminence. What more effective agency is there for the cultivation of the seed wheat of ideals than the university? Where can we find a more promising body of sowers of the grain?

The pioneer's clearing must be broadened into a domain where all that is worthy of human endeavor may find fertile soil on which to grow; and America must exact of the constructive business geniuses who owe their rise to the freedom of pioneer democracy supreme allegiance and devotion to the commonweal. In fostering such an outcome and in tempering the asperities of the conflicts that must precede its fulfilment, the nation has no more promising agency than the state universities, no more hopeful product than their graduates.

→ CHAPTER ELEVEN ←

THE WEST AND AMERICAN IDEALS

TRUE TO AMERICAN TRADITIONS THAT EACH SUCCEEDING GENERATION ought to find in the Republic a better home, once in every year the colleges and universities summon the nation to lift its eyes from the routine of work, in order to take stock of the country's purposes and achievements, to examine its past and consider its future.

This attitude of self-examination is hardly characteristic of the people as a whole. Particularly it is not characteristic of the historic American. He has been an opportunist rather than a dealer in general ideas. Destiny set him in a current which bore him swiftly along through such a wealth of opportunity that reflection and well-considered planning seemed wasted time. He knew not where he was going, but he was on his way, cheerful, optimistic, busy and buoyant.

Today we are reaching a changed condition, less apparent perhaps, in the newer regions than in the old, but sufficiently obvious to extend the commencement frame of mind from the college to the country as a whole. The swift and inevitable current of the upper reaches of the nation's history has borne it to the broader expanse and slower stretches which mark the nearness of the level sea. The vessel, no longer carried along by the rushing waters, finds it necessary to determine its own directions on this new ocean of its future, to give conscious consideration to its motive power and to its steering gear.

It matters not so much that those who address these college men and women upon life, give conflicting answers to the questions of whence and whither: the pause for remembrance, for reflection and for aspiration is wholesome in itself.

Although the American people are becoming more self-conscious, more responsive to the appeal to act by deliberate choices, we should be over-sanguine if we believed that even in this new day these commencement surveys were taken to heart by the general public, or that they were directly and immediately influential upon national thought and action.

But even while we check our enthusiasm by this realization of the common thought, we must take heart. The University's peculiar privilege and distinction lie in the fact that it is not the passive instrument of the state to voice its current ideas. Its problem is not that of expressing tendencies. Its mission is to create tendencies and to direct them. Its problem is that of leadership and of ideals. It is called, of course, to justify the support which the public gives it, by working in close and sympathetic touch with those it serves. More than that, it would lose important element of strength if it failed to recognize the fact that improvement and creative movement often come from the masses themselves, instinctively moving toward a better order. The University's graduates must be fitted to take their places naturally and effectually in the common life of the time.

But the University is called especially to justify its existence by giving to its sons and daughters something which they could not well have gotten through the ordinary experiences of the life outside its walls. It is called to serve the time by independent research and by original thought. If it were a mere recording instrument of conventional opinion and average information, it is hard to see why the University should exist at all. To clasp hands with the common life in order that it may lift that life, to be a radiant center enkindling the society in which it has its being, these are primary duties of the University. Fortunate the state which gives free play to this spirit of inquiry. Let it "grubstake" its intellectual prospectors and send them forth where "the trails run out and stop." A famous scientist holds that the universal ether bears vital germs which impinging upon a dead world would bring life to it. So, at least it is, in the world of thought, where energized ideals put in the air and carried here and there by the waves and currents of the intellectual atmosphere, fertilize vast inert areas.

The University, therefore, has a double duty. On the one hand it must aid in the improvement of the general economic and social environment. It must help on in the work of scientific discovery and of making such conditions of existence, economic, political and social, as will produce more fertile and responsive soil for a higher and better life. It must stimulate a wider demand on the part of the public for right leadership. It must extend its operations more widely among the people and sink deeper shafts through social strata to find new supplies of intellectual gold in popular levels yet untouched. And on the other hand, it must find and fit men and women for leadership. It must both awaken new demands and it must satisfy those demands by trained leaders with new motives, with new incentives to ambition, with higher and broader conception of what constitute the prize in life, of what constitutes success. The University has to deal with both the soil and sifted seed in the agriculture of the human spirit.

Its efficiency is not the efficiency which the business engineer is fitted to appraise. If it is a training ship, it is a training ship bound on a voyage of discovery, seeking new horizons. The economy of the University's consumption can only be rightly measured by the later times which shall possess those new realms of the spirit which its voyage shall reveal. If the ships of Columbus had engaged in a profitable coastwise traffic between Palos and Cadiz they might have saved sail cloth, but their keels would never have grated on the shores of a New World.

The appeal of the undiscovered is strong in America. For three centuries the fundamental process in its history was the westward movement, the discovery and occupation of the vast free spaces of the continent. We are the first generation of Americans who can look back upon that era as a historic movement now coming to its end. Other generations have been so much a part of it that they could hardly comprehend its significance. To them it seemed inevitable. The free land and the natural resources seemed practically inexhaustible. Nor were they aware of the fact that their most fundamental traits, their institutions, even their ideals were shaped by this interaction between the wilderness and themselves.

American democracy was born of no theorist's dream; it was not carried in the *Sarah Constant* to Virginia, nor in the *Mayflower* to Plymouth. It came out of the American forest, and it gained new strength each time it touched a new frontier. Not the constitution, but free land and an abundance of natural resources open to a fit people, made the democratic type of society in America for three centuries while it occupied its empire.

Today we are looking with a shock upon a changed world. The national problem is no longer how to cut and burn away the vast screen of the dense and daunting forest; it is how to save and wisely use the remaining timber. It is no longer how to get the great spaces of fertile prairie land in humid zones out of the hands of the government into the hands of the pioneer; these lands have already passed into private possession. No longer is it a question of how to avoid or cross the Great Plains and the arid desert. It is a question of how to conquer those rejected lands by new method of farming and by cultivating new crops from seed collected by the government and by scientists from the cold, dry steppes of Siberia, the burning sands of Egypt, and the remote interior of China. It is a problem of how to bring the precious rills of water on to the alkali and sage brush. Population is increasing faster than the food supply.

New farm lands no longer increase decade after decade in areas equal to those of European states. While the ratio of increase of improved land declines, the value of farm lands rise and the price of food leaps upward, reversing the old ratio between the two. The cry of scientific farming and the conservation of natural resources replaces the cry of rapid conquest of the wilderness. We have so far won our national home, wrested from it its first rich treasures, and drawn to it the unfortunate of other lands, that we are already obliged to compare ourselves with settled states of the Old World. In place of our attitude of contemptuous indifference to the legislation of such countries as Germany and England, even western states like Wisconsin send commissions to study their systems of taxation, workingmen's insurance, old age pensions and a great variety of other remedies for social ills.

If we look about the periphery of the nation, everywhere we see the indications that our world is changing. On the streets of Northeastern cities like New York and Boston, the faces which we meet are to a surprising extent those of Southeastern Europe. Puritan New England, which turned its capital into factories and mills and drew to its shores an army of cheap labor, governed these people for a time by a ruling class like an upper stratum between which and the lower strata there was no assimilation. There was no such evolution into an assimilated commonwealth as is seen in Middle Western agricultural states, where immigrant and old native stock came in together and built up a homogeneous society on the principle of give and take. But now the Northeastern coast finds its destiny, politically and economically, passing away from the descendants of the Puritans. It is the little Jewish boy, the Greek or the Sicilian, who takes the traveler through historic streets, now the home of these newer people to the Old North Church or to Paul Revere's house, or to Tea Wharf, and tells you in his strange patois the story of revolution against oppression.

Along the southern Atlantic and the Gulf coast, in spite of the preservative influence of the Negro, whose presence has always called out resistance to change on the part of the whites, the forces of social and industrial transformation are at work. The old tidewater aristocracy has surrendered to the up-country democrats. Along the line of the Alleghanies like an advancing column, the forces of northern capital, textile and steel mills, year after year extend their invasion into the lower South. New Orleans, once the mistress of the commerce of the Mississippi Valley, is awakening to new dreams of world commerce. On the southern border, similar invasions of American capital have been entering Mexico. At the same time, the opening of the Panama Canal has completed the dream of the ages of the Straits of Anian between Atlantic and Pacific. Four hundred years ago, Balboa raised the flag of Spain at the edge of the Sea of the West and we are now preparing to celebrate both that anniversary, and the piercing of the continent. New relations have been created between Spanish America and the United States and the world is watching the mediation of Argentina, Brazil and Chile between the contending forces of Mexico and the Union. Once more alien national interests lie threatening at our borders, but we no longer appeal to the Monroe Doctrine and send our armies of frontiersmen to settle our concerns off-hand. We take council with European nations and with the sisterhood of South America, and propose a remedy of social reorganization in place of imperious will and force. Whether the effort will succeed or not, it is a significant indication that an old order is passing away, when such a solution is undertaken by a President of Scotch Presbyterian stock, born in the state of Virginia.

If we turn to the northern border, where we are about to celebrate a century of peace with England, we see in progress, like a belated procession of our own history the spread of pioneers, the opening of new wildernesses, the building of new cities, the growth of a new and mighty nation. That old American advance of the wheat farmer from the Connecticut to the Mohawk, and the Genesee, from the Great Valley of Pennsylvania to the Ohio Valley and the prairies of the Middle West, is now by its own momentum and under the stimulus of Canadian homesteads and the high price of wheat, carried across the national border to the once lone plains where the Hudson Bay dog trains crossed the desolate snows of the wild North Land. In the Pacific Northwest the era of construction has not ended, but it is so rapidly in progress that we can already see the closing of the age of the pioneer. Already Alaska beckons on the north, and pointing to her wealth of natural resources asks the nation on what new terms the new age will deal with her. Across the Pacific looms Asia, no longer a remote vision and a symbol of the unchanging, but borne as by mirage close to our shores and raising grave questions of the common destiny of the people of the ocean. The dreams of Benton and of Seward of a regenerated Orient, when the long march of westward civilization should complete its circle, seem almost to be in process of realization. The age of the Pacific Ocean begins, mysterious and unfathomable in its meaning for our own future.

Turning to view the interior, we see the same picture of change. When the Superintendent of the Census in 1890 declared the frontier line no longer traceable, the beginning of the rush into Oklahoma had just occurred. Here where the broken fragments of Indian nations from the East had been gathered and where the wilder tribes of the Southwest were being settled, came the rush of the land-hungry pioneer. Almost at a blow the old Indian Territory passed away, populous cities came into being and it was not long before gushing oil wells made a new era of sudden wealth. The farm lands of the Middle West taken as free homesteads or bought for a mere pittance, have risen so in value that the original owners have in an increasing degree either sold them in order to reinvest in the newer cheap lands of the West, or have moved into the town and have left the tillage to tenant farmers. The growth of absentee ownership of the soil is producing a serious problem in the former centers of the Granger and the Populist. Along the Old Northwest the Great Lakes are becoming a new Mediterranean Sea joining the realms of wheat and iron ore, at one end with the coal and furnaces of the forks of the Ohio, where the most intense and wide-reaching center of industrial energy exists. City life like that of the East, manufactures and accumulated capital, seem to be reproducing in the center of the Republic the tendencies already so plain on the Atlantic Coast.

Across the Great Plains where buffalo and Indian held sway successive industrial waves are passing. The old free range gave place to the ranch, the ranch to the homestead and now in places in the arid lands the homestead is replaced by the ten or twenty acre irrigated fruit farm. The age of cheap land, cheap corn and wheat, and cheap cattle has gone forever. The federal government has undertaken vast paternal enterprises of reclamation of the desert.

In the Rocky Mountains where at the time of Civil War, the first important rushes to gold and silver mines carried the frontier backward on a march toward the east, the most amazing transformations have occurred. Here, where prospectors made new trails, and lived the wild free life of mountain men, here where the human spirit seemed likely to attain the largest measure of individual freedom, and where fortune beckoned to the common man, have come revolutions wrought by the demand for organized industry and capital. In the regions where the popular tribunal and the free competitive life flourished, we have seen law and order break down in the unmitigated collision of great aggregations of capital, with each other and with organized socialistic labor. The Cripple Creek strikes, the contests at Butte, the Goldfield mobs, the recent Colorado fighting, all tell a similar story, the solid impact of contending forces in regions where civic power and loyalty to the state have never fully developed. Like the Grand Cañon, where in dazzling light the huge geologic history is written so large that none may fail to read it, so in the Rocky Mountains the dangers of modern American industrial tendencies have been exposed.

As we crossed the Cascades on our way to Seattle, one of the passengers was moved to explain his feeling on the excellence of Puget Sound in contrast with the remaining visible Universe. He did it well in spite of irreverent interruptions from those fellow travelers who were unconverted children of the East, and at last he broke forth in passionate challenge,

> Why should I not love Seattle! It took me from the slums of the Atlantic Coast, a poor Swedish boy with hardly fifteen dollars in my pocket. It gave me a home by the beautiful sea; it spread before my eyes a vision of snow-capped peaks and smiling fields; it brought abundance and a new life to me and my children and I love it, I love it! If I were a multi-millionaire I would charter freight cars and carry away from the crowded tenements and noisome alleys of the eastern cities and the Old World the toiling masses, and let them loose in our vast forests and ore-laden mountains to learn what life really is!

And my heart was stirred by his words and by the whirling spaces of woods and peaks through which we passed.

But as I looked and listened to this passionate outcry, I remembered the words of Talleyrand, the exiled Bishop of Autun, in Washington's administration. Looking down from an eminence not far from Philadelphia upon a wilderness which is now in the heart of that huge industrial society where population presses on the means of life, even the cold-blooded and cynical Talleyrand, gazing on those unpeopled hills and forests, kindled with the vision of coming clearings, the smiling farms and grazing herds that were to be, the populous towns that should be built, the newer and finer social organization that should there arise. And then I remembered the hall in Harvard's museum of social ethics through which I pass to my lecture room when I speak on the history of the

Westward movement. That hall is covered with an exhibit of the work in Pittsburgh steel mills, and of the congested tenements. Its charts and diagrams tell of the long hours of work, the death rate, the relation of typhoid to the slums, the gathering of the poor of all Southeastern Europe to make a civilization at that center of American industrial energy and vast capital that is a social tragedy. As I enter my lecture room through that hall, I speak of the young Washington leading his Virginia frontiersmen to the magnificent forest at the forks of the Ohio. Where Braddock and his men, "carving a cross on the wilderness rim," were struck by the painted savages in the primeval woods, huge furnaces belch forth perpetual fires and Huns and Bulgars, Poles and Sicilians struggle for a chance to earn their daily bread, and live a brutal and degraded life. Irresistibly there rushed across my mind the memorable words of Huxley:

> Even the best of modern civilization appears to me to exhibit a condition of mankind which neither embodies any worthy ideal nor even possesses the merit of stability. I do not hesitate to express the opinion that, if there is no hope of a large improvement of the condition of the greater part of the human family; if it is true that the increase of knowledge, the winning of a greater dominion over Nature, which is its consequence, and the wealth which follows upon that dominion, are to make no difference in the extent and the intensity of Want, with its concomitant physical and moral degradation, among the masses of the people, I should hail the advent of some kindly comet, which would sweep the whole affair away, as a desirable consummation.

But if there is disillusion and shock and apprehension as we come to realize these changes, to strong men and women there is challenge and inspiration in them too. In place of old frontiers of wilderness, there are new frontiers of unwon fields of science, fruitful for the needs of the race; there are frontiers of better social domains yet unexplored. Let us hold to our attitude of faith and courage, and creative zeal. Let us dream as our fathers dreamt and let us make our dreams come true.

> Daughters of Time, the hypocritic days,
> Muffled and dumb like barefoot dervishes,
> And marching single in an endless file,
> Bear diadems and fagots in their hands.
> To each they offer gifts after his will

Bread, kingdoms, stars, and sky that hold them all.
I, in my pleachéd garden watched the pomp,
Forgot my morning wishes, hastily
Took a few herbs and apples and the day
Turned and departed silent. I, too late,
Under her solemn fillet, saw the scorn!

What were America's "morning wishes"? From the beginning of that long westward march of the American people America has never been the home of mere contented materialism. It has continuously sought new ways and dreamed of a perfected social type.

In the fifteenth century when men dealt with the New World which Columbus found, the ideal of discovery was dominant. Here was placed within the reach of men whose ideas had been bounded by the Atlantic, new realms to be explored. America became the land of European dreams, its Fortunate Islands were made real, where, in the imagination of old Europe, peace and happiness, as well as riches and eternal youth, were to be found. To Sir Edwin Sandys and his friends of the London Company, Virginia offered an opportunity to erect the Republic for which they had longed in vain in England. To the Puritans, New England was the new land of freedom, wherein they might establish the institutions of God, according to their own faith. As the vision died away in Virginia toward the close of the seventeenth century, it was taken up anew by the fiery Bacon with his revolution to establish a real democracy in place of the rule of the planter aristocracy, that formed along the coast. Hardly had he been overthrown when in the eighteenth century, the democratic ideal was rejuvenated by the strong frontiersmen, who pressed beyond the New England Coast into the Berkshires and up the valleys of the Green Mountains of Vermont, and by the Scotch-Irish and German pioneers who followed the Great Valley from Pennsylvania into the Upland South. In both the Yankee frontiersmen and the Scotch-Irish Presbyterians of the South, the Calvinistic conception of the importance of the individual, bound by free covenant to his fellow men and to God, was a compelling influence, and all their wilderness experience combined to emphasize the ideals of opening new ways, of giving freer play to the individual, and of constructing democratic society.

When the backwoodsmen crossed the Alleghanies they put between themselves and the Atlantic Coast a barrier which seemed to separate them from a region already too much like the Europe they had left, and as they followed the courses of the rivers that flowed to the Mississippi, they called themselves "Men of the western Waters," and their new home in the Mississippi Valley was the "Western World." Here, by the thirties, Jacksonian democracy flourished, strong in the faith of the intrinsic excellence of the common man, in his right to make his own place in the world, and in his capacity to share in government. But while Jacksonian democracy demanded these rights, it was also loyal to leadership as the very name implies. It was ready to follow to the uttermost the man in whom it placed its trust, whether the hero were frontier fighter or president, and it even rebuked and limited its own legislative representatives and recalled its senators when they ran counter to their chosen executive. Jacksonian democracy was essentially rural. It was based on the good fellowship and genuine social feeling of the frontier, in which classes and inequalities of fortune played little part. But it did not demand equality of condition, for there was abundance of natural resources and the belief that the self-made man had a right to his success in the free competition which western life afforded, was as prominent in their thought as was the love of democracy. On the other hand, they viewed governmental restraints with suspicion as a limitation on their right to work out their own individuality.

For the banking institutions and capitalists of the East they had an instinctive antipathy. Already they feared that the "money power" as Jackson called it, was planning to make hewers of wood and drawers of water of the common people.

In this view they found allies among the labor leaders of the East, who in the same period began their fight for better conditions of the wage earner. These Locofocos were the first Americans to demand fundamental social changes for the benefit of the workers in the cities. Like the western pioneers, they protested against monopolies and special privilege. But they also had a constructive policy, whereby society was to be kept democratic by free gifts of the public land, so that surplus labor might not bid against itself, but might find an outlet in the West. Thus to both the labor theorist and the practical pioneer, the existence of what seemed inexhaustible cheap land and unpossessed resources was the condition of democracy. In these years of the thirties and forties, western democracy took on its distinctive form. Travelers like De Tocqueville and Harriet Martineau, came to study and to report it enthusiastically to Europe.

Side by side with this westward marching army of individualistic liberty-loving democratic backwoodsmen, went a more northern stream of pioneers, who cherished similar ideas, but added to them the desire to create new industrial centers, to build up factories, to build railroads, and to develop the country by founding cities and extending prosperity. They were ready to call upon legislatures to aid in this, by subscriptions to stock, grants of franchises, promotion of banking and internal improvements. These were the Whig followers of that other western leader, Henry Clay, and their early strength lay in the Ohio Valley, and particularly among the well-to-do. In the South their strength was found among the aristocracy of the Cotton Kingdom.

Both of these western groups, Whigs and Democrats alike, had one common ideal: the desire to leave their children a better heritage than they themselves had received, and both were fired with devotion to the ideal of creating in this New World a home more worthy of mankind. Both were ready to break with the past, to boldly strike out new lines of social endeavor, and both believed in American expansion.

Before these tendencies had worked themselves out, three new forces entered. In the sudden extension of our boundaries to the Pacific Coast, which took place in the forties, the nation won so vast a domain that its resources seemed illimitable and its society seemed able to throw off all its maladies by the very presence of these vast new spaces. At the same period the great activity of railroad building to the Mississippi Valley occurred, making these lands available and diverting attention to the task of economic construction. The third influence was the slavery question which, becoming acute, shaped the American ideals and public discussion for nearly a generation. Viewed from one angle, this struggle involved the great question of national unity. From another it involved the question of the relations of labor and capital, democracy and aristocracy. It was not without significance that Abraham Lincoln became the very type of American pioneer democracy, the first adequate and elemental demonstration to the world that that democracy could produce a man who belonged to the ages.

After the war, new national energies were set loose, and new construction and development engaged the attention of the westerners as they occupied prairies and Great Plains and mountains. Democracy and capitalistic development did not seem antagonistic.

With the passing of the frontier, western social and political ideals took new form. Capital began to consolidate in even greater masses, and increasingly attempted to reduce to system and control the processes of industrial development. Labor with equal step organized its forces to destroy the old competitive system. It is not strange that the western pioneers took alarm for their ideals of democracy as the outcome of the free struggle for the national resources became apparent. They espoused the cause of governmental activity.

It was a new gospel, for the western radical became convinced that he must sacrifice his ideal of individualism and free competition in order to maintain his ideal of democracy. Under this conviction the Populist revised the pioneer conception of government. He saw in government no longer something outside of him, but the people themselves shaping their own affairs. He demanded therefore an extension of the powers of governments in the interest of his historic ideal of democratic society. He demanded not only free silver, but the ownership of the agencies of communication and transportation, the income tax, the postal savings bank, the provision of means of credit for agriculture, the construction of more effective devices to express the will of the people, primary nominations, direct elections, initiative, referendum and recall. In a word, capital, labor, and the western pioneer, all deserted the ideal of competitive individualism in order to organize their interests in more effective combinations. The disappearance of the frontier, the closing of the era which was marked by the influence of the West as a form of society, brings with it new problems of social adjustment, new demands for considering our past ideals and our present needs.

Let us recall the conditions of the foreign relations along our borders, the dangers that wait us if we fail to unite in the solution of our domestic problems. Let us recall those internal evidences of the destruction of our old social order. If we take to heart this warning, we shall do well also to recount our historic ideals, to take stock of those purposes, and fundamental assumptions that have gone to make the American spirit and the meaning of America in world history.

First of all, there was the ideal of discovery, the courageous determination to break new paths, indifference to the dogma that because an institution or a condition exists, it must remain. All American experience has gone to the making of the spirit of innovation; it is in the blood and will not be repressed.

Then, there was the ideal of democracy, the ideal of a free self-directing people, responsive to leadership in the forming of programs and their execution, but insistent that the procedure should be that of free choice, not of compulsion.

But there was also the ideal of individualism. This democratic society was not a disciplined army, where all must keep step and where the collective interests destroyed individual will and work. Rather it was a mobile mass of freely circulating atoms, each seeking its own place and finding play for its own powers and for its own original initiative. We cannot lay too much stress upon this point, for it was at the very heart of the whole American movement. The world was to be made a better world by the example of a democracy in which there was freedom of the individual, in which there was the vitality and mobility productive of originality and variety.

Bearing in mind the far-reaching influence of the disappearance of unlimited resources open to all men for the taking, and considering the recoil of the common man when he saw the outcome of the competitive struggle for these resources as the supply came to its end over most of the nation, we can understand the reaction against individualism and in favor of drastic assertion of the powers of government. Legislation is taking the place of the free lands as the means of preserving the ideal of democracy. But at the same time it is endangering the other pioneer ideal of creative and competitive individualism. Both were essential and constituted what was best in America's contribution to history and to progress. Both must be preserved if the nation would be true to its past, and would fulfill its highest destiny. It would be a grave misfortune if these people so rich in experience, in self-confidence and aspiration, in creative genius, should turn to some Old World discipline of socialism or plutocracy, or despotic rule, whether by class or by dictator. Nor shall we be driven to these alternatives. Our ancient hopes, our courageous faith, our underlying good humor and love of fair play will triumph in the end. There will be give and take in all directions. There will be disinterested leadership, under loyalty to the best American ideals. Nowhere is this leadership more likely to arise than among the men trained in the Universities, aware of the promise of the past and the possibilities of the future. The times call for new ambitions and new motives.

In a most suggestive essay on the Problems of Modern Democracy, Mr. Godkin has said:

> M. de Tocqueville and all his followers take it for granted that the great incentive to excellence, in all countries in which excellence is found, is the patronage and encouragement of an aristocracy; that democracy is generally content with mediocrity. But where is the proof of this? The incentive to exertion which is widest, most constant, and most powerful in its operations in all civilized

countries, is the desire of distinction; and this may be composed either of love of fame or love of wealth or of both. In literary and artistic and scientific pursuits, sometimes the strongest influence is exerted by a love of the subject. But it may safely be said that no man has ever labored in any of the higher colleges to whom the applause and appreciation of his fellows was not one of the sweetest rewards of his exertions.

What is there we would ask, in the nature of democratic institutions, that should render this great spring of action powerless, that should deprive glory of all radiance, and put ambition to sleep? Is it not notorious, on the contrary, that one of the most marked peculiarities of democratic society, or of a society drifting toward democracy, is the fire of competition which rages in it, the fevered anxiety which possesses all its members to rise above the dead level to which the law is ever seeking to confine them, and by some brilliant stroke become something higher and more remarkable than their fellows? The secret of that great restlessness which is one of the most disagreeable accompaniments of life in democratic countries, is in fact due to the eagerness of everybody to grasp the prizes of which in aristocratic countries, only the few have much chance. And in no other society is success more worshiped, is distinction of any kind more widely flattered and caressed.

In democratic societies, in fact, excellence is the first title to distinction; in aristocratic ones there are two or three others which are far stronger and which must be stronger or aristocracy could not exist. The moment you acknowledge that the highest social position ought to be the reward of the man who has the most talent, you make aristocratic institutions impossible.

All that was buoyant and creative in American life would be lost if we gave up the respect for distinct personality, and variety in genius, and came to the dead level of common standards. To be "socialized into an average" and placed "under the tutelage of the mass of us," as a recent writer has put it, would be an irreparable loss. Nor is it necessary in a democracy, as these words of Godkin well disclose. What is needed is the multiplication of motives for ambition and the opening of new lines of achievement for the strongest. As we turn from the task of the first rough conquest of the continent there lies before us a whole wealth of unexploited resources in the realm of the spirit. Arts and letters, science and better social creation, loyalty and political service to the commonweal, these and a thousand other directions of activity are open to the men, who formerly under the incentive of attaining distinction by amassing extraordinary wealth, saw success only in material display. Newer and finer careers will open to the ambitious when once public opinion shall award the laurels to those who rise above their fellows in these new fields of labor. It has not been the gold, but the getting of the gold, that has caught the imaginations of our captains of industry. Their real enjoyment lay not in the luxuries which wealth brought, but in the work of construction and in the place which society awarded them. A new era will come if schools and universities can only widen the intellectual horizon of the people, help to lay the foundations of a better industrial life, show them new goals for endeavor, inspire them with more varied and higher ideals.

The western spirit must be invoked for new and nobler achievements. Of that matured western spirit, Tennyson's Ulysses is a symbol.

> . . . I am become a name
> For always roaming with an hungry heart,
> Much have I seen and known . . .
> I am a part of all that I have met;
> Yet all experience is an arch, where thro'
> Gleams that untravelled world, whose margin fades
> Forever and forever when I move.
> How dull it is to pause, to make an end.
> To rust unburnished, not to shine in use!
> .   .   .   .
> And this gray spirit yearning in desire
> To follow knowledge like a shining star
> Beyond the utmost bound of human thought.
> . . . Come my friends,
> 'Tis not too late to seek a newer world.
> Push off, and sitting well in order smite
> The sounding furrows; for my purpose holds
> To sail beyond the sunset, and the baths
> Of all the western stars until I die
> .   .   .   .
> To strive, to seek, to find and not to yield.

→ CHAPTER TWELVE ←

SOCIAL FORCES IN AMERICAN HISTORY

THE TRANSFORMATIONS THROUGH WHICH THE UNITED STATES IS PASSING in our own day are so profound, so far-reaching, that it is hardly an exaggeration to say that we are witnessing the birth of a new nation in America. The revolution in the social and economic structure of this country during the past two decades is comparable to what occurred when independence was declared and the constitution was formed, or to the changes wrought by the era which began half a century ago, the era of Civil War and Reconstruction.

These changes have been long in preparation and are, in part, the result of worldwide forces of reorganization incident to the age of steam production and large-scale industry, and, in part, the result of the closing of the period of the colonization of the West. They have been prophesied, and the course of the movement partly described by students of American development; but after all, it is with a shock that the people of the United States are coming to realize that the fundamental forces which have shaped their society up to the present are disappearing. Twenty years ago, as I have before had occasion to point out, the Superintendent of the Census declared that the frontier line, which its maps had depicted for decade after decade of the westward march of the nation, could no longer be described. Today we must add that the age of free competition of individuals for the unpossessed resources of the nation is nearing its end. It is taking less than a generation to write the chapter which began with the disappearance of the line of the frontier—the last chapter in the history of the colonization of the United States, the conclusion to the annals of its pioneer democracy.

It is a wonderful chapter, this final rush of American energy upon the remaining wilderness. Even the bare statistics become eloquent of a new era. They no longer derive their significance from the exhibit of vast proportions of the public domain transferred to agriculture, of wildernesses equal to European nations changed decade after decade into the farm area of the United States. It is true there was added to the farms of the nation between 1870 and 1880 a territory equal to that of France, and between 1880 and 1900 a territory equal to the European area of France, Germany, England, and Wales combined. The records of 1910 are not yet available, but whatever they reveal they will not be so full of meaning as the figures which tell of upleaping wealth and organization and concentration of industrial power in the East in the last decade. As the final provinces of the western empire have been subdued to the purposes of civilization and have yielded their spoils, as the spheres of operation of the great industrial corporations have extended, with the extension of American settlement, production and wealth have increased beyond all precedent.

The total deposits in all national banks have more than trebled in the present decade; the money in circulation has doubled since 1890. The flood of gold makes it difficult to gage the full meaning of the incredible increase in values, for in the decade ending with 1909 over 41,600,000 ounces of gold were mined in the United States alone. Over four million ounces have been produced every year since 1905, whereas between 1880 and 1894 no year showed a production of two million ounces. As a result of this swelling stream of gold and instruments of credit, aided by a variety of other causes, prices have risen until their height has become one of the most marked features and influential factors in American life, producing social readjustments and contributing effectively to party revolutions.

But if we avoid those statistics which require analysis because of the changing standard of value, we still find that the decade occupies an exceptional place in American history. More coal was mined in the United States in the ten years after 1897 than in all the life of the nation before that time. Fifty years ago we mined less than fifteen million long tons of coal. In 1907 we mined nearly 429,000,000. At the present rate it is estimated that the supply of coal would be exhausted at a date no farther in the future than the formation of the constitution is in the past. Iron and coal are the measures of industrial power. The nation has produced three times as much iron ore in the past two decades as in all its previous history; the production of the past ten years was more than double that of the prior decade. Pig-iron production is admitted to be an excellent barometer of manufacture and of transportation. Never until 1898 had this reached an annual total of ten million long tons. But in the five years beginning with 1904 it averaged over twice that. By 1907 the United States had surpassed Great Britain, Germany, and France combined in the production of pig-iron and steel together, and in the same decade a single great corporation has established its domination over the iron mines and steel manufacture of the United States. It is more than a mere accident that the United States Steel Corporation with its stocks and bonds aggregating $1,400,000,000 was organized at the beginning of the present decade. The former wilderness about Lake Superior has, principally in the past two decades, established its position as overwhelmingly the preponderant source of iron ore, present and prospective, in the United States—a treasury from which Pittsburgh has drawn wealth and extended its unparalleled industrial empire in these years. The tremendous energies thus liberated at this center of industrial power in the United States revolutionized methods of manufacture in general, and in many indirect ways profoundly influenced the life of the nation.

Railroad statistics also exhibit unprecedented development, the formation of a new industrial society. The number of passengers carried one mile more than doubled between 1890 and 1908; freight carried one mile has nearly trebled in the same period and has doubled in the past decade. Agricultural products tell a different story. The corn crop has only risen from about two billion bushels in 1891 to two and seven-tenths billions in 1909; wheat from six hundred and eleven million bushels in 1891 to only seven hundred and thirty-seven million in 1909; and cotton from about nine million bales in 1891 to ten and three-tenths million bales in 1909. Population has increased in the United States proper from about sixty-two and one-half millions in 1890 to seventy-five and one-half millions in 1900 and to over ninety millions in 1910.

It is clear from these statistics that the ratio of the nation's increased production of immediate wealth by the enormously increased exploitation of its remaining natural resources vastly exceeds the ratio of increase of population and still more strikingly exceeds the ratio of increase of agricultural products. Already population is pressing upon the food supply while capital consolidates in billion-dollar organizations. The "Triumphant Democracy" whose achievements the iron-master celebrated has reached a stature even more imposing than he could have foreseen; but still less did he perceive the changes in democracy itself and the conditions of its life which have accompanied this material growth.

Having colonized the Far West, having mastered its internal resources, the nation turned at the conclusion of the nineteenth and the beginning of the twentieth century to deal with the Far East, to engage in the world-politics of the Pacific Ocean. Having continued its historic expansion into the lands of the old Spanish empire by the successful outcome of the recent war, the United States became the mistress of the Philippines at the same time that it came into possession of the Hawaiian Islands, and the controlling influence in the Gulf of Mexico. It provided early in the present decade for connecting its Atlantic and Pacific coasts by the Isthmian Canal, and became an imperial republic with dependencies and protectorates—admittedly a new world-power, with a potential voice in the problems of Europe, Asia, and Africa.

This extension of power, this undertaking of grave responsibilities in new fields, this entry into the sisterhood of world-states, was no isolated event. It was, indeed, in some respects the logical outcome of the nation's march to the Pacific, the sequence to the era in which it was engaged in occupying the free lands and exploiting the resources of the West. When it had achieved this position among the nations of the earth, the United States found itself confronted, also, with the need of constitutional readjustment, arising from the relations of federal government and territorial acquisitions. It was obliged to reconsider questions of the rights of man and traditional American ideals of liberty and democracy, in view of the task of government of other races politically inexperienced and undeveloped.

If we turn to consider the effect upon American society and domestic policy in these two decades of transition we are met with palpable evidences of the invasion of the old pioneer democratic order. Obvious among them is the effect of unprecedented immigration to supply the mobile army of cheap labor for the centers of industrial life. In the past ten years, beginning with 1900, over eight million immigrants have arrived. The newcomers of the eight years since 1900 would, according to a writer in 1908, "repopulate all the five older New England States as they stand today; or, if properly disseminated over the newer parts of the country they would serve to populate no less than nineteen states of the Union as they stand." In 1907 "there were one and one-quarter million arrivals. This number would entirely populate both New Hampshire and Maine, two of our oldest states." "The arrivals of this one year would found a state with more inhabitants than any one of twenty-one of our other existing commonwealths which could be named." Not only has the addition to the population from Europe been thus extraordinary, it has come in increasing measure from southern and eastern Europe. For the year 1907, Professor Ripley, whom I am quoting, has redistributed the incomers on the basis of physical type and finds that one-quarter of them were of the Mediterranean race, one-quarter of the Slavic race, one-eighth Jewish, and only one-sixth of the Alpine, and one-sixth of the Teutonic. In 1882 Germans had come to the amount of two hundred fifty thousand; in 1907 they were replaced by three hundred thirty thousand South Italians. Thus it is evident that the ethnic elements of the United States have undergone startling changes; and instead of spreading over the nation these immigrants have concentrated especially in the cities and great industrial centers in the past decade. The composition of the labor class and its relation to wages and to the native American employer have been deeply influenced thereby; the sympathy of the employers with labor has been unfavorably affected by the pressure of great numbers of immigrants of alien nationality and of lower standards of life.

The familiar facts of the massing of population in the cities and the contemporaneous increase of urban power, and of the massing of capital and production in fewer and vastly greater industrial units, especially attest the revolution. "It is a proposition too plain to require elucidation," wrote Richard Rush, Secretary of the Treasury, in his report of 1827, "that the creation of capital is retarded rather than accelerated by the diffusion of a thin population over a great surface of soil." Thirty years before Rush wrote these words Albert Gallatin declared in Congress that "if the cause of the happiness of this country were examined into, it would be found to arise as much from the great plenty of land in proportion to the inhabitants which their citizens enjoyed as from the wisdom of their political institutions." Possibly both of these Pennsylvania financiers were right under the conditions of the time; but it is at least significant that capital and labor entered upon a new era as the end of the free lands approached. A contemporary of Gallatin in Congress had replied to the argument that cheap lands would depopulate the Atlantic coast by saying that if a law were framed to prevent ready access to western lands it would be tantamount to saying that there is some class which must remain "and by law be obliged to servo the others for such wages as they pleased to give." The passage of the arable public domain into private possession has raised this question in a new form and has brought forth new answers. This is peculiarly the era when competitive individualism in the midst of vast unappropriated opportunities changed into the monopoly of the fundamental industrial processes by huge aggregations of capital as the free lands disappeared. All the tendencies of the large-scale production of the twentieth century, all the trend to the massing of capital in large combinations, all of the energies of the age of steam, found in America exceptional freedom of action and were offered regions of activity equal to the states of all western Europe. Here they reached their highest development.

The decade following 1897 is marked by the work of Mr. Harriman and his rivals in building up the various railroads into a few great groups, a process that had gone so far that before his death Mr. Harriman was ambitious to concentrate them all under his single control. High finance under the leadership of Mr. Morgan steadily achieved the consolidation of the greater industries into trusts or combinations and effected a community of interests between them and a few dominant banking organizations, with allied insurance companies and trust companies. In New York City have been centered, as never before, the banking reserves of the nation, and here, by the financial management of capital and speculative promotion, there has grown up a unified control over the nation's industrial life. Colossal private fortunes have arisen. No longer is the per capita wealth of the nation a real index to the prosperity of the average man. Labor on the other hand has shown an increasing self-consciousness, is combining and increasing its demands. In a word, the old pioneer individualism is disappearing, while the forces of social combination are manifesting themselves as never before. The self-made man has become, in popular speech, the coal baron, the steel king, the oil king, the cattle king, the railroad magnate, the master of high finance, the monarch of trusts. The world has never before seen such huge fortunes exercising combined control over the economic life of a people, and such luxury as has come out of the individualistic pioneer democracy of America in the course of competitive evolution.

At the same time the masters of industry, who control interests which represent billions of dollars, do not admit that they have broken with pioneer ideals. They regard themselves as pioneers under changed conditions, carrying on the old work of developing the natural resources of the nation, compelled by the constructive fever in their veins, even in ill-health and old age and after the accumulation of wealth beyond their power to enjoy, to seek new avenues of action and of power, to chop new clearings, to find new trails, to expand the horizon of the nation's activity, and to extend the scope of their dominion. "This country," said the late Mr. Harriman in an interview a few years ago, "has been developed by a wonderful people, flush with enthusiasm, imagination and speculative bent. . . . They have been magnificent pioneers. They saw into the future and adapted their work to the possibilities. . . . Stifle that enthusiasm, deaden that imagination and prohibit that speculation by restrictive and cramping conservative law, and you tend to produce a moribund and conservative people and country." This is an appeal to the historic ideals of Americans who viewed the republic as the guardian of individual freedom to compete for the control of the natural resources of the nation.

On the other hand, we have the voice of the insurgent West, recently given utterance in the New Nationalism of ex-President Roosevelt, demanding increase of federal authority to curb the special interests, the powerful industrial organizations, and the monopolies, for the sake of the conservation of our natural resources and the preservation of American democracy.

The past decade has witnessed an extraordinary federal activity in limiting individual and corporate freedom for the benefit of society. To that decade belong the conservation congresses and the effective organization of the Forest Service, and the Reclamation Service. Taken together these developments alone would mark a new era, for over three hundred million acres are, as a result of this policy, reserved from entry and sale, an area more than equal to that of all the states which established the constitution, if we exclude their western claims; and these reserved lands are held for a more beneficial use of their forests, minerals, arid tracts, and water rights, by the nation as a whole. Another example is the extension of the activity of the Department of Agriculture, which seeks the remotest regions of the earth for crops suitable to the areas reclaimed by the government, maps and analyzes the soils, fosters the improvement of seeds and animals, tells the farmer when and how and what to plant, and makes war upon diseases of plants and animals and insect pests. The recent legislation for pure food and meat inspection, and the whole mass of regulative law under the Interstate Commerce clause of the constitution, further illustrates the same tendency.

Two ideals were fundamental in traditional American thought, ideals that developed in the pioneer era. One was that of individual freedom to compete unrestrictedly for the resources of a continent—the squatter ideal. To the pioneer government was an evil. The other was the ideal of a democracy—"government of the people, by the people and for the people." The operation of these ideals took place contemporaneously with the passing into private possession of the free public domain and the natural resources of the United States. But American democracy was based on an abundance of free lands; these were the very conditions that shaped its growth and its fundamental traits. Thus time has revealed that these two ideals of pioneer democracy had elements of mutual hostility and contained the seeds of its dissolution. The present finds itself engaged in the task of readjusting its old ideals to new conditions and is turning increasingly to government to preserve its traditional democracy. It is not surprising that socialism shows noteworthy gains as elections continue; that parties are forming on new lines; that the demand for primary elections, for popular choice of senators, initiative, referendum, and recall, is spreading, and that the regions once the center of pioneer democracy exhibit these tendencies in the most marked degree. They are efforts to find substitutes for that former safeguard of democracy, the disappearing free lands. They are the sequence to the extinction of the frontier.

It is necessary next to notice that in the midst of all this national energy, and contemporaneous with the tendency to turn to the national government for protection to democracy, there is clear evidence of the persistence and the development of sectionalism. Whether we observe the grouping of votes in Congress and in general elections, or the organization and utterances of business leaders, or the association of scholars, churches, or other representatives of the things of the spirit, we find that American life is not only increasing in its national intensity but that it is integrating by sections. In part this is due to the factor of great spaces which make sectional rather than national organization the line of least resistance; but, in part, it is also the expression of the separate economic, political, and social interests and the separate spiritual life of the various geographic provinces or sections. The votes on the tariff, and in general the location of the strongholds of the Progressive Republican movement, illustrate this fact. The difficulty of a national adjustment of railway rates to the diverse interests of different sections is another example. Without attempting to enter upon a more extensive discussion of sectionalism, I desire simply to point out that there are evidences that now, as formerly, the separate geographical interests have their leaders and spokesmen, that much Congressional legislation is determined by the contests, triumphs, or compromises between the rival sections, and that the real federal relations of the United States are shaped by the interplay of sectional with national forces rather than by the relation of state and nation. As time goes on and the nation adjusts itself more durably to the conditions of the differing geographic sections which make it up, they are coming to a new self-consciousness and a revived self-assertion. Our national character is a composite of these sections.

Obviously in attempting to indicate even a portion of the significant features of our recent history we have been obliged to take note of a complex of forces. The times are so close at hand that the relations between events and tendencies force themselves upon our attention. We have had to deal with the connections of geography, industrial growth, politics, and government. With these we must take into consideration the changing social composition, the inherited beliefs and habitual attitude of the masses of the people, the psychology of the nation and of the separate sections, as well as of the leaders. We must see how these leaders are shaped partly by their time and section, and how they are in part original, creative, by virtue of their own genius and initiative. We cannot neglect the moral tendencies and the ideals. All are related parts of the same subject and can no more be properly understood in isolation than the movement as a whole can be understood by neglecting some of these important factors, or by the use of a single method of investigation. Whatever be the truth regarding European history, American history is chiefly concerned with social forces, shaping and reshaping under the conditions of a nation changing as it adjusts to its environment. And this environment progressively reveals new aspects of itself, exerts new influences, and calls out new social organs and functions.

I have undertaken this rapid survey of recent history for two purposes. First, because it has seemed fitting to emphasize the significance of American development since the passing of the frontier, and, second, because in the observation of present conditions we may find assistance in our study of the past.

It is a familiar doctrine that each age studies its history anew and with interests determined by the spirit of the time. Each age finds it necessary to reconsider at least some portion of the past, from points of view furnished by new conditions which reveal the influence and significance of forces not adequately known by the historians of the previous generation. Unquestionably each investigator and writer is influenced by the times in which he lives and while this fact exposes the historian to a bias, at the same time it affords him new instruments and new insight for dealing with his subject.

If recent history, then, gives new meaning to past events, if it has to deal with the rise into a commanding position of forces, the origin and growth of which may have been inadequately described or even overlooked by historians of the previous generation, it is important to study the present and the recent past, not only for themselves but also as the source of new hypotheses, new lines of inquiry, new criteria of the perspective of the remoter past. And, moreover, a just public opinion and a statesmanlike treatment of present problems demand that they be seen in their historical relations in order that history may hold the lamp for conservative reform.

Seen from the vantage-ground of present developments what new light falls upon past events! When we consider what the Mississippi Valley has come to be in American life, and when we consider what it is yet to be, the young Washington, crossing the snows of the wilderness to summon the French to evacuate the portals of the great valley, becomes the herald of an empire. When we recall the huge industrial power that has centered at Pittsburgh, Braddock's advance to the forks of the Ohio takes on new meaning. Even in defeat, he opened a road to what is now the center of the world's industrial energy. The modifications which England proposed in 1794 to John Jay in the northwestern boundary of the United States from the Lake of the Woods to the Mississippi, seemed to him, doubtless, significant chiefly as a matter of principle and as a question of the retention or loss of beaver grounds. The historians hardly notice the proposals. But they involved, in fact, the ownership of the richest and most extensive deposits of iron ore in America, the all-important source of a fundamental industry of the United States, the occasion for the rise of some of the most influential forces of our time.

What continuity and meaning are furnished by the outcome in present times of the movements of minor political parties and reform agitations! To the historian they have often seemed to be mere curious side eddies, vexatious distractions to the course of his literary craft as it navigated the stream of historical tendency. And yet, by the revelation of the present, what seemed to be side eddies have not seldom proven to be the concealed entrances to the main current, and the course which seemed the central one has led to blind channels and stagnant waters, important in their day, but cut off like ox-bow lakes from the mighty river of historical progress by the mere permanent and compelling forces of the neglected currents.

We may trace the contest between the capitalist and the democratic pioneer from the earliest colonial days. It is influential in colonial parties. It is seen in the vehement protests of Kentucky frontiersmen in petition after petition to the Congress of the Confederation against the "nabobs" and men of wealth who took out titles to the pioneers' farms while they themselves were too busy defending those farms from the Indians to perfect their claims. It is seen in the attitude of the Ohio Valley in its backwoods days before the rise of the Whig party, as when in 1811 Henry Clay denounced the Bank of the United States as a corporation which throve on special privileges—"a special association of favored individuals taken from the mass of society, and invested with exemptions and surrounded by immunities and privileges." Benton voiced the same contest twenty years later when he denounced the bank as

> . . . a company of private individuals, many of them foreigners, and the mass of them residing in a remote and narrow corner of the Union, unconnected by any sympathy with the fertile regions of the Great Valley in which the natural power of this Union, the power of numbers, will be found to reside long before the renewed term of the second charter would expire.

"And where," he asked, "would all this power and money center? In the great cities of the Northeast, which have been for forty years and that by force of federal legislation, the lion's den of southern and western money—that den into which all the tracks point inward; from which the returning track of a solitary dollar has never yet been seen." Declaring, in words that have a very modern sound, that the bank tended to multiply nabobs and paupers, and that "a great moneyed power is favorable to great capitalists, for it is the principle of capital to favor capital," he appealed to the fact of the country's extent and its sectional divergences against the nationalizing of capital.

> What a condition for a confederacy of states! What grounds for alarm and terrible apprehension when in a confederacy of such vast extent, so many rival commercial cities, so much sectional jealousy, such violent political parties, such fierce contests for power, there should be but one moneyed tribunal before which all the rival and contending elements must appear.

Even more vehement were the words of Jackson in 1837. "It is now plain," he wrote, "that the war is to be carried on by the monied aristocracy of the few against the democracy of numbers; the [prosperous] to make the honest laborers hewers of wood and drawers of water through the credit and paper system."

Van Buren's administration is usually passed hastily over with hardly more than mention of his Independent Treasury plan, and with particular consideration of the slavery discussion. But some of the most important movements in American social and political history began in these years of Jackson and Van Buren. Read the demands of the obscure labor papers and the reports of labor's open-air meetings anew, and you will find in the utterances of so-called labor visionaries and the Locofoco champions of "equal rights for all and special privileges for none," like Evans and Jacques, Byrdsall and Leggett, the finger points to the currents that now make the main channel of our history; you will find in them some of the important planks of the platforms of the triumphant parties of our own day. As Professor Commons has shown by his papers and the documents which he has published on labor history, an idealistic but widespread and influential humanitarian movement, strikingly similar to that of the present, arose in the years between 1830 and 1850, dealing with social forces in American life, animated by a desire to apply the public lands to social amelioration, eager to find new forms of democratic development. But the flood of the slavery struggle swept all of these movements into its mighty inundation for the time. After the war, other influences delayed the revival of the movement. The railroads opened the wide prairies after 1850 and made it easy to reach them; and decade after decade new sections were reduced to the purposes of civilization and to the advantages of the common man as well as the promotion of great individual fortunes. The nation centered its interests in the development of the West. It is only in our own day that this humanitarian democratic wave has reached the level of those earlier years. But in the meantime there are clear evidences of the persistence of the forces, even though under strange guise. Read the platforms of the Greenback-Labor, the Granger, and the Populist parties, and you will find in those platforms, discredited and reprobated by the major parties of the time, the basic proposals of the Democratic party after its revolution under the leadership of Mr. Bryan, and of the Republican party after its revolution by Mr. Roosevelt. The Insurgent movement is so clearly related to the areas and elements that gave strength to this progressive assertion of old democratic ideals with new weapons, that it must be regarded as the organized refusal of these persistent tendencies to be checked by the advocates of more moderate measures.

I have dealt with these fragments of party history, not, of course, with the purpose of expressing any present judgment upon them, but to emphasize and give concreteness to the fact that there is disclosed by present events a new significance to these contests of radical democracy and conservative interests; that they are rather a continuing expression of deep-seated forces than fragmentary and sporadic curios for the historical museum.

If we should survey the history of our lands from a similar point of view, considering the relations of legislation and administration of the public domain to the structure of American democracy, it would yield a return far beyond that offered by the formal treatment of the subject in most of our histories. We should find in the squatter doctrines and practices, the seizure of the best soils, the taking of public timber on the theory of a right to it by the labor expended on it, fruitful material for understanding the atmosphere and ideals under which the great corporations developed the West. Men like Senator Benton and Delegate Sibley in successive generations defended the trespasses of the pioneer and the lumberman upon the public forest lands, and denounced the paternal government that "harassed" these men, who were engaged in what we should call stealing government timber. It is evident that at some time between the middle of the nineteenth century and the present time, when we impose jail sentences upon Congressmen caught in such violations of the land laws, a change came over the American conscience and the civic ideals were modified. That our great industrial enterprises developed in the midst of these changing ideals is important to recall when we write the history of their activity.

We should find also that we cannot understand the land question without seeing its relations to the struggle of sections and classes bidding against each other and finding in the public domain a most important topic of political bargaining. We should find, too, that the settlement of unlike geographic areas in the course of the nation's progress resulted in changes in the effect of the land laws; that a system intended for the humid prairies was ill-adjusted to the grazing lands and coal fields and to the forests in the days of large-scale exploitation by corporations commanding great capital. Thus changing geographic factors as well as the changing character of the forces which occupied the public domain must be considered, if we would understand the bearing of legislation and policy in this field. It is fortunate that suggestive studies of democracy and the land policy have already begun to appear.

The whole subject of American agriculture viewed in relation to the economic, political, and social life of the nation has important contributions to make. If, for example, we study the maps showing the transition of the wheat belt from the East to the West, as the virgin soils were conquered and made new bases for destructive competition with the older wheat states, we shall see how deeply they affected not only land values, railroad building, the movement of population, and the supply of cheap food, but also how the regions once devoted to single cropping of wheat were forced to turn to varied and intensive agriculture and to diversified industry, and we shall see also how these transformations affected party politics and even the ideals of the Americans of the regions thus changed. We shall find in the overproduction of wheat in the provinces thus rapidly colonized, and in the overproduction of silver in the mountain provinces which were contemporaneously exploited, important explanations of the peculiar form which American politics took in the period when Mr. Bryan mastered the Democratic party, just as we shall find in the opening of the new gold fields in the years immediately following, and in the passing of the era of almost free virgin wheat soils, explanations of the more recent period when high prices are giving new energy and aggressiveness to the demands of the new American industrial democracy.

Enough has been said, it may be assumed, to make clear the point which I am trying to elucidate, namely that a comprehension of the United States of today, an understanding of the rise and progress of the forces which have made it what it is, demands that we should rework our history from the new points of view afforded by the present. If this is done, it will be seen, for example, that the progress of the struggle between North and South over slavery and the freed Negro, which held the principal place in American interest in the two decades after 1850, was, after all, only one of the interests in the time. The pages of the Congressional debates, the contemporary newspapers, the public documents of those twenty years, remain a rich mine for those who will seek therein the sources of movements dominant in the present day.

The final consideration to which I ask your attention in this discussion of social forces in American life, is with reference to the mode of investigating them and the bearing of these investigations upon the relations and the goal of history. It has become a precedent, fairly well established by the distinguished scholars who have held the office which I am about to lay down, to state a position with reference to the relations of history and its sister-studies, and even to raise the question of the attitude of the historian toward the laws of thermodynamics and to seek to find the key of historical development or of historical degradation. It is not given to all to bend the bow of Ulysses. I shall attempt a lesser task.

We may take some lessons from the scientist. He has enriched knowledge especially in recent years by attacking the no-man's lands left unexplored by the too sharp delimitation of spheres of activity. These new conquests have been especially achieved by the combination of old sciences. Physical chemistry, electro-chemistry, geo-physics, astrophysics, and a variety of other scienic unions have led to audacious hypotheses, veritable flashes of vision, which open new regions of activity for a generation of investigators. Moreover they have promoted such investigations by furnishing new instruments of research. Now in some respects there is an analogy between geology and history. The new geologist aims to describe the inorganic earth dynamically in terms of natural law, using chemistry, physics, mathematics, and even botany and zoölogy so far as they relate to paleontology. But he does not insist that the relative importance of physical or chemical factors shall be determined before he applies the methods and data of these sciences to his problem. Indeed, he has learned that a geological area is too complex a thing to be reduced to a single explanation. He has abandoned the single hypothesis for the multiple hypothesis. He creates a whole family of possible explanations of a given problem and thus avoids the warping influence of partiality for a simple theory.

Have we not here an illustration of what is possible and necessary for the historian? Is it not well, before attempting to decide whether history requires an economic interpretation, or a psychological, or any other ultimate interpretation, to recognize that the factors in human society are varied and complex; that the political historian handling his subject in isolation is certain to miss fundamental facts and relations in his treatment of a given age or nation; that the economic historian is exposed to the same danger; and so of all of the other special historians?

Those who insist that history is simply the effort to tell the thing exactly as it was, to state the facts, are confronted with the difficulty that the fact which they would represent is not planted on the solid ground of fixed conditions; it is in the midst and is itself a part of the changing currents, the complex and interacting influences of the time, deriving its significance as a fact from its relations to the deeper-seated movements of the age, movements so gradual that often only the passing years can reveal the truth about the fact and its right to a place on the historian's page.

The economic historian is in danger of making his analysis and his statement of a law on the basis of present conditions and then passing to history for justificatory appendixes to his conclusions. An American economist of high rank has recently expressed his conception of "the full relation of economic theory, statistics, and history" in these words:

> A principle is formulated by *a priori* reasoning concerning facts of common experience; it is then tested by statistics and promoted to the rank of a known and acknowledged truth; illustrations of its action are then found in narrative history and, on the other hand, the economic law becomes the interpreter of records that would otherwise be confusing and comparatively valueless; the law itself derives its final confirmation from the illustrations of its working which the records afford; but what is at least of equal importance is the parallel fact that the law affords the decisive test of the correctness of those assertions concerning the causes and the effects of past events which it is second nature to make and which historians almost invariably do make in connection with their narrations.

There is much in this statement by which the historian may profit, but he may doubt also whether the past should serve merely as the "illustration" by which to confirm the law deduced from common experience by *a priori* reasoning tested by statistics. In fact the pathway of history is strewn with the wrecks of the "known and acknowledged truths" of economic law, due not only to defective analysis and imperfect statistics, but also to the lack of critical historical methods, of insufficient historical-mindedness on the part of the economist, to failure to give due attention to the relativity and transiency of the conditions from which his laws were deduced.

But the point on which I would lay stress is this. The economist, the political scientist, the psychologist, the sociologist, the geographer, the student of literature, of art, of religion—all the allied laborers in the study of society—have contributions to make to the equipment of the historian. These contributions are partly of material, partly of tools, partly of new points of view, new hypotheses, new suggestions of relations, causes, and emphasis. Each of these special students is in some danger of bias by his particular point of view, by his exposure to see simply the thing in which he is primarily interested, and also by his effort to deduce the universal laws of his separate science. The historian, on the other hand, is exposed to the danger of dealing with the complex and interacting social forces of a period or of a country, from some single point of view to which his special training or interest inclines him. If the truth is to be made known, the historian must so far familiarize himself with the work, and equip himself with the training of his sister-subjects that he can at least avail himself of their results and in some reasonable degree master the essential tools of their trade. And the followers of the sister-studies must likewise familiarize themselves and their students with the work and the methods of the historians, and coöperate in the difficult task.

It is necessary that the American historian shall aim at this equipment, not so much that he may possess the key to history or satisfy himself in regard to its ultimate laws. At present a different duty is before him. He must see in American society with its vast spaces, its sections equal to European nations, its geographic influences, its brief period of development, its variety of nationalities and races, its extraordinary industrial growth under the conditions of freedom, its institutions, culture, ideals, social psychology, and even its religions forming and changing almost under his eyes, one of the richest fields ever offered for the preliminary recognition and study of the forces that operate and interplay in the making of society.

CHAPTER THIRTEEN

MIDDLE WESTERN PIONEER DEMOCRACY

IN TIME OF WAR, WHEN ALL THAT THIS NATION HAS STOOD FOR, ALL THE things in which it passionately believes, are at stake, we have met to dedicate this beautiful home for history.

There is a fitness in the occasion. It is for historic ideals that we are fighting. If this nation is one for which we should pour out our savings, postpone our differences, go hungry, and even give up life itself, it is not because it is a rich, extensive, well-fed and populous nation; it is because from its early days America has pressed onward toward a goal of its own; that it has followed an ideal, the ideal of a democracy developing under conditions unlike those of any other age or country.

We are fighting not for an Old World ideal, not for an abstraction, not for a philosophical revolution. Broad and generous as are our sympathies, widely scattered in origin as are our people, keenly as we feel the call of kinship, the thrill of sympathy with the stricken nations across the Atlantic, we are fighting for the historic ideals of the United States, for the continued existence of the type of society in which we believe, because we have proved it good, for the things which drew European exiles to our shores, and which inspired the hopes of the pioneers.

We are at war that the history of the United States, rich with the record of high human purposes, and of faith in the destiny of the common man under freedom, filled with the promises of a better world, may not become the lost and tragic story of a futile dream.

Yes, it is an American ideal and an American example for which we fight; but in that ideal and example lies medicine for the healing of the nations. It is the best we have to give to Europe, and it is a matter of vital import that we shall safeguard and preserve our power to serve the world, and not be overwhelmed in the flood of imperialistic force that wills the death of democracy and would send the freeman under the yoke. Essential as are our contributions of wealth, the work of our scientists, the toil of our farmers and our workmen in factory and shipyard, priceless as is the stream of young American manhood which we pour forth to stop the flood which flows like moulten lava across the green fields and peaceful hamlets of Europe toward the sea and turns to ashes and death all that it covers, these contributions have their deeper meaning in the American spirit. They are born of the love of Democracy.

Long ago in prophetic words Walt Whitman voiced the meaning of our present sacrifices:

> Sail, sail thy best, ship of Democracy,
> Of value is thy freight, 'tis not the Present only,
> The Past is also stored in thee,
> Thou holdest not the venture of thyself alone, not of the western Continent alone,
> Earth's résumé entire floats on thy keel, O ship, is steadied by thy spars,
> With thee Time voyages in trust, the antecedent nations sink or swim with thee,
> With all their ancient struggles, martyrs, heroes, epics, wars, thou bear'st the other continents,
> Theirs, theirs as much as thine, the destination-port triumphant.

Shortly before the Civil War, a great German, exiled from his native land for his love of freedom, came from his new home among the pioneers of the Middle West to set forth in Faneuil Hall, the "cradle of liberty," in Boston, his vision of the young America that was forming in the West, "the last depository of the hopes of all true friends of humanity." Speaking of the contrast between the migrations to the Mississippi Valley and those of the Old World in other centuries, he said:

> It is now not a barbarous multitude pouncing upon old and decrepit empires, not a violent concussion of tribes accompanied by all the horrors of general destruction, but we see the vigorous elements of all nations . . . peaceably congregating and mingling together on virgin soil . . . ; led together by the irresistible attraction of free and broad principles; undertaking to commence a new era

in the history of the world, without first destroying the results of the progress of past periods; undertaking to found a cosmopolitan nation without marching over the dead bodies of slain millions.

If Carl Schurz had lived to see the outcome of that Germany from which he was sent as an exile, in the days when Prussian bayonets dispersed the legislatures and stamped out the beginnings of democratic rule in his former country, could he have better pictured the contrasts between the Prussian and the American spirit? He went on to say:

> Thus was founded the *great colony of free humanity,* which has not old England alone, but the *world* for its mother country. And in the colony of free humanity, whose mother country is the world, they established the Republic of equal rights where the title of manhood is the title to citizenship. My friends, if I had a thousand tongues, and a voice as strong as the thunder of heaven, they would not be sufficient to impress upon your minds forcibly enough the greatness of this idea, the overshadowing glory of this result. This was the dream of the truest friends of man from the beginning; for this the noblest blood of martyrs has been shed; for this has mankind waded through seas of blood and tears. There it is now; there it stands, the noble fabric in all the splendor of reality.

It is in a solemn and inspiring time, therefore, that we meet to dedicate this building, and the occasion is fitting to the time. We may now see, as never before, the deeper significance, the larger meaning of these pioneers, whose plain lives and homely annals are glorified as a part of the story of the building of a better system of social justice under freedom, a broader, and as we fervently hope, a more enduring foundation for the welfare and progress under individual liberty of the common man, an example of federation, of peaceful adjustments by compromise and concession under a self-governing Republic, where sections replace nations over a Union as large as Europe, where party discussions take the place of warring countries, where the *Pax Americana* furnishes an example for a better world.

As our forefathers, the pioneers, gathered in their neighborhood to raise the log cabin, and sanctified it by the name of home, the dwelling place of pioneer ideals, so we meet to celebrate the raising of this home, this shrine of Minnesota's historic life. It symbolizes the conviction that the past and the future of this people are tied together; that this Historical

Society is the keeper of the records of a noteworthy movement in the progress of mankind; that these records are not unmeaning and antiquarian, but even in their details are worthy of preservation for their revelation of the beginnings of society in the midst of a nation caught by the vision of a better future for the world.

Let me repeat the words of Harriet Martineau, who portrayed the American of the thirties:

> I regard the American people as a great embryo poet, now moody, now wild, but bringing out results of absolute good sense; restless and wayward in action, but with deep peace at his heart; exulting that he has caught the true aspect of things past and the depth of futurity which lies before him, wherein to create something so magnificent as the world has scarcely begun to dream of. There is the strongest hope of a nation that is capable of being possessed with an idea.

And recall her appeal to the American people to "cherish their high democratic hope, their faith in man. The older they grow the more they must reverence the dreams of their youth."

The dreams of their youth! Here they shall be preserved, and the achievements as well as the aspirations of the men who made the state, the men who built on their foundations, the men with large vision and power of action, the lesser men in the mass, the leaders who served the state and nation with devotion to the cause. Here shall be preserved the record of the men who failed to see the larger vision and worked impatiently with narrow or selfish or class ends, as well as of those who labored with patience and sympathy and mutual concession, with readiness to make adjustments and to subordinate their immediate interests to the larger good and the immediate safety of the nation.

In the archives of such an old institution as that of the Historical Society of Massachusetts, whose treasures run to the beginnings of the Puritan colonization, the students cannot fail to find the evidence that a state Historical Society is a Book of Judgment wherein is made up the record of a people and its leaders. So, as time unfolds, shall be the collections of this Society, the depository of the material that shall preserve the memory of this people. Each section of this widely extended and varied nation has its own peculiar past, its special form of society, its traits and its leaders. It were a pity if any section left its annals solely to the collectors of a remote region, and it were a pity if its collections were not transformed into printed documents and monographic studies which can go to the libraries of all the parts of the Union and thus enable the student to see the nation as a whole in its past as well as in its present.

This Society finds its special field of activity in a great state of the Middle West, so new, as history reckons time, that its annals are still predominantly those of the pioneers, but so rapidly growing that already the era of the pioneers is a part of the history of the past, capable of being handled objectively, seen in a perspective that is not possible to the observer of the present conditions.

Because of these facts I have taken as the special theme of this address the Middle Western Pioneer Democracy, which I would sketch in some of its outstanding aspects, and chiefly in the generation before the Civil War, for it was from those pioneers that the later colonization to the newer parts of the Mississippi Valley derived much of their traits, and from whom large numbers of them came.

The North Central states as a whole is a region comparable to all of Central Europe. Of these states, a large part of the old Northwest, Ohio, Indiana, Illinois, Michigan and Wisconsin; and their sisters beyond the Mississippi—Missouri, Iowa and Minnesota—were still, in the middle of the nineteenth century, the home of an essentially pioneer society. Within the lifetime of many living men, Wisconsin was called the "Far West," and Minnesota was a land of the Indian and the fur traders, a wilderness of forest and prairie beyond the "edge of cultivation." That portion of this great region which was still in the pioneering period of settlement by 1850 was alone about as extensive as the old thirteen states, or Germany and Austria-Hungary combined. The region was a huge geographic mold for a new society, modeled by nature on the scale of the Great Lakes, the Ohio Valley, the upper Mississippi and the Missouri. Simple and majestic in its vast outlines it was graven into a variety that in its detail also had a largeness of design. From the Great Lakes extended the massive glacial sheet which covered that mighty basin and laid down treasures of soil. Vast forests of pine shrouded its upper zone, breaking into hardwood and the oak openings as they neared the ocean-like expanses of the prairies. Forests again along the Ohio Valley, and beyond, to the west, lay the levels of the Great Plains. Within the earth were unexploited treasures of coal and lead, copper and iron in such form and quantity as were to revolutionize the industrial processes of the world. But nature's revelations are progressive, and it was rather the marvelous adaptation of the soil to the raising of corn and wheat that drew the pioneers to this land of promise, and made a new era of colonization. In the unity with variety of this pioneer empire and in its broad levels we have a promise of its society.

First had come the children of the interior of the South, and with ax and rifle in hand had cut their clearings in the forest, raised their log cabins, fought the Indians and by 1830 had pushed their way to the very edge of the prairies along the Ohio and Missouri Valleys, leaving unoccupied most of the Basin of the Great Lakes.

These slashers of the forest, these self-sufficing pioneers, raising the corn and live stock for their own need, living scattered and apart, had at first small interest in town life or a share in markets. They were passionately devoted to the ideal of equality, but it was an ideal which assumed that under free conditions in the midst of unlimited resources, the homogeneous society of the pioneers *must* result in equality. What they objected to was arbitrary obstacles, artificial limitations upon the freedom of each member of this frontier folk to work out his own career without fear or favor. What they instinctively opposed was the crystallization of differences, the monopolization of opportunity and the fixing of that monopoly by government or by social customs. The road must be open. The game must be played according to the rules. There must be no artificial stifling of equality of opportunity, no closed doors to the able, no stopping the free game before it was played to the end. More than that, there was an unformulated, perhaps, but very real feeling, that mere success in the game, by which the abler men were able to achieve preëminence gave to the successful ones no right to look down upon their neighbors, no vested title to assert superiority as a matter of pride and to the diminution of the equal right and dignity of the less successful.

If this democracy of southern pioneers, this Jacksonian democracy, was, as its socialist critics have called it, in reality a democracy of "expectant capitalists," it was not one which expected or acknowledged on the part of the successful ones the right to harden their triumphs into the rule of a privileged class. In short, if it is indeed true that the backwoods democracy was based upon equality of opportunity, it is also true that it resented the conception that opportunity under competition should result in the hopeless inequality, or rule of class. Ever a new clearing must be possible. And because the wilderness seemed so unending, the menace to the enjoyment of this ideal seemed rather to be feared from government, within or without, than from the operations of internal evolution.

From the first, it became evident that these men had means of supplementing their individual activity by informal combinations. One of the things that impressed all early travelers in the United Slates was the capacity for extra-legal, voluntary association. This was natural enough; in all America we can study the process by which in a new land social customs form and crystallize into law. We can even see how the personal leader becomes the governmental official. This power of the newly arrived pioneers to join together for a common end without the intervention of governmental institutions was one of their marked characteristics. The log rolling, the house-raising, the husking bee, the apple paring, and the squatters' associations whereby they protected themselves against the speculators in securing title to their clearings on the public domain, the camp meeting, the mining camp, the vigilantes, the cattle-raisers' associations, the "gentlemen's agreements," are a few of the indications of this attitude. It is well to emphasize this American trait, because in a modified way it has come to be one of the most characteristic and important features of the United States of today. America does through informal association and understandings on the part of the people many of the things which in the Old World are and can be done only by governmental intervention and compulsion. These associations were in America not due to immemorial custom of tribe or village community. They were extemporized by voluntary action.

The actions of these associations had an authority akin to that of law. They were usually not so much evidences of a disrespect for law and order as the only means by which real law and order were possible in a region where settlement and society had gone in advance of the institutions and instrumentalities of organized society.

Because of these elements of individualistic competition and the power of spontaneous association, pioneers were responsive to leadership. The backwoodsmen knew that under the free opportunities of his life the abler man would reveal himself, and show them the way. By free choice and not by compulsion, by spontaneous impulse, and not by the domination of a caste, they rallied around a cause, they supported an issue. They yielded to the principle of government by agreement, and they hated the doctrine of autocracy even before it gained a name.

They looked forward to the extension of their American principles to the Old World and their keenest apprehensions came from the possibility of the extension of the Old World's system of arbitrary rule, its class wars and rivalries and interventions to the destruction of the free states and democratic institutions which they were building in the forests of America.

If we add to these aspects of early backwoods democracy, its spiritual qualities, we shall more easily understand them. These men were emotional. As they wrested their clearing from the woods and from the savages who surrounded them, as they expanded that clearing and saw the beginnings of commonwealths, where only little communities had been, and as they saw these commonwealths touch hands with each other along the great course of the Mississippi River, they became enthusiastically optimistic and confident of the continued expansion of this democracy. They had faith in themselves and their destiny. And that optimistic faith was responsible both for their confidence in their own ability to rule and for the passion for expansion. They looked to the future. "Others appeal to history: an American appeals to prophecy; and with Malthus in one hand and a map of the back country in the other, he boldly defies us to a comparison with America as she is to be," said a London periodical in 1821. Just because, perhaps, of the usual isolation of their lives, when they came together in associations whether of the camp meeting or of the political gathering, they felt the influence of a common emotion and enthusiasm. Whether Scotch-Irish Presbyterian, Baptist, or Methodist, these people saturated their religion and their politics with feeling. Both the stump and the pulpit were centers of energy, electric cells capable of starting widespreading fires. They *felt* both their religion and their democracy, and were ready to fight for it.

This democracy was one that involved a real feeling of social comradeship among its widespread members. Justice Catron, who came from Tennessee to the Supreme Court in the presidency of Jackson, said: "The people of New Orleans and St. Louis are next neighbors—if we desire to know a man in any quarter of the union we inquire of our next neighbor, who but the other day lived by him." Exaggerated as this is, it nevertheless had a surprising measure of truth for the Middle West as well. For the Mississippi River was the great highway down which groups of pioneers like Abraham Lincoln, on their rafts and flat boats, brought the little neighborhood surplus. After the steamboat came to the western waters the voyages up and down by merchants and by farmers shifting their homes, brought people into contact with each other over wide areas.

This enlarged neighborhood democracy was determined not by a reluctant admission that under the law one man is as good as another; it was based upon "good fellowship," sympathy and understanding.

They were of a stock, moreover, which sought new trails and were ready to follow where the trail led, innovators in society as well as finders of new lands.

By 1830 the southern inundation ebbed and a different tide flowed in from the northeast by way of the Erie Canal and steam navigation on the Great Lakes to occupy the zone unreached by southern settlement. This new tide spread along the margins of the Great Lakes, found the oak openings and small prairie islands of southern Michigan and Wisconsin; followed the fertile forested ribbons along the river courses far into the prairie lands; and by the end of the forties began to venture into the margin of the open prairie.

In 1830 the Middle West contained a little over a million and a half people; in 1840, over three and a third millions; in 1850, nearly five and a half millions. Although in 1830 the North Atlantic states numbered between three and four times as many people as the Middle West, yet in those two decades the Middle West made an actual gain of several hundred thousand more than did the old section. Counties in the newer states rose from a few hundred to ten or fifteen thousand people in the space of less than five years. Suddenly, with astonishing rapidity and volume, a new people was forming with varied elements, ideals and institutions drawn from all over this nation and from Europe. They were confronted with the problem of adjusting different stocks, varied customs and habits, to their new home.

In comparison with the Ohio Valley, the peculiarity of the occupation of the northern zone of the Middle West, lay in the fact that the native element was predominantly from the older settlements of the Middle West itself and from New York and New England. But it was from the central and western counties of New York and from the western and northern parts of New England, the rural regions of declining agricultural prosperity, that the bulk of this element came.

Thus the influence of the Middle West stretched into the Northeast, and attracted a farming population already suffering from western competition. The advantage of abundant, fertile, and cheap land, the richer agricultural returns, and especially the opportunities for youth to rise in all the trades and professions, gave strength to this competition. By it New England was profoundly and permanently modified.

This Yankee stock carried with it a habit of community life, in contrast with the individualistic democracy of the southern element. The colonizing land companies, the town, the school, the church, the feeling of local unity, furnished the evidences of this instinct for communities. This instinct was accompanied by the creation of cities, the production of a surplus for market, the reaching out to connections with the trading centers of the East, the evolution of a more complex and at the same time a more integrated industrial society than that of the southern pioneer.

But they did not carry with them the unmodified New England institutions and traits. They came at a time and from a people less satisfied with the old order than were their neighbors in the East. They were the young men with initiative, with discontent; the New York element especially was affected by the radicalism of Locofoco democracy which was in itself a protest against the established order.

The winds of the prairies swept away almost at once a mass of old habits and prepossessions. Said one of these pioneers in a letter to friends in the East:

> *If you value ease more than money or prosperity, don't come. . . . Hands are too few for the work, houses for the inhabitants, and days for the day's work to be done. . . . Next if you can't stand seeing your old New England ideas, ways of doing, and living and in fact, all of the good old Yankee fashions knocked out of shape and altered, or thrown by as unsuited to the climate, don't be caught out here. But if you can bear grief with a smile, can put up with a scale of accommodations ranging from the soft side of a plank before the fire (and perhaps three in a bed at that) down through the middling and inferior grades; if you are never at a loss for ways to do the most unpracticable things without tools; if you can do all this and some more come on. . . . It is a universal rule here to help one another, each one keeping an eye single to his own interest.*

They knew that they were leaving many dear associations of the old home, giving up many of the comforts of life, sacrificing things which those who remained thought too vital to civilization to be left. But they were not mere materialists ready to surrender all that life is worth for immediate gain. They were idealists themselves, sacrificing the ease of the immediate future for the welfare of their children, and convinced of the possibility of helping to bring about a better social order and a freer life. They were social idealists. But they based their ideals on trust in the common man and the readiness to make adjustments, not on the rule of a benevolent despot or a controlling class.

The attraction of this new home reached also into the Old World and gave a new hope and new impulses to the people of Germany, of

England, of Ireland, and of Scandinavia. Both economic influences and revolutionary discontent promoted German migration at this time; economic causes brought the larger volume, but the quest for liberty brought the leaders, many of whom were German political exiles. While the latter urged, with varying degrees of emphasis, that their own contribution should be preserved in their new surroundings, and a few visionaries even talked of a German state in the federal system, what was noteworthy was the adjustment of the emigrants of the thirties and forties to Middle Western conditions; the response to the opportunity to create a new type of society in which all gave and all received and no element remained isolated. Society was plastic. In the midst of more or less antagonism between "bowie knife southerners," "cow-milking Yankee Puritans," "beer-drinking Germans," "wild Irishmen," a process of mutual education, a giving and taking, was at work. In the outcome, in spite of slowness of assimilation where different groups were compact and isolated from the others, and a certain persistence of inherited *morale*, there was the creation of a new type, which was neither the sum of all its elements, nor a complete fusion in a melting pot. They were American pioneers, not outlying fragments of New England, of Germany, or of Norway.

The Germans were most strongly represented in the Missouri Valley, in St. Louis, in Illinois opposite that city, and in the Lake Shore counties of eastern Wisconsin north from Milwaukee. In Cincinnati and Cleveland there were many Germans, while in nearly half the counties of Ohio, the German immigrants and the Pennsylvania Germans held nearly or quite the balance of political power. The Irish came primarily as workers on turnpikes, canals and railroads, and tended to remain along such lines, or to gather in the growing cities. The Scandinavians, of whom the largest proportion were Norwegians, founded their colonies in northern Illinois, and in southern Wisconsin about the Fox and the head waters of Rock River, whence in later years they spread into Iowa, Minnesota and North Dakota.

By 1850 about one-sixth of the people of the Middle West were of North Atlantic birth, about one-eighth of southern birth, and a like fraction of foreign birth, of whom the Germans were twice as numerous as the Irish, and the Scandinavians only slightly more numerous than the Welsh, and fewer than the Scotch. There were only a dozen Scandinavians in Minnesota. The natives of the British Islands, together with the natives of British North America in the Middle West, numbered nearly as many as the natives of German lands. But in 1850 almost three-fifths of the population were natives of the Middle West itself, and over a third of the population lived in Ohio. The cities were especially a mixture of peoples. In the five larger cities of the section natives and foreigners were nearly balanced. In Chicago the Irish, Germans and natives of the North Atlantic states about equaled each other. But in all the other cities, the Germans exceeded the Irish in varying proportions. There were nearly three to one in Milwaukee.

It is not merely that the section was growing rapidly and was made up of various stocks with many different cultures, sectional and European; what is more significant is that these elements did not remain as separate strata underneath an established ruling order, as was the case particularly in New England. All were accepted and intermingling components of a forming society, plastic and absorptive. This characteristic of the section as "a good mixer" became fixed before the large immigrations of the eighties. The foundations of the section were laid firmly in a period when the foreign elements were particularly free and eager to contribute to a new society and to receive an impress from the country which offered them a liberty denied abroad. Significant as is this fact, and influential in the solution of America's present problems, it is no more important than the fact that in the decade before the Civil War, the southern element in the Middle West had also had nearly two generations of direct association with the northern, and had finally been engulfed in a tide of Northeastern and Old World settlers.

In this society of pioneers men learned to drop their old national animosities. One of the Immigrant Guides of the fifties urged the newcomers to abandon their racial animosities. "The American laughs at these steerage quarrels," said the author.

Thus the Middle West was teaching the lesson of national cross-fertilization instead of national enmities, the possibility of a newer and richer civilization, not by preserving unmodified or isolated the old component elements, but by breaking down the line-fences, by merging the individual life in the common product—a new product, which held the promise of world brotherhood. If the pioneers divided their allegiance between various parties, Whig, Democrat, Free Soil or Republican, it does not follow that the western Whig was like the eastern Whig. There was an infiltration of a western quality into all of these. The western Whig supported Harrison more because he was a pioneer than because he was a Whig. It saw in him a legitimate successor of Andrew Jackson. The campaign of 1840 was a Middle Western camp meeting on a huge scale. The log cabins, the cider and the coonskins were the symbols of the triumph of Middle Western ideas, and were carried with misgivings by the merchants, the bankers and the manufacturers of the East. In like fashion, the Middle Western wing of the Democratic party was as different from the southern wing wherein lay its strength, as Douglas was from Calhoun. It had little in common with the slaveholding classes of the South, even while it felt the kinship of the pioneer with the people of the southern upland stock from which so many westerners were descended.

In the later forties and early fifties most of the Middle Western states made constitutions. The debates in their conventions and the results embodied in the constitutions themselves tell the story of their political ideals. Of course, they based the franchise on the principle of manhood suffrage. But they also provided for an elective judiciary, for restrictions on the borrowing power of the state, lest it fall under the control of what they feared as the money power, and several of them either provided for the extinguishment of banks of issue, or rigidly restrained them. Some of them exempted the homestead from forced sale for debt; married women's legal rights were prominent topics in the debates of the conventions, and Wisconsin led off by permitting the alien to vote after a year's residence. It welcomed the newcomer to the freedom and to the obligations of American citizenship.

Although this pioneer society was preponderantly an agricultural society it was rapidly learning that agriculture alone was not sufficient for its life. It was developing manufactures, trade, mining, the professions, and becoming conscious that in a progressive modern state it was possible to pass from one industry to another and that all were bound by common ties. But it is significant that in the census of 1850, Ohio, out of a population of two millions, reported only a thousand servants, Iowa only ten in two hundred thousand and Minnesota fifteen in its six thousand.

In the intellectual life of this new democracy there was already the promise of original contributions even in the midst of the engrossing toil and hard life of the pioneer.

The country editor was a leader of his people, not a patent-insides recorder of social functions, but a vigorous and independent thinker and writer. The subscribers to the newspaper published in the section were higher in proportion to population than in the state of New York and not greatly inferior to those of New England, although such eastern papers as the *New York Tribune* had an extensive circulation throughout the Middle

West. The agricultural press presupposed in its articles and contributions a level of general intelligence and interest above that of the later farmers of the section, at least before the present day.

Farmer boys walked behind the plow with their book in hand and sometimes forgot to turn at the end of the furrow; even rare boys, who, like the young Howells, "limped barefoot by his father's side with his eyes on the cow and his mind on Cervantes and Shakespeare."

Periodicals flourished and faded like the prairie flowers. Some of Emerson's best poems first appeared in one of these Ohio Valley magazines. But for the most part the literature of the region and the period was imitative or reflective of the common things in a not uncommon way. It is to its children that the Middle West had to look for the expression of its life and its ideals rather than to the busy pioneer who was breaking a prairie farm or building up a new community. Illiteracy was least among the Yankee pioneers and highest among the southern element. When illiteracy is mapped for 1850 by percentages there appear two contrasting zones, the one extending from New England, the other from the South.

The influence of New England men was strong in the Yankee regions of the Middle West. Home missionaries, and representatives of societies for the promotion of education in the West, both in the common school and denominational colleges, scattered themselves throughout the region and left a deep impress in all these Stales. The conception was firmly fixed in the thirties and forties that the West was the coming power in the Union, that the fate of civilization was in its hands, and therefore rival sects and rival sections strove to influence it to their own types. But the Middle West shaped all these educational contributions according to her own needs and ideals.

The state universities were for the most part the result of agitation and proposals of men of New England origin; but they became characteristic products of Middle Western society, where the community as a whole, rather than wealthy benefactors, supported these institutions. In the end the community determined their directions in accord with popular ideals. They reached down more deeply into the ranks of the common people than did the New England or Middle state colleges; they laid more emphasis upon the obviously useful, and became coëducational at an early date. This dominance of the community ideals had dangers for the Universities, which were called to raise ideals and to point new ways, rather than to conform.

Challenging the spaces of the West, struck by the rapidity with which a new society was unfolding under their gaze, it is not strange that the pioneers dealt in the superlative and saw their destiny with optimistic eyes. The meadow lot of the small intervale had become the prairie, stretching farther than their gaze could reach.

All was motion and change. A restlessness was universal. Men moved, in their single life, from Vermont to New York, from New York to Ohio, from Ohio to Wisconsin, from Wisconsin to California, and longed for the Hawaiian Islands. When the bark started from their fence rails, they felt the call to change. They were conscious of the mobility of their society and gloried in it. They broke with the Past and thought to create something finer, more fitting for humanity, more beneficial for the average man than the world had ever seen.

"With the Past we have literally nothing to do," said B. Gratz Brown in a Missouri Fourth of July oration in 1850, "save to dream of it. Its lessons are lost and its tongue is silent. We are ourselves at the head and front of all political experience. Precedents have lost their virtue and all their authority is gone. . . . Experience can profit us only to guard from antequated delusions."

"The yoke of opinion," wrote Channing to a western friend, speaking of New England, "is a heavy one, often crushing individuality of judgment and action," and he added that the habits, rules, and criticisms under which he had grown up had not left him the freedom and courage which are needed in the style of address best suited to the western people. Channing no doubt unduly stressed the freedom of the West in this respect. The frontier had its own conventions and prejudices, and New England was breaking its own cake of custom and proclaiming a new liberty at the very time he wrote. But there was truth in the eastern thought of the West, as a land of intellectual toleration, one which questioned the old order of things and made innovation its very creed.

The West laid emphasis upon the practical and demanded that ideals should be put to work for useful ends; ideals were tested by their direct contributions to the betterment of the average man, rather than by the production of the man of exceptional genius and distinction.

For, in fine this was the goal of the Middle West, the welfare of the average man; not only the man of the South, or of the East, the Yankee, or the Irishman, or the German, but all men in one common fellowship. This was the hope of their youth, of that youth when Abraham Lincoln rose from rail-splitter to country lawyer, from Illinois legislator to congressman and from congressman to President.

It is not strange that in all this flux and freedom and novelty and vast spaces, the pioneer did not sufficiently consider the need of disciplined devotion to the government which he himself created and operated. But the name of Lincoln and the response of the pioneer to the duties of the Civil War, to the sacrifices and the restraints on freedom which it entailed under his presidency, reminds us that they knew how to take part in a common cause, even while they knew that war's conditions were destructive of many of the things for which they worked.

There are two kinds of governmental discipline: that which proceeds from free choice, in the conviction that restraint of individual or class interests is necessary for the common good; and that which is imposed by a dominant class, upon a subjected and helpless people. The latter is Prussian discipline, the discipline of a harsh machine-like, logical organization, based on the rule of a military autocracy. It assumes that if you do not crush your opponent first, he will crush you. It is the discipline of a nation ruled by its General Staff, assuming war as the normal condition of peoples, and attempting with remorseless logic to extend its operations to the destruction of freedom everywhere. It can only be met by the discipline of a people who use their own government for worthy ends, who preserve individuality and mobility in society and respect the rights of others, who follow the dictates of humanity and fair play, the principles of give and take. The Prussian discipline is the discipline of Thor, the War God, against the discipline of the White Christ.

Pioneer democracy has had to learn lessons by experience: the lesson that government on principles of free democracy can accomplish many things which the men of the middle of the nineteenth century did not realize were even possible. They have had to sacrifice something of their passion for individual unrestraint; they have had to learn that the specially trained man, the man fitted for his calling by education and experience, whether in the field of science or of industry, has a place in government; that the rule of the people is effective and enduring only as it incorporates the trained specialist into the organization of that government, whether as umpire between contending interests or as the efficient instrument in the hands of democracy.

Organized democracy after the era of free land has learned that popular government to be successful must not only be legitimately the choice of the whole people; that the offices of that government must not only be open to all, but that in the fierce struggle of nations in the field of economic competition and in the field of war, the salvation and perpetuity of the republic depend upon recognition of the fact that specialization of the organs of the government, the choice of the fit and the capable for office, is quite as important as the extension of popular control. When we lost our free lands and our isolation from the Old World, we lost our immunity from the results of mistakes, of waste, of inefficiency, and of inexperience in our government.

But in the present day we are also learning another lesson which was better known to the pioneers than to their immediate successors. We are learning that the distinction arising from devotion to the interests of the commonwealth is a higher distinction than mere success in economic competition. America is now awarding laurels to the men who sacrifice their triumphs in the rivalry of business in order to give their service to the cause of a liberty-loving nation, their wealth and their genius to the success of her ideals. That craving for distinction which once drew men to pile up wealth and exhibit power over the industrial processes of the nation, is now finding a new outlet in the craving for distinction that comes from service to the Union, in satisfaction in the use of great talent for the good of the republic.

And all over the nation, in voluntary organizations for aid to the government, is being shown the pioneer principle of association that was expressed in the "house raising." It is shown in the Red Cross, the Y. M. C. A., the Knights of Columbus, the councils and boards of science, commerce, labor, agriculture; and in all the countless other types, from the association of women in their kitchen who carry out the recommendations of the Food Director and revive the plain living of the pioneer, to the Boy Scouts who are laying the foundations for a self-disciplined and virile generation worthy to follow the trail of the backwoodsmen. It is an inspiring prophecy of the revival of the old pioneer conception of the obligations and opportunities of neighborliness, broadening to a national and even to an international scope. The promise of what that wise and lamented philosopher, Josiah Royce called, "the beloved community." In the spirit of the pioneer's "house raising" lies the salvation of the Republic.

This then is the heritage of pioneer experience, a passionate belief that a democracy was possible which should leave the individual a part to play in free society and not make him a cog in a machine operated from above; which trusted in the common man, in his tolerance, his ability to adjust differences with good humor, and to work out an American type from the contributions of all nations—a type for which he would fight against those who challenged it in arms, and for which in time of war he would make sacrifices, even the temporary sacrifice of individual freedom and his life, lest that freedom be lost forever.

INDEX

A

Absentee proprietors, 34, 200
Achievement, 208
Adams, Henry, 139
Adams, J. Q., 16, 124, 151
Agriculture, 212, 222; Middle West, 94, 95
Agriculture, Department of, 216
Alamance, 73, 74
Alaska, 199
Albany, 27, 32
Albany congress of 1754, 9
Algonquin Indians, 81
Aliens, land tenure by, 68
Alleghany Mountains, 5, 11, 42; as barrier to be overcome, 126
Allen, Ethan, 33
Allen, W. V., 144
American Historical Assoc., 102
American history, social forces, 210; survey of recent, 210
American life, distinguishing feature, 1
American people, 230
American spirit, 206, 228, 229
"American System," 110
Americanization, effective, 3
Arid lands, 5, 93, 143, 158, 162, 186
Aristocracy, 166, 169, 171, 184
Army posts, frontier, 10; prototypes, 29
Asia, 199
Association, voluntary, 233, 243
Astor's American Fur Co., 4, 90

Atlantic coast, as early frontier, 3; Mississippi Valley and, 123, 124; northern, History, 199
Atlantic frontier, composition, 7
Atlantic states, 135
Augusta, Ga., 60
Autocracy, 233

B

Back country, 42, 44; democracy of, 164; New England, 47
Backwoods society, 138
Backwoodsmen, 103, 105
Bacon, Francis, 192
Bacon's Rebellion, 52, 164, 166, 203
Baltimore, trade, 67
Bancroft, George, 108
Bank, 110, 169, 220
Bedford, Pa., 3
Beecher, Lyman, 22
Bell, John, 124
Benton, T. H., 16, 22, 124, 220, 222
Berkshires, 37, 45, 48
Beverley, Robert, 53, 57; manor, 57
"Birch seal," 49
Black Hills, 91
Blank patents, 59
Blood-feud, 168
Blount, William, 121
Blue Ridge, 56, 61
Boone, A. J., 11
Boone, Daniel, 11, 65, 77, 106, 134
Boston, trade, 66

Boutmy, E. G., 137
Braddock, Edward, 117, 219
Brattle, Thomas, 35
British and Middle West, 237
Brown, B. Gratz, 241
Brunswick County, Va., 56
Bryan, W. J., 132, 156, 157, 163, 188, 221, 223
Bryce, James, 105, 133, 138, 190
Buffalo, N. Y., 85, 95, 96
Buffalo herds, 90
Buffer state, 82, 84
Burke, Edmund, 21; on the Germans, 67
Byrd, Col. William, 53, 54, 61

C

Calhoun, J. C., 1, 65, 89, 112, 134, 159; on representation, 72; policy of obtaining western trade for the South, 127
California, 5; gold, 90
Canada, 33, 149; barrier between, and the United States, 82; border warfare, 28; homesteads, 199; Middle West and, 79; wheat fields, 186
Canadians, 149
Canals, deep water, 95
Capital, 185, 205, 219; concentration and combinations, 162, 174, 177, 188, 205–06
"Capitalistic classes," 191
Capitalists, 13; "expectant," 232
Capitals, state, transfers, 75
Captains of industry, 172, 173
Carnegie, Andrew, 173, 176
Caroline cow-pens, 10
Catron, John, 234
Cattle raising in Virginia, 55, 57
Census, first, frontier at, 4
Census of 1820, frontier, 4
Census of 1890, extinction of frontier, 1, 5, 24, 25, 200

Center of nation, 146
Channing, W. E., 241
Charleston, S. C., 55, 67, 127
Chase, S. P., 64, 89
Cherry Valley, 64
Chicago, 86, 95, 96, 116, 238; character, 153
Chillicothe, 83, 147
Cincinnati, 83, 96, 103, 147, 153
Cincinnati and Charleston R. R., 112
Cities, 200, 214–15; northeastern, 198–99; seaboard, 125, 126, 127; three periods of development, 126
Civil War, 242; Middle West and, 89; Mississippi Valley and, 130; Northwest and, 141
Clark, G. R., 81, 107, 120
Class distinctions, 188, 191
Clay, Henry, 16, 108, 110, 111, 112, 124, 127, 134, 139, 141, 149, 159, 205, 220
Cleaveland, Gen. Moses, 83, 146, 171
Cleveland, 83, 95, 147, 153
Clinton, De Witt, 126, 127
Coal supply, 211
Coast, Atlantic, 134; destiny, 198; interior and, antagonisms, 68
Coeducation, 240
Colden, Cadwallader, 50
Colonial life, 6
Colonial system, 79
Colonization, 210; English and French contrasted, 8–9; peaceful, 109
Colony of free humanity, 229–30
Columbus, Ohio, 103, 151
Combinations of capital and of labor, 162
Commencement seasons, 195
Commons, J. R., 221
Community, "beloved community," 243; life, 235; type of settlement, 46, 77
Competition, 98, 132, 186, 208, 210

Compromise, 112, 128, 151, 156; slavery, 88, 90
Concentration of power and wealth, 162, 174, 177, 188
Concord, Mass., 25
Concurrent majority, 72
Congregational church, 46, 69
Congress and frontiersmen, 167–68
Connecticut, frontier towns, 27, 28, 33; land policy, 47
Connecticut River, 32, 33, 45
Connecticut Valley, 39, 46
Conquest, 180
Conscience, American, 222
Constitution, U. S., 136, 162
Constitutional convention of 1787, 165
Constitutions, state, 74, 167, 239; reconstruction, 124
Cooperation, voluntary, 106, 171, 172
Corn, areas, 94; belt, 96
Corporations, 177, 222
Cotton culture, 18, 87, 169; early extension, 4; transfer from the East to Mississippi Valley, 125
"Cotton Kingdom," 112, 122, 125, 128
Coureurs de bois, 118
Cow pens, 10, 55
Crockett, Davy, 65
Crops, migration, 94
Currency, 93; evil, 20; expansion, 136
Cutler, Manasseh, 89

D

Dairy interests in Wisconsin, 154, 156
Dakotas, settlement, 91, 92
Darien, Ga., 60
Davis, Jefferson, 65, 87, 112
De Bow, J. D. B., 128
De Bow's *Review*, 142
Debs, E. V., 188
Dedham, 25, 36
Deerfield, 30, 32, 36, 44
Democracy, 20, 33, 206; doubts of, 188; established in Old West, 66; free land and, 183; frontier, early, 65; frontier and, 19, 164, 165; Gookin on, 207; in early 18th century, 61; Jacksonian, 124, 204, 232–33; Jeffersonian, 166, 167; magnitude of achievement in the West, 172; Middle West, 97; Mississippi Valley, 118; neighborhood, 234; new type in West, 136, 141; Ohio Valley, influence, 110; Ohio Valley and, 112; organized, 242; origin, 197; outcome of American experiences, 177; pressure on the universities, 190; significance of Mississippi Valley in promoting, 123; Upland South, 106; western contributions, 161; western ideals, 174; see *also* Pioneer democracy
Democratic party, 221, 223; basis, 165; Middle Western wing, 239
Democratic-Republican party, 166
Denver, Colo., 12
De Tocqueville. *See* Tocqueville
Detroit, 85, 95
Development, American, 133, 144; four changes, 162; personal, 182; significant decade, 163–64; study of, 6; true point of view, 2; western, 142
D'Iberville. *See* Iberville
Discovery, 182, 197, 203, 206
Doddridge, Joseph, 71
Dogs for hunting Indians, 28
Douglas, S. A., 88; Lincoln debates, 152
Douglass, William, 67
Down east, 49
Dracut, 69
Dreams, 203, 230
Duel, 168
Duluth, 95, 155
Dunkards, 175
Dunstable, 30, 35
Duquesne, Abraham, 8
Dwight, Timothy (1752–1817), 39; fears of pioneer class, 167

E

East, efforts to restrict advance of frontier, 20, 21; fears of the West, 136; out of touch with West, 11
Economic forces and political institutions, 161
Economic historian, 224
Economic legislation and Ohio Valley, 109
Education, 189; Middle West, 99
Edwards, Jonathan, 39
Egleston, Melville, 34
Eliot, C. W., on corporation, 177; on democracy and slavery, 170
Emerson, R. W., 240; on Lincoln, 170
England, decrease of dependence on, 14; Mississippi Valley and, 116, 120; Old Northwest and, 81, 84
English pioneers, 181
English settlers in Michigan and Wisconsin, 149
English stock and English speech, 14
Equality, 184; New England, 37, 38, 39; western settlers, 138
Erie Canal, 4, 85, 126, 128
Europe, American democracy and, 189; how America reacted on, 2; Southeastern, 198, 214
Europeans, 178
Evolution, American, as key to history, 6
Expansion, 134, 143, 205, 234; Ohio Valley and, 106; world politics, 163
Experts, 191, 192

F

"Fall line," 3, 5, 43; efforts to establish military frontier on, 52
Fairfax, Lord, 57, 75
Far East, 213
Far West, 213, 231
Farm lands, 200
Farm machinery, 185
Farmers, 158
Farmer's frontier, 7, 10, 11
Federal colonial system, 108
Federal Reserve districts, 217
Fertility, 80
Field, Marshall, 176
Finance, 215; pioneer ideas, 94
Firearms and Indians, 8
Firmin, Giles, 35
Food supply, 187, 198, 212
Foreign parentage, Indiana and Illinois, 153; Michigan, 154; western states, 156; Wisconsin, 153–54
Foreign policy, 107, 143
Foreign Service, 216
Forest philosophy, 134
"Foresters," 39
Forests, 180, 197; Middle West, 81
Fortified houses, 44
Fourierists, 175
France, efforts to revive empire in America, 107; Middle West and, 81; Mississippi Valley and, 116, 120; western exploration, 104; Franchise, 165–66, 167
Franklin, Benjamin, Mississippi Valley and, 117; on the Germans, 67
Free Soil Party, 88, 112, 142
French explorers, 104
French Huguenots, 65
French settlers in Michigan and Wisconsin, 149
Frontier, conservative attitude toward advance, 39; definition, 2, 26; demand for independent statehood, 165; efforts to check and restrict it, 21; evil effects, 20; extinction, 1, 5, 24, 25, 217; farmers, 158, 159; first official, 25, 33; importance as a military training school, 9; influence toward democracy, 164, 165; kinds and modes of advance, 7; Massachusetts, 40; military, of Old

West, 65–66; religious aspects, 23; towns in Massachusetts, 27, 28, 33, 44; various comparisons, 6
Frontiersmen, 134, 136, 138; in Congress, 167–68; Mississippi Valley, 117; Virginia idea, 54
Fulton, Robert, 110
Fur trade, 7; England after Revolution, 81; Hudson River, 50; southern, Old West, 54

G

Gallatin, Albert, 124, 168, 214
Galveston, 131
Garfield, J. A., 160
Geographic factors, 222
Geographic provinces, 101
Georgia, 112, 127; restriction of land tenure, 60; settlement, 60
Germanic germs, 3
Germans, 175; in New York in early times, 3; Middle West and, 86–87, 92; Palatine, 3, 51, 62, 67, 76; political exiles, 237; sectaries, 105; Wisconsin, 14, 149, 156; zone of settlement in Great Valley, 63
Glarus, 156
Godkin, E. L., 207
Glenn, James, 14, 67
Goochland County, Va., 58
Government, 217; paternal, 222; popular, 242
Government discipline, 242
Government expeditions, 10
Government intervention, 233
Government ownership, 94
Government powers, 207
Government regulation, 188
Granger movement, 94, 132, 143, 185, 188
Grant, U. S., 89
Granville, Lord, 59, 75
Great Lakes, 79, 94, 95, 112, 200
Great Plains, 5, 79, 93; Indian trade and war, 91

Great Valley, 62; colonization, 62–63
Greater South, 112
Greeley, Horace, 64
Green Mountain Boys, 49
Greenback movement, 93, 132, 143, 185
Greenway manor, 57
Groseilliers, 116
Groton, 30, 35
Grund, F. J., 4
Grundy, Felix, 124
Gulf coast, 198
Gulf states, 89; occupation, 87

H

Hammond, J. H., on slavery problem in the Mississippi Valley, 128
Hanna, Marcus, 176
Harriman, E. H., 188, 215
Harrison, W. H., 108, 111, 122, 124, 139, 169
Hart, A. B., 114
Hartford, 48
Haverhill, 32, 39
Hayes, R. B., 160
Henry, Patrick, 58
Heroes, 169, 170; western, 139
High thinking, 192
Higher law, 158
Hill, J. J., 173
Historian, 225
Historic ideals, 206, 227
Historical societies, 102–03, 230
History, character, 224–25; new viewpoints, 223
Holland, J. G., 46
Holst, H. E. von, 15
Home markets, 66, 141
Home missions, 23, 240
Homestead law of 1862, 91, 185
Hoosier State, 147
Housatonic River, 45
Housatonic Valley, 45
Houston, Sam, 65
Howells, W. D., 240

Hudson River, 33, 50; frontier, 27; fur trade, 50
Humanitarian movement, 221
Huxley, T. H., on modern civilization, 202

I

Iberville, P. le M. d', 116
Icarians, 175
Idealists, America the goal, 174; social, 236
Ideals, 158; American, and the West, 195; American, loyalty to, 207; American historic, 206, 227; immigrants, 176; Middle West, 97; Mississippi Valley, 132; pioneer, and the state university, 180; readjustment, 217, 222; western, 136, 139, 178; western democracy and, 174
Illinois, composite nationality, 153; elements of settlement, 148; settlement, 85
Illiteracy in Middle West, 240
Immigrants, 186; idealism, 176
Immigration, 92, 140, 214
Indian guides, 10
Indian policy, 6
Indian question, early, 5
Indian reservations, 186
Indian trade, 4, 8; Middle West, 90, 91
Indian wars, 5; New England and, 43; Ohio Valley and, 107
Indiana, character, 153; constitution, 189; elements in settlement, 147–48; settlement, 84
Indianapolis, 103, 151
Indians, buffer state for England, 82, 84; congresses to treat with, 9; effects of trades on, 8; hunting Indians with dogs, 59; influence on Puritans and New England, 28; Middle West and, 83; society, 8
Individualism, 19, 20, 24, 49, 77, 88, 132, 169, 172, 182, 183, 203, 206; in the Old West, 66; reaction against, 207; Upland South, 106
Industrial conditions, 187, 188, 191; Middle West, 94, 97; Mississippi Valley, 125, 130; Ohio Valley and, 112
Industry, captains of, and large undertakings, 172, 173; control, 215
Inland waterways, 113
Insurgent movement, 221
Intellectual life and the frontier, 23
Intercolonial congresses, 9
Interior and coast, antagonisms, 68
Internal commerce, 110, 121
Internal improvements, 17, 18, 68, 109, 110, 141, 171; after 1812 to break down barrier to West, 126; Old West, 67
Internal trade, Old West, 66, 67
Iowa, 89, 90; elements and growth, 151; settlement, 86
Ipswich, 35
Irish, 238
Iron mines in Middle West, 96
Iron ore, 211
Iroquois Indians, 8, 50
Irrigation, 172, 187
Isms, 158
Izard, Ralph, 184

J

Jackson, Andrew, 65, 108, 111, 122, 134, 139, 141, 159, 168, 179, 220; personification of frontier traits, 168, 169
Jackson, Stonewall, 65
Jacksonian democracy, 124, 204, 232–33
James River, 53, 56; settlement, 57
Jefferson, Thomas, 58, 65, 70, 178; conception of democracy, 166, 167; on England and the Mississippi, 120; on the pioneer in Congress, 168; on the importance of the Mississippi Valley, 121

"Jim River" Valley, 91
Johnson, R. M., 124
Johnson, Sir William, 51, 64
Justice, direct forms in the West, 138

K

Kansas, 89, 91, 92, 96; Populists, 157; settlers, 156
Kansas City, 96
Kentucky, 11, 75, 103, 107, 108, 124, 148, 168; slavery, 112
King Philip's War, 25, 29, 43
Kipling, Rudyard, "Toreloper," 181; "Son of the English," 174

L

Labor, combinations, 163; composition of laboring class, 214
Labor theorists, 204, 220
Lamar, L. Q. C. (1825–1893), 16
Lancaster, Mass., 30, 35, 38
Land, 221–22; abundance, 183; abundance, as basis of democracy, 123, 124; alien tenure, 68; free, exhausted, 162–63; free western, 137, 172; fundamental fact in western society, 137; "mongering," 37; *see also* Public lands
Land companies, 76, 235
Land grants, 5; for schools and colleges, 47; to railroads, 185
Land Ordinance of 1785, 82
Land policies, 6
Land system, "equality" principle in New England, 37, 38, 39; Georgia, 60; later federal, 75; New England, 33; New England conflicts, 47; New York State, 50; North Carolina, 59; Old West, 75; Pennsylvania, 62; Virginia, 56; Virginia grants to societies, 53
La Salle, 116
Laurentide glacier, 80
Law and order, 201, 233

Leadership, 139, 196, 197, 207; educated, 192
Lease, Mary Ellen, 159
Legislation, 186, 207; frontier and, 15; Leicester, 36; Leigh, B. W., 71
Lewis and Clark, 8, 10
Liberty, Bacon on, 192; for universities, 192; individual, 139; western, 138
Life as a whole, 193
Lincoln, Abraham, 65, 84, 89, 112, 134, 139, 142, 148, 159, 179, 205, 241; Douglas debates, 152; embodiment of pioneer period, 169–70; Ohio Valley, influence of, 112
Lincoln, C. H., 69
Litchfield, 45, 48, 76
Livingston manor, 51
Locofocos, 204, 221, 236
Log cabin, 229
"Log cabin campaign," 111
London Company, 203
Loria, Achille, 6
Louisiana, 116, 135
Louisiana Purchase, 16, 22, 88, 107, 139, 166; effect on Mississippi Valley, 122–23
Louisville, 103
Lowell, J. R., on Lincoln, 169
Loyal Land Co., 76, 117
Lumber industry, 96; Wisconsin, 154–55
Lumbermen, 182, 183
Lynch law, 138, 182; New England, 49

M

McKinley, William, 156, 157, 160
Magnitude, 172, 173, 185
Maine, 32–33
Maine coast, 49
Mallet brothers, 116
Manila, battle of, 164
Manorial practice in New York, 51
Marietta, 76, 83, 147, 171
"Mark colonies," 44

Marquette, Jacques, 116
Martineau, Harriet, 140, 204, 230
Massachusetts, attempt to locate frontier line, 25; frontier, 40; frontier towns, 27, 28, 33, 44; locating towns before settlement, 48
Mather, Cotton, attitude as to advancing frontier, 39
Mesabi mines, 96, 155
Mendon, 35
Methodists, 157
Mexico, 199
Michigan, 84–85, 86; development and resources, 153; settlement, 149, 150
Middle region, 17; in formation of the Old West, 49; typical American, 17
Middle West, agriculture, 95; Canada and, 79; Civil War and, 89; early society, 97–98; education, 189; elements of settlement— northern and southern, 235, 238; Europe and, 189; flow of population into, 82–83; forests, 81; Germans and, 86–87; Germans and Scandinavians, 92; idealism, 97; immigrants of varied nationalities, 237; importance, 78, 79; increase of settlement in the fifties, 89–90; industrial organism, 94; meaning of term, 78; nationalism, 89; natural resources, 80; New England element, 86; peculiarity and influence, 235; pioneer democracy, 227; settlement, 85, 233; slavery question and, 87; southern zone, 87
Migration, 13, 157, 228; communal vs. individual, 77; crops, 94; interstate, 148; labor, 38; New England, and land policy, 48
Militant expansive movement, 65

Military frontier, 26, 29; early form, 30; Old West, significance, 65–66; Virginia in later 17th century, 52
Milwaukee, 86, 149, 156, 238
Miner's frontier, 7
Mining camps, 5
Mining laws, 6
Minneapolis, 86, 95, 155
Minnesota, 90, 91, 156; economic development, 155; Historical Society, 229–30
Missions to the Indians, 49
Mississippi Company, 76, 117
Mississippi River, 4, 89, 118, 151, 234
Mississippi Valley, 6, 87, 106–07, 219; beginning of stratification, 128; Civil War and, 130; democracy and, 123; early population, 118; economic progress after 1812, 125; England's efforts to control, 116–17; extent, 115; French explorers in, 116; frontiersmen's allegiance, 120–21; idealism, social order, 131–32; industrial growth after the Civil War, 130–31; political power and growth from 1810 to 1840, 124; primitive history, 116; question of severance from the Union, 121; significance in American history, 114, 119; slavery struggle and, 130; social forces, early, 118
Missouri, 124
Missouri Compromise, 88, 112, 149
Missouri Valley, 84
Mohawk Valley, 42, 51
Monroe, James, 95
Monroe Doctrine, 199; germ, 107
Monticello, 58
Moravians, 59, 63
Morgan, J. P., 215
Mormons, 175
Morris, Gouverneur, 134

N

Nashaway, 35
National problem, 197
Nationalism, 18; evils of, 100; Middle West and, 89
Nationalities, mixture, 17; replacement in Wisconsin, 155
Naturalization, 68
Nebraska, 91, 92, 143; settlers, 156
Negro, 198
New England, 17, 203; back lands, 47; coast vs. interior, 68; colonies from, 76; culmination of frontier movement, 49; early official frontier line, 27; economic life, 49; effect on the West, 23; foreign element, 198; frontier protection, 29–30; frontier types, 27–28; Greater New England, 41, 44; ideas, and Middle West, 235; Indian wars, 43; land system, 33; Middle West and, 235; Ohio settlement and, 147; Old West and, 42; Old West and interior New England, 44; pioneer type, 158; streams of settlement from, 140; two New Englands of the formative period of the Old West, 49–50
New Englanders in the Middle West, 86; in Wisconsin and the lake region, 150; three movements of advance from the coast, 85; westernized, 140, 141
New Glarus, 156
New Hampshire, 43, 45, 48, 68
New Hampshire grants, 48
New Northwest, 146
New Orleans, 85, 86, 107, 121, 122, 142, 199
New South, 143; Old West and, 62
New West, 171
New York City, 85, 126, 215
New York State, early frontier, 27; lack of expansive power, 50; land system, 50; settlement from New England, 52; western, 151
Newspapers of the Middle West, 239
Nitrates, 187
Norfolk, 126
North Carolina, 54, 65; coast vs. upland, 71; in Indiana Settlement, 148; public lands, 59; settlement, 58, 59; slavery, 75; taxation, 72, 73
North Central states, 78; region as a whole, 231
North Dakota, development, 157
Northampton, 39
Northfield, 33
Northwest, democracy, 242; Old and New, 146; *see also* Old Northwest
Northwest Territory, 146
Northwestern boundary, 219
Norwegians, 154
Nullification, 72, 169

O

Ohio, diversity of interests, 152–53; elements of settlement, 147; history, 82–83; New England element, 147; southern contribution to settlement, 147
Ohio Company, 76, 83, 89, 117, 146
Ohio River, 3, 103
Ohio Valley, 64; as a highway, 103; economic legislation and, 109; effects on national expansion, 106; in American history, 100; influence on Lincoln, 112; part in making of the nation, 102; physiography, 102–03; relation to the South, 112; religious spirit, 105, 106; stock and settlement, 105
Oil wells, 200
Oklahoma, 186, 200
Old National road, 85
Old Northwest, 81, 82, 85, 144; as a whole, 159–60; defined, 142;

elements of settlement, 146; political position, 156; social origin, 146–47; southern element in settlement, 147, 148–49; turning point of control, 151
"Old South," 106
Old West, colonization of areas beyond the mountains, 76; consequences of formation, 65; New South and, 62; summary of frontier movement in 17th and early 18th centuries, 60; term defined, 42
Old World, 174, 178, 198, 201, 233, 236; effect of American frontier, 14; West and, 134, 137
Opportunity, 24, 138, 158, 173, 174, 175, 181–82, 232
Orangeburg, 60
Ordinance of 1787, 16, 82, 108, 123, 147
Oregon country, 90
Orient, 199
Osgood, H. L., 19

P

Pacific coast, 108, 143, 205
Pacific Northwest, 199
Pacific Ocean, 200, 213
Packing industries, 96
Palatine Germans, 3, 14, 62, 67, 76; New York State and, 51
Palisades, 44
Panama Canal, 199
Panics, 186–87
Paper money, 20, 68, 75, 136
Parkman, Francis, 44, 45, 91, 104
"Particular plantations," 26
Past, lessons of, 241
Patroon estates, 50
Paxton Boys, 69
Pecks *New Guide to the West*, 12
Penn, William, 175
Pennsylvania, 14, 17; coast and interior, antagonisms, 69; German settlement, 51, 63; Great Valley of, 42, 105; land grants, 63; new Pennsylvania of the Great Valley, 62; Scotch-Irish, 63, 64; settlement of Old West part, 52
Pennsylvania Dutch, 14, 62, 68
Perrot, Nicolas, 116
Philadelphia, 65; trade, 66
Physiographic provinces, 79
Piedmont, 43; Virginia, 54, 55
Pig iron, 96, 211
Pine, 96
Pine belt in Middle West, 90
Pioneer democracy, lessons learned, 242; Middle West, 227
Pioneer farmers, 13, 134, 171
Pioneers, conservative fears about, 167; contest with capitalist, 219; contrast of conditions, 187; deeper significance, 229; essence, 181; ideals and the state university, 180; Middle West, 92, 98; Ohio Valley, 107; old ideals, 94; sketch, 11
Pittsburgh, 64, 78, 85, 98–99, 103, 176, 202, 212, 219
Plain people, 170, 178
Political institutions, 161; frontier and, 15
Political parties, 163, 219
Polk, J. K., 65, 124, 169
Pontiac, 81, 91
Poor whites, 147
Population center, 146
Populists, 20, 78, 93, 98, 132, 144, 164, 186, 188, 206; Kansas, 157
Prairie Plains, 80
Prairie states, 158
Prairies, 142, 156, 185, 236; settlement, 91, 94
Presbyterians, 63, 65, 67, 105
Presidency, 169; Mississippi Valley and, 124; Ohio Valley and, 112; Old Northwest and, 146
Prices, 211

Princeton college, 65
Pritchett, H. S., 189
Privilege, 124; conflict against, 74
Proclamation of 1763, 117
Progressive Republican movement, 217
Prohibitionists, 158
"Proletariat," 191
Property, 136; as basis of suffrage, 165
Prosperity, 188
Protection. See Tariff Provinces, geographic, 110
Provincialism, desirable, 100, 102
Prussianism, 229, 242
Public lands, 16, 82, 204; policy of America, 16, 109; western lands, first debates on, 123
Public schools, 178, 189
Puget Sound, 201
Puritan ideals, 46, 47, 49; German conflict with, 86
Puritanism, 17
Puritans and Indians, 28
Purrysburg, 60
Pyrichon, John, 32

Q

Quakers, 65, 69, 105; in settlement of Indiana, 147
Quebec, Province of, 81
Quincy, Josiah, 135

R

Radisson, Sieur de, 116
Railroads, Chicago and, 95; continental, 164; in early fifties, 86; land grants to, 185; Mississippi Valley, 205; northwestern, 92; origin, 8; speculative movement, 185; statistics, 212; western, 142
Rancher's frontier, 7, 10
Ranches, 5, 10; Virginia, 55
Rappahannock River, 53, 56; settlement, 58
Reclamation, 200

Reclamation Service, 216
Red Cloud (Indian), 91
Red River valley, 91
Redemptioners, 14, 56, 60, 62
Reformers, 188, 219; social, 274–75
Regulation, War of the, 164
Regulators, 72, 73, 74, 138
Religion of the Middle West, 234
Religious freedom of the Old West, 74
Religious spirit, Ohio Valley, 105, 106; Upland South, 105, 106
Rensselaerswyck, 50
Representation, 70, 72, 74
Republican party, 221
Research, 191, 192, 224
Revolution, American, 19
Rhodes, J. F., 15
Richmond, Va., 67
Rights, equal, 220–21, 229; of man, 124
Ripley, W. Z., 214
Robertson, James, 65, 121
Rockefeller, J. D., 173, 175–76
Rocky Mountains, 5, 6, 200
Roosevelt, Theodore, 131, 132, 188, 216, 221; on the Mississippi Valley, 115; *Winning of the West*, 42
Root, Elihu, 101
Roxbury, 36
Royce, Josiah, 100, 243
Rush, Richard, 214

S

St. Louis, 96, 103, 151
St. Paul, 86, 155
Salisbury, Mass., 35
Salt, 10; annual pilgrimage to coast for, 11
Salt springs, 10, 11
Salzburgers, 60
Sandys, Sir Edwin, 203
Sault Ste. Marie Canal, 95
Scalps, Massachusetts bounty for, 28
Scandinavians, 175, 237; Middle West, 92; western life, 153–54

Schools, early difficulties, 66; *see also* Public schools Schurz, Carl, 229
Science, 191, 223–24
Scientific farming, 198
Scotch Highlanders, 64; Georgia, 60
Scotch-Irish, 3, 14, 45; migration in Great Valley and Piedmont, 63; Pennsylvania, 64; South Carolina, 61; Virginia, 54, 56–57
Scotch-Irish Presbyterians, 64, 67, 105
Scovillites, 72
Seaboard cities, 125, 126, 127
Seattle, 201
"Section" of land, 75, 82
Sectionalism, 17, 18, 100, 140, 144, 217
Sections, relation, 101
Self-government, 108, 123, 134, 165, 170
Self-made man, 143, 215
Servants, 37, 239
Service to the Union, 243
Settlement, community type, 46
Settler, 13
Sevier, John, 65, 121
Seward, W. H., 89; on the Northwest, 152; on the slavery issue in the Mississippi Valley, 129, 130
Shays' Rebellion, 69, 73, 75, 165
Sheffield, 45
Sheldon, George, 36
Shenandoah Valley, 43, 56, 57, 61, 64
Sherman, W. T., 89
Sibley, H. H. (1811–1891), 182, 183, 222
Silver movement, 157, 158, 222
Simsbury, 39
Singletary, Amos, 159
Sioux Indians, 81
Six Nations, 9, 52
Slavery question, 15, 18, 61, 68, 87, 205, 223; compromise movement, 112; democracy and, 170; expansion, 112; Middle West and, 87; Mississippi Valley and, 128, 130; Northwest and, 151; slaves as property, 70; Virginia and North Carolina, 75
Smith, Major Lawrence, 53
Social control, 186
Social forces, in American history, 210; mode of investigating, 223; on the Atlantic coast, 200; political institutions and, 161
Social mobility, 241
Social order, Mississippi Valley, 131–32; new, 175
Social reformers, 174–75
Socialism, 163, 185, 207, 217
Society, backwoods, 138; rebirth of in the West, 133
Soils, 187; search for, 11
Solid South, 141
South, 17, 106, 142; contribution to settlement of Old Northwest (Ohio, Indiana, Illinois), 147, 148–49; Ohio Valley and, 112; solid, 141; transforming forces, 198; West and, 127; *see also* Upland South
South Carolina, 112; condition of antagonism between coast and interior, 60; land system, townships, 60; trade, 66
South Dakota, development, 157
Southeastern Europe, 198, 202, 214
Southerners and the Middle West, 82–83, 84, 85, 87
Southwest, 200
Spain, 107, 117, 163; Mississippi Valley and, 119
Spangenberg, A. G., 10
Spanish America, 117, 199
Spanish War, 163
Speculation, 216
Spoils system, 20, 169
Spotswood, Alexander, 14, 55, 56, 56, 69, 164; Mississippi Valley and, 116
Spotsylvania County, Va., 56

Spreckles, Claus, 176
Squatter-sovereignty, 88
Squatters, 182, 233; doctrines, 183, 222; ideal, 216; Middle West, 86; Ohio Valley, 109; Pennsylvania in 1726, 62
Stark, John, 63–64
State historical societies, 230
State lines, 79
State universities, 144, 240; as safeguard of democracy, 192; Michigan, 154; peculiar power, 189–90; pioneer ideals and, 180, 188
States, checkerboard, 142; frontier pioneers' demand for statehood, 165; groups, 101; new states vs. Atlantic states, 135; System of, 108
Staunton, Va., 57
Steam navigation, 4, 235
Steel, 212
Steel and iron industry, 96
Stockbridge, 49
Stoddard, Solomon, 28
Success, 193, 208
Sudbury, 25
Suffrage, 124, 141; basis, 165; frontier and extension, 19; manhood, 166, 239
Superior, Lake, 116, 212; iron mines, 96
Swedes, 154
Symmes Purchase, 147

T

Talleyrand, 201
Taney, R. B., 89
Tariff, 15, 17, 109, 110, 127, 141
Taylor, Zachary, 169
Tecumthe, 84, 91
Tennessee, 75, 108, 121, 148, 168; democracy, 124
Tennyson's "Ulysses," 209
Territories, system of, 108

Texas, 108
Thomas, J. B., 112
Tocqueville, A. C. H. C. de, 97, 184, 204
Toledo, Ohio, 153
Toleration, 241
Town meeting, 38
Towns, legislating into existence, 77; locating, Massachusetts, 47; New England and Virginia, 26; new settlements in New England, 34; South Carolina, 59; typical form of establishing in New England, 46; Virginia, 53, 54
Trader's frontier, 7; effects following, 7; rapidity of advance, 7, 8
Trading posts, 9
Transportation, 93; Great Lakes, 95
Tryon, William, 75
Tuscarora War, 58, 59

U

Ulstermen, 64
Unification of the West, 140
United States, collection of nations, 102; development since 1890, 210; federal aspect, 101; fundamental forces, 210; original contribution to society, 189–90; wealth, 211
U. S. Steel Corporation, 96–97, 164, 177, 212
Universities, duties, 196; function, 193; influence of university men, 191; need of freedom, 192; pressure of democracies on, 190; state and, 192; *see also* state universities
Upland South, 105; religious spirit, 105, 106

V

Van Buren, Martin, 169, 221
Van Rensselaer manor, 51
Vandalia, 151

Verendryes, the, 116
Vermont, 43, 45, 48, 49, 69, 75, 85
Vermonters in Wisconsin and Michigan, 150
Vicksburg, 130
Vigilance committees, 138
Vinton, S. F., 89, 151
Virginia, 203; early attempt to establish frontier, 26; Indian wars, 43–44; inequalities, coast vs. interior, 69; interest in Mississippi Valley, 117; land grants, 57; land grants to societies, 53; Piedmont, society, 59; Piedmont portions, 54, 55; settlement in latter part of 17th century, 52; slavery, 75; two Virginias in later 17th century, 58; western democracy and, 123
Virginia Convention of 1829–30, 18, 19
Visions, 181, 224, 229–30
Voyageurs, 10

W

Wachovia, 59
Walker, F. A., 79
War of 1812, 108, 139
Washington, George, 57, 76, 81; Mississippi Valley and, 117, 125, 127, 219; Ohio Valley and, 104, 107
Wealth, 138–39, 143, 193, 215; democracy versus, 124; in politics, 111; United States, 211
Wells (town), 29
"Welsh tract," 60
Wentworth, Benning, 48
West, American ideals and, 195; beginning of, 4; center of interest, 221; constructive force, 133; contributions to democracy, 161; factor in American history, 1, 3; ideals, 136, 140, 178; indefiniteness of term, 78; insurgent voice, 216; main streams of settlement, 140; mark of New England, 23; phase of division, 140–41; population, 22; problem of, 133; South and, 127, 128; warnings against, 135, 136; Middle West; *see also* Old West; Old Northwest
West Virginia, 71
Westchester County, N. Y., 51
Western colleges, 23
Western life, dominant forces, 146
Western Reserve, 76, 83
Western spirit, 209
"Western Waters," 103, 134, 204; men of freedom and independence, 118
"Western World," 103, 106, 134, 204; basis of its civilization, 114
Wheat, 223; areas, 94
Whig party, 17, 111, 205, 220, 238
White, Abraham, 159
White, Hugh, 124
Whitman, Walt, 228
Wilderness, 174, 180, 181, 187
Wilkinson, James, 108, 120
Williams, John (1664–1729), 44
Williams, Roger, 175
Windsor, 48
Winthrop, John, 38
Wisconsin, 86, 87, 143, 198, 231; development and elements, 153–54; German element, 149, 150, 156; New England element, 151; settlement, 149
Wood, Abraham, 61
Woodstock, 36
World's fairs, 99
World-politics, 163, 213
Wyoming Valley, 49, 76

Y

Yemassee War, 59
"Young America" doctrine, 88

SUGGESTED READING

BARNHART, JOHN D. *Valley of Democracy: The Frontier versus the Plantation in the Ohio Valley, 1775–1818.* Bloomington: Indiana University Press, 1953.
BARTLETT, RICHARD A. *The New Country: A Social History of the American Frontier, 1776–1890.* New York: Oxford University Press, 1974.
BENNETT, JAMES D. *Frederick Jackson Turner.* Boston: Twayne Publishers, 1975.
GROSSMAN, JAMES R., ED. *The Frontier in American Culture: Essays by Richard White and Patricia Nelson Limerick.* Berkeley: University of California Press, 1994.
SLOTKIN, RICHARD. *Regeneration through Violence: The Mythology of the American Frontier, 1600–1800.* Middletown: Wesleyan University Press, 1973.